ACCIDENTAL PLAYBOY

ACCIDENTAL PLAYBOY

CAUGHT IN THE ULTIMATE MALE FANTASY

LEIF UELAND

WARNER BOOKS

An AOL Time Warner Company

Warner Books, Inc., 1271 Avenue of the Americas, New York, NY 10020
Visit our Web site at www.twbookmark.com.

 An AOL Time Warner Company

Printed in the United States of America
First Printing: November 2002
10 9 8 7 6 5 4 3 2 1

Library of Congress Cataloging-in-Publication Data

Ueland, Leif.
    Accidental playboy : caught in the ultimate male fantasy / Leif Ueland.
      p. cm.
    ISBN 0-446-52700-9
      1. Playboy (Chicago, Ill.) 2. Ueland, Leif. I. Title.

PN4900.P5 U45 2002
051—dc21   2002024037

For Sigurd and Sissy Ueland,

My exquisite, much-beloved parents

Mom and Dad, please do not read beyond this point.

Author's Note

In the summer of 1998, I was invited to spend six months aboard *Playboy* magazine's Playmate 2000 Search bus and chronicle my adventures as it trekked across America, searching for the Playmate of the Millennium. The following is my account of that trip.

With the exception of the few celebrities mentioned, the names and other identifying details of persons in this book have been obscured. For the sake of narrative cohesion, I did create one fictitious individual: Vegas, the Playboy production assistant. However, all of the events of which he was a part did occur.

As for my own role in the story, much as I may have been tempted to cast some of my misadventures in a more flattering light, I have resisted the urge. It also bears noting that what follows is not a novel, though it may at times read like one. Such was the odd and appealing nature of life on the Playboy bus, where life had a way of unfolding as it would in a book.

—Leif Ueland
July 2001

You have to understand, I've been living out the dreams of a great many men for a very long time.

—Hugh Hefner

Prologue

◆

So," she asks, "do you do this in every city?"

"Do what?" I respond, smiling through a piña colada haze.

"This," she says, gesturing to the surroundings. "Tell a bunch of women it's your birthday and ask them to come back to your hotel room for a slumber party."

"Oh, that." I nod, playing slow. "No, it really *is* my birthday." But cue *2001: A Space Odyssey* theme music, because the most adolescent region of my brain is now piping up, *Hey, why didn't I think of that?*

"Besides," I add, "we couldn't do this in every city. I'd be dead by now."

What surrounds us is little less than a circus. My two queen-size beds have been dragged to the middle of the hotel room and pushed together. A long strand of white Christmas lights has been wrapped several times around the beds, which, with the only other light in the room coming from many scattered tea candles, gives the scene a look that is part spaceship, part flying carpet.

A candidate dressed in a bright pink baby-doll negligee sits at the center of the bed in front of my computer, struggling with some software glitch so I can resume my "chat" with the diehard readers of my online dispatches. To the side is our Playboy photographer of the moment, Raj, kicked back on the sofa, drink in one hand, camera in the other, as one of the other candidates cavorts in front of him, opening up her pajama top and hiking up her men's boxers. Photos of her randy voguing are being instantly posted online.

There's more. Someone ordered pizza, and not only is the delivery person female, but she's feeling yet another candidate's bare breasts, unable to believe they're fake. Meanwhile, a technician from the hotel is stringing telephone cord all over the room, trying to give us a second line so we can have two computers in on the chat, while a second hotel employee is bringing in a birthday cake. Vegas, the tour gofer—shirt off, puffing on a cigar, eyes the narrow slits of the blindly inebriated—is standing at an ironing board, blending up a fresh pitcher of piña coladas. Sophia, our excellent PR woman, who has been wearing a ten-minute heat mask for over an hour (and whose skin tomorrow will look amazing, incidentally), keeps shaking her head. "You," she will say to me, "are an evil genius."

Did I mention I'm wearing jammies?

And here's the disturbing thing: This event, this Fearless Reporter Live Chat Slumber Party Birthday Extravaganza, is all my doing. Even more disturbing: Its creation wasn't prescripted. Rather, the whole spectacle came to me in a vision, the same way at a certain point I'll just know that I must lie on the bed, open my shirt, set a piece of cake—with burning candle—on my chest, choreograph fork-wielding women around me, and have the picture recorded for tomorrow's dispatch.

These are the sorts of things that are spontaneously arriving in my mind. No sudden epiphanies for the novel I should be writing. No moments of insight into the human condition. No, I'm channeling Bacchus and the night is young.

And there's more to come. By the end of the weekend I'll refer to myself as mini-Hefner, or Hef-lite. But this isn't right. This isn't who I'm supposed to be. I'm no evil genius.

What the hell has happened to me?

Los Angeles, California

◈

The call, when it comes, is nothing more than an amusing bright blip in the dark tempest of my depression. The phone rings and, as is only natural under the circumstances, I'm terrified. What if it's someone I owe money to? Or worse, someone with whom I have an emotional tie? I'm a writer, in the midst of writing what I darkly tell everyone is a bestseller, and understandably I'm averse to distraction.

Ah, the gay, romantic pleasures of the writing life—a succession of perfectly turned epigrams dashed off on Odeon cocktail napkins while some working girl whom Hemingway has sent over purrs dirty French limericks into my ear. So good, it's almost cliché!

The reality is, it's seven at night. I'm washing a sinkful of dishes, dressed only in my musty old bathrobe. The bestseller is, after nearly a full calendar year . . . well, it's not done. As far as *quantity* of writing, I've long since written the length of a novel. Who knew I'd keep writing the first several chapters over and over and over? I didn't.

In the last twelve months I've earned a grand total of two hundred and fifty dollars. To pay the bills, I've liquidated the stock portfolio I prudently built up in my youth, money I imagined going to a down payment on a house. I have, in essence, robbed a child's piggy bank to pay for the dream that seems to be slipping away. Worse than that, these were funds accumulated while suffering the ultimate humiliation: modeling kiddie underwear.

Where was I?

Right, phone ringing, me screening. Out of the squawking answering machine comes the voice of a good friend, Max, who is in a much worse place than I and thus fair game for a conversation. To make a medium-length story short, he was hit by a bus. *He* was hit. Not his car, his person. To him, with his one hundred thousand dollars of hospital debt and looming bankruptcy, my two hundred and fifty dollars in income looks huge. How can I not take his call?

A year ago, Max and I came up with an idea for a television show, which we pitched around town, though we had neither agent nor lawyer, and we now get a kick out of watching our ideas crop up on the shows that happen to be produced by the very same executives we pitched to. So these calls usually pick up my spirits, albeit in an embittered way.

But this call is different. Max has heard of a job. The details are sketchy, but from what he's picked up . . . something about Playboy . . . traveling around the country . . . a search . . . Miss Millennium . . . Playboy's website . . . writing . . . photography. Max thinks I'm a natural.

Here's the cruelest aspect of the writing life: Even in a joking spirit, it's difficult to listen to Max talking up this opportunity. The mere act of *considering* a side job feels like a betrayal, and with it comes a queasy stomach—it's sort of like a priest picturing life without the collar.

And yet, Max and I are laughing. As I heroically continue on with the dishes, we're cracking each other up at the thought of me on this trip, whatever it is. The right person for the job, it would seem to us, would be a writer/actor who was about to take a part on a soap opera when he received the call. Instead of playing Phallus, the roguishly handsome investigative reporter on *As the Universe Expands,* he takes the Playboy gig, churning out prose like, "Next up was Tina, who like Daphne before, and Alexis before her, also had above-average breasts. Very above average."

The fact is, I've never been the Playboy guy. To wit, that two-hundred-and-fifty-dollar windfall was payment for a piece I wrote, "Trials of a Gay-Seeming Straight Male." And with lines like, "Though I'm incredibly heterosexual, I can't resist sucking the occasional cock," I have a hard time envisioning Hugh Hefner appreciating my worldview, even if that line was facetious.

While I have no intention of getting into it with Max, "gay-seeming straight male" is not even accurate. The fact is, I'm not especially sure about the male thing. That's not to suggest these are the words of a woman trapped in a man's body. But I'm not ready to state they're the work of a man trapped in a man's body, either, at least as currently defined. I don't really know how to explain it, other than the hesitancy I experience when faced with the male/female option on a form. I feel *other.*

As for sexual activity, I've been a nonparticipant for longer than I'm willing/able to acknowledge. Long enough that of late I feel comfortable in suggesting I've reclaimed my virginity, become a virtual virgin. Actually, if I'm really going to spill it, *virtual virgin's* not accurate. The truth is, I've started to think it's something worse, having to do with that word that begins with an *I* and is the least frequently uttered word in the male vocabulary.

Me cavorting with Playmates—it's the proverbial fish-out-of-water story. Sort of like Arnold Schwarzenegger teaching kindergarten . . . or experiencing childbirth! That's what I'm hearing—sexually desperate confused me . . . cavorting with Playmates! As Max and I continue goofing on the idea of my chronicling a Playmate Search, I'm struck by the irony that this is a job I might actually have a good shot at getting.

That "Gay-Seeming Straight Male" piece was written for *nerve,* a website that is highly regarded in the Internet community, particularly the erotic Internet community. I know from an inside source that Playboy.com has been actively poaching *nerve's* writers. And then there was my previous writing job, coauthoring a book about MTV's *Road Rules*. My background sounds dangerously similar to this Playboy gig: writing, photography, travel.

I've finished the dishes and am wiping the tears of laughter from my eyes, trying to bring the conversation to a close so that I can get back to struggling to write my bestseller, when Max asks, "So what should I tell my friend? Are you interested?"

My journal from this day only makes passing reference to the conversation, a sentence amid paragraphs of writerly woe. Understandable, really. First, friends-whose-friends-know-a-guy leads are as likely to pay off as discarded lottery tickets, especially when the job in question is one I imagine every normal male writer would go to extreme lengths to land. Second, I have no intention of giving up on the novel. Third, there's no way I'm descending to the world of she-had-very-above-average-breasts writing. Not with current life expectancy rates and lack of convincing evidence for reincarnation.

And yet . . . *Miss Millennium.* The title alone is so rich, so historic, it would be difficult to dismiss it outright. I mean, if Lewis and Clark called up looking for a writer-photographer to chronicle their expedition, would I say without a moment's hesitation, *No way. I've got a bestseller to write?*

"I don't know, Max. Fine, I guess, maybe, I don't know, whatever."

Chicago, Illinois

———————◆———————

Richard asks me to take a seat as he closes the door. The latch sounds like the bolt of a rifle engaging. Which is to say, I've never been especially comfortable with authority figures—teachers, guidance counselors, bosses, prospective employers—especially once doors are closed. It's an issue I'll save for therapy . . . *whoops,* the secret's out: I'm also in therapy.

Richard, who was recently named head of Playboy's Playmate 2000 Search project and is reputedly a rising star in the company, is the latter—prospective boss—and consequently cause of the aneurysmlike throbbing in my frontal lobe. Door shut, he takes his seat behind the desk.

"Well, the reason I wanted to talk to you . . ." he begins, then pauses. His speech is measured, deliberate, in a way that suggests not a word escapes his mouth that hasn't been preloaded. His face, too, is held in a position that has been scrubbed of emotion and labeled purposeful. "Was . . ."

The phone rings.

"Will you excuse me for a moment?" he asks. Picking up the receiver, he murmurs a series of assents and denials that give no glimpse of the subject at hand. Rather, they leave my mind free to imagine a standard Richard midday work call: *Richard, we've got a major situation here. The feathers in the pillows, for the pillow fight shot, you know? They're too small, man, don't have the necessary loft, what should we do?*

It should be noted that I'm not surprised to be in his office. Indeed, I'd seen this talk coming—seen it with the clarity that a damsel tied to a pair of train tracks spies an approaching locomotive. But seeing the approach is not the same as knowing what will happen when the thing arrives. For that—what Richard will say—I must wait for him to finish his phone call.

I'm in Chicago. I'd been flown in by Playboy, put up at a swank where-guests-of-Oprah-stay hotel, given a generous per diem. All this after agreeing to meet some guy for coffee in LA, the guy Max's friend knew. Actually, before that there were weeks of not hearing anything, other than Max's increasingly distracting, "Has he called yet?"

Finally the Playboy guy, Herman, called, said he was in town, wanted to meet for coffee. Once we were face-to-face, he gave me the vaguest understanding of the job (when pressed as to what I would be doing, he kept saying, "We think you should just have a good time, that the more fun you have, the more interesting the material will be"), and when I referred to already having a project (the best-seller), he mentioned Playboy's intention to contract with the writer for the first half of the trip, give him and them a chance to decide if he (and they) would like to go the distance.

"Do this," he finally suggested. "Fly to Chicago, check out the home office, and at least talk with the higher-ups about the possibility of taking the job."

But since my arrival at the headquarters this morning, Herman, instead of running me through interviews, has been introducing me around the office as "the reporter we're sending on the road." He's also included me in production meetings relating to the bus. Given that we've yet to discuss if I want to go, if the magazine wants me to go, or what money they'll pay if we get past those first two considerations, the assumption has given the morning an odd spin, more Kafka than Dilbert.

It was in one of the production meetings that Richard and I shared a fleeting moment that foreshadowed his calling me into this office. The group was discussing some brand-new, very expensive digital equipment that would accompany the bus on the road. As various issues were considered, the problem shifted to a question of continuity.

According to the then plan, aside from the bus driver, a security man, a production assistant, and the New Media reporter (*me?*), everyone else working the Search—photographer, photographer's assistant, public relations person—would be periodically rotated off the bus. Something about the inevitable *burnout factor*. So the question was: Who would be responsible for teaching incoming photographers about the equipment, taking care of various details the photographers wouldn't have time for, and looking after the equipment in between photographers?

The bus driver and security guy wouldn't understand the technical details, the group agreed. And the production assistant, someone said with a laugh, was "of no use." And so the answer was clear. They were initially tentative when they expressed it, but each repetition accrued confidence until it was virtually automatic: Leif. Won't Leif be there for that? Oh, and Leif can take care of that.

It's hard not to be flattered hearing one's name put forward as the solution to any problem, but as the group continued proffering me and the monosyllabic word *Leif* began sounding like a new wonder cleaning product guaranteed to get out even the toughest stains, the perversity of the situation struck me like an unwelcome beer bottle to the side of the head. Here a company as formidable as Playboy was planning a multimillion-dollar, six-month project . . . and the glue holding it all together? One neurotic struggling writer.

Jesus Christ! I thought. *How the f--k did this happen?* That's when Richard and I had our momentary mind-meld and I foresaw this tête-à-tête.

"So, I realize," he says, hanging up the phone, "that we haven't had a chance to talk."

The walls and shelves of Richard's office are covered with photos and mementos. There are pictures from *Playboy* shoots, including ones where the naked model is joined by Richard and the rest of the crew. There are attractively framed photos of Richard with smiling friends. Richard with closely trimmed goatee, his sandy brown hair beginning to thin, large brown eyes obscured behind glasses, but looking more soulful than his flat voice would suggest. There are toys from movies starring Pee-Wee Herman and Austin Powers. Everything is hung just right, or set just so, creating the sort of office I would imagine myself having, were I a different person. The effect is a kaleidoscope of novelty with seemingly toast-dry Richard as the neutral center, a revealing contradiction I don't appreciate at this precise moment.

"Why don't you tell me about yourself, get me up to speed on what brought you here?"

I launch into my story, tell him about my graduate writing degree from USC, about paying my way through school researching for the writers of Greg Kinnear's show at NBC, about my first break out of school coauthoring a book for MTV.

I don't tell him that though I finished the graduate program I never got around to the paperwork that would lead to actually getting a degree, or that my NBC job amounted to being paid to watch television all day, or that the MTV book wasn't so much writing as editing. Rather, my overview is the highly condensed most-flattering-light-possible spin we give to prospective employers, or, for that matter, anyone who suggests, "Tell me about yourself." And I leave out the bestseller.

He gives this tale a sliver of his attention. Having been raised in part by a wonderful father who, as an overworked corporate executive, struggled at times to leave his egg-timer attention span at the office, I can easily sense listeners tuning out. So I take a break in my life story. The pause has its intended effect.

"Let me tell you what I wanted to talk to you about," Richard says.

He begins by speaking of Playboy. He refers to the obvious, the extremely sensitive nature of the work that goes on at such a company. There's a protocol that has been developed over time and he thinks it's only fair that I understand the system. Think of it as an apprenticeship, he suggests, an apprenticeship that has been developed as a means of establishing trust. Yes, trust, and in the normal Playboy scheme, it's a trust that takes years to develop.

I'm nodding my head in agreement, because what other choice do I have? Trust. Years. Years being very different from the mere week in which I could prove myself before the trip.

There's something about Richard's prefabricated remarks—it's tough not to do my own mental wandering. There's another of his framed photos, this one to my right. It is actually a series of three shots, all mounted side by side in one frame, of the same naked woman lying on a beach.

"But because of the structure of this project," he continues, "with different crews rotating in and out of the bus, what arises is the possibility of you as one of the few constants on the road," bringing us back to the *Jesus Christ* moment Richard and I had shared.

He goes on to explain what I cannot yet appreciate. He's seen it before: Playboy, with its connection to the great beauties of our time—the Marilyn Monroes, the Pam Andersons, the Jenny McCarthys—rolls into town, and there to greet the bus will be the "candidates," girls who were always the prettiest in high school. The catch is, the Playboy Aura, involving as it does women who are the "Michael Jordans of beauty," will tend to make these girls feel insecure and extremely vulnerable.

In the framed picture, the woman on the beach is stretched out on the sand with the grace of a cat burglar. As she moves from one frame to the next, sand is revealed, clinging to patches of tawny skin like powdered sugar on a donut.

Richard has paused, for the first time betraying uncertainty as to what he'll say next.

Her body is such an assemblage of curves that—combined with the manner in which she arches and twists, and in the context of the sand's hills and valleys—it helps me for the briefest moment to understand cubism.

"What we're talking about . . ." Richard says, still on unstable ground, "basically, what we're talking about is giving you the keys to the kingdom."

The woman's face, an unidentifiable mingling of ethnicities, radiates in such a way that the shots themselves almost seem capable of movement, as though they and she were . . . panting.

Heat radiates up through my chest and down past my waist. I've ceased looking at the photographs, but I know she's there, am somewhat in awe of the fact I've picked this moment—after an entire day at the photo-filled Playboy offices—to become not quite aroused but lusty.

Richard presses his lips together and nods his head in a way that suggests punctuation, as though he were done speaking. *But what?* What was he driving at? Am I to speak, to somehow respond to Marilyn Monroe and apprenticeships and keys to whatever? Did he realize it was an absurd proposition, placing an unknown writer in a position of responsibility, and I've just gotten the ax? I have, right? It's all over, yes?

Or is it something else? Because he could be telling me that I'm actually in, but under special circumstances, and this spiel has been a warning about contact with women. Or possibly it's a third message: I'm in and contact with women is okay, but just be sensitive to their insecurities?

Fighting off the lust fog, I stutter out a response about the long line of past employers who can vouch for me and blah, blah, blah. It's all true—close friends, especially female, can confirm that this is one of my biggest faults: excessive scruples.

I can't help noticing, as I make my case, what I'm so obviously doing. I'm lobbying for this job that I very recently considered a joke.

It's not long, though, before my sensors again kick in. Richard has heard enough. Suddenly he's standing up and we're shaking hands in a man-to-man-understanding fashion. If only I could say what that understanding was.

I find Herman back by the printer retrieving pages emblazoned with the Playboy letterhead.

"I'm printing up your contract," he says, adding, "Richard talk to you?"

"Yep," I say, still stunned by the way I just acted.

"How did it go?"

"Good, I guess."

Los Angeles, California II

Something's, um, happened."

I'm in the chair, facing Burt, my therapist. He rests his clipboard on his lap. I'm looking down at my hands, suddenly struck by a really interesting hangnail. I've been sitting in this chair an hour a week, off and on for four years. I first came to this man when I noticed the mental health phone number on the back of my insurance card. I found myself dialing the number, telling the voice on the other end of the line that I couldn't sleep.

At the first session, after I'd gotten over Burt's first-glance resemblance to Dr. Jack Kevorkian, I added to the insomnia complaint my sneaking concern that I was no longer feeling emotions. Toward the end of the hour, Burt said, "It seems to me you're very lonely." After I protested, pointing out that, if anything, I had *too* many friends, and after he replied that it's not the same thing, that it's possible to have lots of friends and still be lonely, I started bawling uncontrollably. Burt said, "Well, at least we've cured you of not feeling emotions." I was hooked.

"So, are you going to tell me what?" Burt says, responding to my something's-happened gambit.

I manage to drag my attention away from that fascinating hangnail and catch him up on things, reminding him how last time I was freaking out about my lack of funds, the fact that I've been writing the same chapters forever, that I have no life, that I'm living in a shack high up in the hills over crumbling LA barrio Echo Park, that I still at this advanced age of thirty-two (here Burt counters that I look twenty-six) have no clue if this writing thing is going to work out, and, f--k, I'm not the kind of person who wants to do something if I'm not meant to be doing it, I'm not one of the deluded types, I just need to know once and for all—

"Leif?"

"Yes?"

"I got that part. I'm the guy sitting across from you every week, remember?"

"Right. Sorry. Anyway . . ."

Bathrobe, dirty dishes, scary ringing phone—I catch him up.

"Next thing I know, I'm in Chicago, signing a contract. . . ."

Burt smiles. It's the mellow, beatific, all-things-happen-for-a-reason smile I suspected and feared. I wanted outrage, at least a pencil snapped in tension, followed by, *How could you? You're in the middle of writing a bestseller!*

"Shanghaied. And it's my fault. I doubted myself. I blinked."

He's still smiling, assailing me with sickening amounts of understanding and empathy, so much so that I want to shout, *Burt, this isn't Tuesdays with Morrie.*

"Weren't you saying to me—and keep in mind this stuff you see me doing with pen and paper is me taking notes—weren't you saying last time how you needed to make changes, to make some money to give you a little breathing room, to establish that you could be paid to write, to interact with the world?"

"Venting. I was venting."

"Don't you think this is just a little amazing, that something like this would seek you out just at the moment you needed it most? Has a sense of amazement been part of your reaction, that you're the type of person to whom such things happen?"

I know where this is going. Dominating this man's view of the world is the deceptively simple notion that as long as you're making efforts to deal with your hang-ups and following your heart, all that's really needed is faith and openness to opportunity. Because life, when self-sabotage is eliminated from the picture, has a funny way of working out.

"It's a mystery, isn't it?" Burt queries.

I hear what he's saying, but I don't really consider it a practical way to go through life. You just can't, I protest, sit around your apartment in a bathrobe, wondering how the hell you're going to pay the rent, and expect the phone to ring with the answer to your problems! Who could live like that?

"And we both know," Burt says, "as far as women, the word *godsend* comes to mind."

We continue talking. He's done a good job convincing me I can come back to my novel, that it's not going anywhere. But there's something else, something less easily dismissed than my concerns about the bestseller.

It begins with my great-grandmother, Clara, whom I didn't know, but who was a pioneer in the women's suffrage movement in Minnesota, first president of our chapter of the League of Women Voters. I recall the proud little kid I was when, during a field trip to the state capital, I made my entire class look at the plaque in the rotunda honoring Clara. Her spirit has loomed large for ensuing generations.

Then there's my great-aunt Brenda, daughter of Clara. She was a writer, best known for writing a book called *If You Want to Write.* Brenda had gone off to Greenwich Village in the twenties, hung out with the likes of John Reed. She took her mother's feminism a step further, to a sort of postfeminism, decades before the mainstream movement. Men, Brenda would cheerily tell me as a very little kid, make great pets.

Brenda's nieces, my dad's older twin sisters, both grew up to be professors back when the jobs available to female Ph.D.s were in less savory locales—no offense to Bemidji and Detroit. These women were and continue to be—in terms of intelligence, sense of humor, passion for life—among my favorite role models. They, too, were imbued with that sense of not having time for sexism. Again, for a kid, the image of "woman" that I received was of someone who didn't need help from men, lapsed into foreign languages, and wrote books about Simone de Beauvoir.

Even the women who married into the family have been legends. My grandmother, a famous local beauty in her day, who still looked great in a dress in her ninety-fourth year, was an ever-questing lover and liver of life until the very end. A Christian Scientist who hadn't been to a doctor in fifty years, she died in a Christian Science hospice, her body succumbing to congestive heart failure, sitting up in a chair, only tea to comfort the pain, with a resilience the memory of which—years later—continues to inspire awe in me.

My mother, too, is a woman to be reckoned with. At twenty, with a kid and a bad marriage, she woke up one morning and decided to start over, taking the kid and only a couple hundred dollars. This was still a time when a young divorced woman with a kid and no college education was not exactly embraced by the mainstream. Mom hit the road undeterred and she gave up not an ounce of her intense originality in the process.

I pause, letting this sink in, giving Burt a chance to digest while I reach for the industrial-size, conveniently placed tissue box.

"Those are great stories, and again you're fortunate, but . . . so?"

"So? So I *know* better, have always known better. I'm surrounded by feminist goddesses and I'm going to work for Playboy?"

"Updike, Mailer, Talese—I was under the impression a lot of great writers—"

"Hefner's savvy, he knows great writers confer legitimacy."

"Well, maybe you bring a little of yourself, of these great women in your family, to Playboy. It seems to me there's something very hopeful about you at this job."

See? This is what therapy is—arguing away the panic, making life palatable.

"What if it's the other way around? What if Playboy changes me? What if next time you see me I'm calling myself Phallus and waxing on about some woman's very-above-average breasts?"

"Phallus?"

"What if there is a serious pig within, just waiting to get out?"

Burt reaches for the appointment book, signaling the end of the session.

"Well, pig, sounds like you're beginning some kind of adventure."

We're waiting, waiting with the pregnant anticipation of hunters sensing their prey.

Except that, rather than the bleary-eyed, crack-of-dawn hour of hunters, it's midday, and instead of a mosquito-ridden bayou, we inhabit a lush sun-filled enclave that, considering the roaming peacocks and screeching monkeys, may as well be the Garden of Eden. And where hunters tend to be stoic, even surly, we're all in high spirits, smiling openly. Not just us, but even the service staff. Everyone is in such unabashedly good spirits that if Disneyland hadn't already staked the claim, one would call this the happiest place on earth.

Oh, and—no offense to hunters—we're not drunk.

The place is the Playboy Mansion and the day is the kickoff party for the Playmate 2000 Search. It's quickly become apparent that *party* in the current context is a festive synonym for *media event,* with all the photographers and videographers milling about. I'm the only one in the mix who doesn't seem to know everyone else. And with my little just-issued digital camera, with its fey wrist strap, I'm humbled next to the multiple cameras with embarrassingly long lenses. I'm also the only one who doesn't know what is going on.

We're sending off the bus, I know that much. The milling that's taking place is all in the shadow of the beast. It's parked in the circular drive in front of the Mansion. The thing is massive (they rented a crane to help maneuver it up the Mansion's curvy driveway) and is painted glossy black, with the words PLAYMATE 2000 SEARCH and the huge bunny-head logo, all in a design that looks like liquid mercury. There's talk the vehicle was formerly Aretha Franklin's rig and that the renovation cost a million dollars.

Inside, there's more black, a lounge with a long leather couch running down each side, a huge TV hanging precariously from the ceiling, a galley/wet bar, a two-person shower, a staging area with two changing stalls and well-lit makeup vanity, and, all the way in the rear, a mobile photo studio tricked out with the electric doors from *Star Trek* and a white photo backdrop, also electronic. Had someone thought to include a helicopter pad on the roof, the thing would look a great deal like the ultimate ride kids back in the seventies dreamed of when conversion vans were all the rage.

According to my press kit, though, the bus was partly inspired by Hugh Hefner's jet, which he owned before he ensconced himself in the Mansion West and was still going back and forth between Chicago and LA. The aircraft was known as the *Big Bunny*, a name that the bus will adopt. Placed as it is amid this sunny Eden, this *Big Bunny* is about as quiet as a roller-coaster ride filled with kids who don't make it up to the height line. It's hard not to giggle at the thought of this monster pulling into Any-Town, USA. Someone, it seems to me, has a darkish sense of humor.

It's not just the waiting that's like hunting, but also the end of the waiting. Suddenly, *blam!*, the pack is off, skittering across the lawn, cameras jouncing, all before I even notice, before I shake off the thought, *What am I doing here?* So, without exactly knowing what we're after or why, I'm running, giving chase. Fortunately, we're not in pursuit of migrating ducks and I quickly catch up, but the boys aren't about to do the gracious thing—part and let the new guy have a clear shot—so I have to peel off around to the side for what will be an inferior vantage.

When finally I come around the edge and get my clear view, what appears in my sights is so overwhelming that for a moment I lose my breath. There are two of them. They're dressed in brightly colored bikinis, one yellow, one orange, the colors of M&Ms. On an average woman the swimsuits would be adequate, but on these women, with remarkably assertive busts, hips, and asses, they struggle at coverage. *Ohmygod,* my mind helpfully offers, *Playmates!*

In combination with the bikinis, they wear high heels on their feet and full-on photo-shoot makeup on their faces and are tanned with an evenness that is more Barbie-doll skin than human. It should be mentioned that this combination alone, bikini with heels and makeup, is something I've never encountered before, no matter how many times I may have sketched it out to girlfriends as an ideal getup for vacuuming. Indeed, outside of Miss America judges, who has seen this?

They walk slowly, a step up from slow motion, a speed that if it were on a blender would be labeled delicious, and though the shutters clatter like locusts and the photographers shout at them to look this way and that, they maintain their apparently whimsical conversation as they go. Juggling knives would be no more surprising, given the context.

Oh, and there's the little matter of fighting that nagging I-know-you-from-someplace feeling, only to realize that it's not that I went to high school with them or met them randomly at a cocktail party. Rather, it's that I know their images, have seen them repeatedly. Had the women the ability to look out from their pages, I would have reason to blush from ear to ear, for they would have seen me— along with several million of my fellow *Playboy* "reading" comrades—in a highly compromised, totally unflattering position. If you get my meaning.

They seem to replicate. Coming from different directions, always in twos, and at first glance so similar—except for the "let's-be-sure-not-to-wear-the-same-outfit!" different-colored suits—that you want to say, *Hey, Hef, that rascal, he's cloning!* Their numbers swell until there are ten of them, but ten of them, because of everything they are, seems like more. There are four men to every woman on the grounds and yet we men seem outnumbered.

A few Playmates climb inside the bus for a look, while photographers call out others' names, pull them aside for a shot, pose them in a certain light, and the Playmates respond with enraptured smiles, crinkled-up noses, and sparkly eyes, all seemingly synced to the camera shutter. Ever so out of place, I opt for the documentary photo, over other photographers' shoulders, parasiting off their moment. *Hey, Karen, over here!*—I just can't bring myself to say it.

And then there's a change, something that interrupts the Playmate-photographer tango. It's coming from the direction of the Mansion and causes us to drop the Playmates and scurry off in pursuit once again. He's dressed in black silk pajamas and smoking jacket, and steps into the dazzling light of day with a friendly succession of nods to the photographers, before jauntily setting off with an appraising eye for the new *Big Bunny. Good god, he's real.*

The Playmates have been wrangled into a picturesque line right in front of the bus and with a few kisses and "Hey, Hef's" he steps into his place in the center. The photo and video guys are getting riled up, with everyone shouldering in for a shot and, like in grade school, no one trusting the calls for everyone to take a step back. Finally one of the boys suggests that photo guys go first and then video, narrowly avoiding a photographer melee.

I'm no longer shooting from the edge, have assumed a position dead center. It finally occurred to me that, unlike nearly all the others, I actually work for Playboy. These are my people. I can shoot from wherever I want. And from where I crouch, shooting up at the lineup, the Playmates look like giants. The other boys are screaming for the women to look their way, I'm fighting the urge to call for a kick line.

After the video guys have had their chance, Hef breaks away to check out the bus and hold court with the news cameras. He quickly reveals himself as a master of the sound bite, his decades as an icon not for nothing. Will Hef go out on the road with the bus? "No, the bus'll come to me." What does he hope it will bring? "A lot of beautiful ladies." How can just an average guy get on this bus? "They can't, only gorgeous girls allowed."

He finishes each bite with a laugh that is only a touch less quirky than Burgess Meredith's Penguin on the old Batman and Robin series. And with all his references to beautiful ladies and gorgeous girls, part of me expects a media handler to come running up and interrupt with, *I think the point Mr. Hefner is trying to make is that the bus is a unique opportunity for young women of all races, ages, appearance, and economic background to come out and . . .* Such candor from a corporate figurehead—even Playboy—in this day and age seems, well, pornographic.

I will write of Hef that he seems like a pleasure Buddha, a man who couldn't erase the smile from his face in the worst of moods. It's tempting to want to put Band-Aids at the corners of his mouth. Standing there in that glowing satisfaction, I can't help thinking about the disparity between us. My life has been in so many ways blessed, has included more than my share of pleasure, but compared to Hugh Hefner, there is little difference between me and your average coma victim.

Insignificant as I may feel in comparison, I react to certain of Hef's words as though they were a shot of adrenaline. The question about men on the bus, and Hef's "Only gorgeous girls allowed" was not totally accurate. That's gorgeous girls and me. As Hef said, not even he will be along on the ride. For a moment, my knees go weak at the suddenly real possibility. So this is what it would have felt like to get the college of my choice!

When fans of *Playboy* think Mansion, they imagine three things: the game room, the Grotto, and volleyball. Life at the Mansion, we civilians have been led to believe, is one long volleyball game, interrupted only for swimming, pinball, and sex. And sure enough, an actual volleyball game has spontaneously broken out, and seeing as I'm contractually bound to take pictures of such moments, I must venture over.

The other photographers are firing away, their camera motors whirring almost to the point of smoking, but when I try to get out there and bag my share of photos, I can't seem to make myself raise the camera. The posing around the bus was challenging enough, but taking pictures of Playmates in bikinis playing volleyball? I mean, come on, why don't we just break out those eighties jogging trampolines and have the girls bounce away to an aerobics tape? More bouncing! More bouncing! You're with me here, aren't you? A little dirty-old-mannish, isn't it?

But finally I edge up to the volleyball court and begin snapping a few shots. The Playmates have even—and how could they not?—kicked aside their high heels. Laughing, playing, heels off—there's some demystification, a sudden possibility that they're not otherworldly creatures at all, but women, young women, barely beyond girls, not totally different from the girls I grew up with, went to high school and college with.

I'm quickly rewarded for my picture-taking efforts. A Playmate takes a big swing and completely whiffs. She starts laughing, cracking up, sending me a look that says, *So, I suck at volleyball,* and is totally adorable. I feel like the nerdy kid who has just been asked by the Homecoming Queen if he will help her cheat on the big test. But do I forget that I'm wearing a camera on my face? Was it me or the camera that received the look?

Whatever the case, I'm now on the court, crouching under the net for the good shot.

Instinctively, I'm most interested in capturing the moment when they're striking the ball, but my efforts are repeatedly frustrated by the new digital technology. There's a deceptive lag time between the moment I press the button and the actual release of the electronic shutter. The camera has a small screen on the back that reviews each shot after I take it, revealing each time that I miss. Either the Playmate has already hit it and the ball has disappeared, or the ball hasn't yet entered the frame and she's just waiting.

And then I get it. Stacey Sanchez, who I believe was Playmate of the Year three years back. She's gained a few pounds and is wearing this crocheted bikini, the small top of which is driving her to distraction. There's something reckless about the way she plays, the way she laughs, and I can't help liking her. The ball is soaring over the net to her, but coming in low. Stacey has to lunge with a forceful stride of her long, powerful legs. Her eyes are tracking the ball, and maybe a full second before you would normally take the picture, I press the button.

I flip the camera over to have a look at the preview, impatiently waiting for it to appear. In the upper corner of the frame is the blurry image of the plummeting white ball. Staring at the white streak, fiercely focusing, is Stacey. Her body takes up the rest of the frame, caught in that lunge, hands rising to meet the ball, muscles all tensed, and full Playmate-of-the-Year breasts pressed together by swinging arms and looming huge. Though my knowledge of photography is primitive, I can't help thinking, *That's not bad.* I'm thrilled by the composition and turned on by the sexuality. And as good as these Playmates are at turning it on for the camera, I'm elated that the picture has all their charm without the artifice.

Before describing the end of the party, I must, unfortunately, paint a picture of my Los Angeles love life. I don't know how much you know about dating in LA, where I've lived for the last four years, but it's not good. See, that's me up there on the TV screen, just behind Sally Struthers, with the flies buzzing around my lips. But don't be alarmed. I'm not about to claim that my dating life is any more messed up than anyone else's. I have too much respect for the competition.

I met Nina on Halloween. Being the sort of person who treasures Halloween for the opportunity to choose a costume that conceals my identity and justifies my natural reticence, I'd chosen the garb of a down-and-out mime: beard growth poking through sweaty makeup, cheap cigar, protuberant and low-riding belly, and method-actor extreme intoxication.

Nina was a devil, or had dressed as a devil. Not the usual sexy devil, as in sexy nurse, as in Halloween is a chance for women to dress sexy without being called trashy. Nina was a Donna Reed devil, red and white tea-length dress, and red hair band with satin horns. Amid the nurses, maids, and witches, her retro thing got me. Hey, the fifties—kinky!

Unfortunately, due to the aforementioned real-life drunkenness, I was unable to speak to her. So in good bad-mime fashion I resorted to the only thing I had. Showing my stumbling mastery of the art, I was trapped inside a box for Nina. I pulled a rope for Nina. And then I rode the bike for Nina.

Mime biking makes your standard field sobriety test look like a church cakewalk. It entails keeping one's upper body in place, while the legs work the pedals below, an illusion created by rising up on the ball of one foot and bending knee while opposite leg partially straightens, then going down on heel as straight leg bends, and at the same time looking around indifferently, perhaps waving at a passing stranger.

Out of tricks, I contented myself with sitting by Nina for the rest of the night, most often on the arm of a couch she was sitting on, which put me high up over her shoulder as she talked to a guy who someone told me was big on some soap opera I should have heard of. Whenever they looked up at me, I smiled, oblivious to how really creepy I must have looked, given the costume, but at least she didn't appear scared of me. Which was something.

My friend Estella came and found me when it was time to go. Assessing the situation with just a look, Estella whispered in Nina's ear and then told me to ask her for her number. I did. "Can I . . . uh . . . have number?" Suave. And yet, she gave it to me.

Out in the car, I asked Estella what she said to bring that about.

"I told her we used to go out. I said you were the best lover I've ever had."

Before wrapping up this story I need to establish something: I had no car. I'd given myself an ultimatum—write the bestseller or hang up the pen—and it had occurred to me that an ideal way to avoid distractions for a person who lives high on a hill in a city where walking is anathema is to divest oneself of one's "wheels." Since my brother was in need, I signed my car over to him. You see the logic.

So I made the call to Nina and, given the auto issue, cleverly suggested meeting at a favorite raucous French bar/bistro, LA's version of American expatriate life in the twenties—albeit with cast members from *Buffy the Vampire Slayer* and *That Seventies Show* substituted for famous writers and artists.

Inside the restaurant, I actually approached two no-my-name's-not-Nina's before she finally showed. Amazing what a near blackout will do to one's memory of a girl's face. She generously admitted to being relieved to see what was under my makeup. I said something similar. And I wasn't kidding. (Nina, if you're reading this, you're simply beautiful.)

Strangely enough, the date went well. She told a lot of funny stories about growing up in a middle-class suburban high school where the girls wore their hair huge and weren't afraid to fight. Yes, Donna Reed with big hair and brawling.

There were some classic positive-date signs, talk about doing such-and-such in the future. We went to another bar, with a romantic view of Hollywood, where we had even bigger drinks. I couldn't believe how well it was going. Which is why, I guess, at some fatal moment I felt comfortable enough to mention my lack of a car and the whole self-imposed ultimatum.

Around two in the morning we were parked on Hollywood Boulevard, at a bus stop, with Nina's car idling. The glitter-filled asphalt twinkled deceptively in her headlights. For those who don't know, Hollywood Boulevard at such a time of night is not a safe place.

"I really don't want you to have to take the bus," Nina said, with her pretty tough-girl voice, "but I also really don't want to drive you all the way to Echo Park."

I laughed at her frankness. She'd repeatedly asked me if I "really" lived in Echo Park, having watched a documentary about the neighborhood's gangs. Our two homes were in opposite directions, and we both knew she had to be up in four hours and I had the option to sleep in. Even if she'd offered, I wasn't about to let her drive me home.

Without hesitation, I leaned over and kissed her, fully, deeply, aggressively, and she reciprocated. I was beaming as I said good-bye, and stepped out into the dangerous night. I then waited for a good forty-five minutes before finally boarding the wrong bus, hopping out in an unknown neighborhood, and finally drunkenly flagging down a passing cab. The next day we talked briefly, thanked each other for the nice time, made tentative plans for the weekend, and then never spoke again, though I phoned several times.

When I finally came to grips with what had happened, I laid into myself for possibly offending her by laughing too hard at her stories about the big hair and fighting, or was it the too-aggressive kiss that sent her away? But my friends were there to assure me I was off the mark. It was the combination: Echo Park, unemployed writer, and—most damningly—the lack of car. Too much information, Leif, they informed me, too much information.

I also told my mom the story and she, a disturbingly sunny woman and profanity novice, turned uncharacteristically outraged. "She didn't even wait with you until the bus came? And she never returned your calls, though you kissed? Why, that little . . . that little . . . that little bitch!"

But I'm on Nina's side. I can't help it, I admire her for not equivocating. And as for my feelings about myself in the matter, I throw up my hands. I don't know what to tell me. The fact is, when it comes to women, I really am a down-and-out mime.

That said, I will say of the day at the Mansion, when I tell friends about the experience, and when I tell them again, calling up in the middle of the night to remind them, simply this: The Playmate of the Year wanted me.

Eventually we the media have had our fill of shooting Playmates. A couple of the photographers set down their cameras and join in the volleyball game, while the rest of us take our places in line for food. The food is upscale cookout and prepared in abundance. All day long Playboy people have been reminding me to eat plenty and to drink plenty and be sure to have a good time. This may not be the party I was expecting, more scripted media event than Playboy free-for-all, but they're not kidding about wanting everyone to enjoy themselves.

As I polish off my once-heaping paper plate and try to return to earth from the day's events, some of the other photographers are posing for photos with the Playmates. It makes me think of a friend whose Christmas card is always a shot of him and some random celebrity—Latoya Jackson one year, Ed McMahon the next. Funny, but I've never had the urge.

And yet, fifteen minutes later, as I'm finishing off a wedge of watermelon and talking over the day's coverage with Herman, I shock myself when the current Playmate of the Year walks by and I call out, "Hey, Karen, can I get a picture?"

"Of course," she replies.

I hand my camera off to Herman and then, in the middle of the Mansion's impeccably manicured lawn, as I wrap one arm around the firm, slightly oiled-up waist of the Playmate of the Year, I give the spent watermelon rind a toss over my shoulder, sending it flying with the indifference of a sovereign lord who likes to watch his subjects scramble. It's such a bad idea that we start laughing, including Karen. And then Herman can't get the camera to work, so we're standing in our embrace, with lots of joking about whether she's starting to get nervous.

Finally, picture taken, we part. Later, as she's leaving, I pass her, and she says something like, "See you around," and gives me what I swear is not an innocent look. I tell my friends the story as a joke, as in, "Can you freaking believe how scary I'm getting after one day? I'm already thinking Ms. Playmate of the Year wants me—me, Mr. Depressed and Impoverished Struggling Writer!" I leave out "sexually troubled." My friends don't need to know everything.

In the Air

We're flying up to Vancouver, Herman and I. It's been a while since I've traveled for work, so I'm not feeling the accumulated burden of people who travel frequently, just the mild sense of privilege—that feeling kids have when they tell adults they want a job that involves travel. I'm apparently significant enough to be flown somewhere.

Even more grown-up—and modern—we're working on the plane. Our two laptop computers are open and we're going through the photos from the kickoff party. "Photo editing," as the professionals put it. Since I'm sitting on the aisle, and the pictures we're reviewing are of Playmates in the act of frolicking, the experience is a little awkward. I don't want to be known to my fellow travelers as the Porn Freak in 12C.

On the other hand, I can't help noticing that the passengers with a view—the person in the seat directly across the aisle, as well as the one in the seat behind—are both men, and while they don't actually have blocks for heads, it's clear from whence the term derived.

Kidding!

But they are big, big guys, cruelly constricted in coach airline seats. They remind me of why as a kid growing up in Minnesota I eventually had to quit playing hockey. Still vivid are the memories of skating into the corner after the puck, the sound of skates in pursuit digging into the ice, like knife blade to whetstone, closing in to crumple my lighter frame against the boards.

I check my natural sheepishness and leave the computer where it is. I may even tilt the screen back a smidgen. And as I do, and Herman and I continue flipping through bikini shots, photo editing, I note the photos' gravitational effect. Hovering on my periphery are the large presences rising up in their seats. Soon they're leaning into the aisle, necks craned, to the point that, were the flight attendant to push the beverage cart a little faster, there might be a midflight decapitation.

A moment of mild blushing ensues as the female flight attendant passes on, but quickly we're back to work, as are our neighbors with their eaves-viewing, until finally one of them blurts out, "Is that . . . ?"

No, it's some other senior citizen in black satin pajamas, surrounded by bikini-wearing Kewpie dolls with Jessica Rabbit cartoon bodies, and laughing so hard his head is thrown back like a broken Pez dispenser.

Herman speaks up, offers the explanation—the six-month-long search for Miss Millennium, the Mansion kickoff party. His delivery is Joe Friday serious and stops just short of claiming we are on a mission from god. But if you look closely behind Herm's thickish glasses, there is in those eyes the strain of barely contained mirth.

Herm is along for the first two cities. He's the guy with whom I first discussed the job in LA, the one who assured me my prime directive would be to "just have fun." His title is manager of events for New Media and he is my direct manager on the project. He's along to help familiarize me with the position's technological demands.

Herm is a short figure, with a tendency to launch into manic discourses on the inner workings of the Internet and computers, which I can't begin to interest myself in. At first this is all I can see of Herm, the presumed former Dungeons and Dragons enthusiast who's landed in his techie dream job. But watching him lay on the Playboy spiel to these guys, I sense we're more like-minded than I had first imagined.

Our neighbors—who turn out to be incredibly polite, nice, small-town guys—not only were the Canadian hockey players growing up I'd figured them to be, they're on their way back from Los Angeles, where they attended the bachelor party of their one buddy who made it to the NHL. The friend, as a well-paid professional athlete, threw a bachelor party that featured the kind of stuff these guys had previously only heard of, including the nirvana of bachelor parties, the girl-on-girl show.

This was obviously the high point in their personal debauchery, and here they were happily on their way home to recount the sordid tale to their self-loathing friends who hadn't been invited, when we came along. They look stricken as they consider the almost inconceivably sexy odyssey we're about to begin. For a moment, the bigger of the two seems about to be sick. Reaching for an air sickness bag just in case, I almost regret the way we've behaved.

"That's . . ." begins the bigger of the two, stopping as his eyes look up, taking in the cosmos, me getting the bag ready, "that's the greatest job in the world."

Eventually we return to work, trying to sort through the photos, the bikinis, legs, bellies, breasts. And it's funny, when you think about it, for a writer, to have this sort of ammunition.

"Herm, we can't miss. I could scatter shots of Stacey taking a whack at the volleyball through an edition of *Ulysses* and it would shoot to the top of the bestseller list."

But Herm's mischievous glee has suddenly vanished. He turns in his seat, sits up.

"That's a complicated issue you've touched on there," he says, just before being interrupted by a voice on the intercom. It's time to fasten seat belts, turn off portable devices, return trays to their upright locked blah-blah-blah. The plane is easing into its descent.

"Complicated?" I ask, wondering why he's using the we're-on-a-mission-from-Playboy voice.

"Well, let's call them *considerations*. We've got a great opportunity, of course, and we're undoubtedly going to kick ass, big time, but there remain issues. A company like Playboy, it's stratified, and we're obviously the new kid, if you know what I mean, we at New Media. Especially on this bus. There were times when . . . That you're going to be on the bus every day, this was something I had to fight for. I've no doubt they're going to see the light, but there's already been a struggle. . . ."

Herm pauses, adjusts his glasses, breathes in. His words accelerate geometrically as he becomes more nervous.

"It's all going to be awesome, awesome. Absolutely, but we have to earn it. The magazine, these guys have done searches, they've got their system, and understandably have proprietary feelings, need to be won over to the synergies of the situation, and the primary way to win them over is to reassure that we won't be poaching. What they don't want to feel is that they're making the investment and along comes New Media and gives away the show on the Internet."

The plane is in deep descent now, coming back to earth.

"Herm, what are you saying? I can be there, I just can't write about it?"

"No, not at all. Come on! I'm just talking about a degree of political savvy, okay?"

I really am trying to cooperate, want to understand what he's saying, just don't get what this has to do with photos of women in bikinis playing volleyball, unless . . .

"But *they* get the sexy stuff? That's what you're saying? Save the bikinis and the cute women for the magazine?"

The plane touches down hard, with a heart-skipping bounce.

"Herm?"

"We just need to be sensitive. That's all I'm saying. Proceed with caution."

Hmmm . . . a nice time to be revealing these things.

The door is finally open and passengers begin moving up the aisle. Herm sneaks looks at me, gauging my silence, while we create a bottleneck with our carry-on bags.

"Hey, Playboy guys!"

Hey, not so loud.

Herm and I, wrestling the digital tape recorder from overhead, can't help but look. It's the hockey players on their way out, calling back.

"Where do we go to read about your trip?"

Two-thirds of the plane are in on this exchange, but Herm, the promoter, is unfazed, "Playboy.com. It'll be called the daily dispatch."

"We'll be watching. Don't do anything we wouldn't do."

Can we please get out of this plane?

Vancouver, British Columbia

◆

I emerge from the hotel in the morning surrounded by angels. They hover around me, serenading me with music from these little harps that, it must be admitted, sound heavenly.

Or, more accurately, my vision is blurred both by swollen, sleep-deprived eyes (Herm and I were up all night tangled up in high-tech snags) and the mist drizzling down from a low-hanging gray sky that is the Pacific Northwest's meteorological curse. When I'd envisioned this whole thing, it was always sunny.

As I rub my eyes, the scene slowly comes into focus: bus, looking ever extraterrestrial, surrounded by equally eccentric smaller vehicles, a posse of satellite-dish-topped, gadget-heavy action-news vans. They're parked at haphazard angles around the bus, seemingly poised to mate with the thing.

I pull open the heavy door and step up into the bus, and am about to take another step up, at last about to see what I've gotten myself into, but reflexively stop short, in the nick of time, narrowly avoiding a collision with the massive jeans-clad ass that's backing its way out. I back out myself, returning to the gray drizzle, followed by the titanic ass, which is followed by the ass owner, a news station cameraman built like a steelworker.

It's true what they say about near-death experiences: Life is an impermanent, fleeting gift, so enjoy each day as though it were your last.

"Whew," says he of the gargantuan ass. "Tight in there."

My second assault on the bus is more successful.

They sit on the couch, sandwiched in behind the built-in table on the left. Three of them. Women. Young women. Playmate wanna-bes. Miss Millennium Search candidates. The subject of this media attention, this corporate expenditure, my life change. And my first reaction is this: joy, extreme joy, luminous giddy I-can-see-the-light beaming. Only after a few seconds' observation does it register that they're not particularly attractive.

One has a narrow sparrowlike head, with beak nose, eyes too close together, to the point that her sense of depth must be off, eliminating competitive horseshoe tossing from her future. The second is extremely plain in a way that makes it hard to recall her features. She compensates for her featurelessness—or tries to—with brightly colored makeup, enough for a dozen mannequins. In the split-second calculation that we all go through, consciously or not, I arrive at the answer. No, I wouldn't, sober or drunk.

Only the third truly contends for the term *attractive.* Too slender, I'm guessing, for Playboy, she's nevertheless unambiguously cute. Has been probably since she was born and has a naturally happy disposition to match. Not overtly sexy, never threatening, she's surely passed through life being adored by virtually everyone she's come in contact with, even all the other cheerleaders on the squad. Like, seriously.

Across from the candidates sits a different cameraman, his video camera propped on his knee. He's hunched over, looking through the eyepiece as his reporter partner next to him nods and smiles at the girls, off camera, encouraging them to keep speaking.

They all work at Hooters and are really tired from the bikini contest last night, and the photographer was great and makes you feel beautiful, and their parents all totally support them, are behind this one hundred percent, and it's not about the money, though the money would be nice, you know, two hundred thousand dollars? But it's not about that. Mostly it's about *Playboy*, which is a great magazine and great company, and the whole thing has been the best experience.

From where I stand, it's impossible to see their secret earpieces through which Hugh Hefner, back at the Mansion, is feeding them their lines, but one assumes.

Sophia, our PR coordinator, stands just beyond the reporter, looking on. Her dark curly hair is back in a ponytail and covered by a Playboy baseball cap. She wears small black designer glasses and a black leather jacket. Her face is accented by a nose of a sort that no Playmate has likely ever had, in a culture at war with prominence in noses, but it's an elegant feature. Were I a real photographer, it's a face I'd want to spend some time capturing.

One would expect someone in Sophia's position to be on edge, but when she saw me walk in, she flashed a smile that I couldn't help but think looked extremely relaxed and that was followed by a theatrical yawn. She comes off as simultaneously engaged, ready for anything, and underutilized.

And how does she regard this prospect—traveling around the country looking for whatever exactly we're looking for? Not only will women working the bus be in situations that will constantly call to mind their own tangled feelings of physical attractiveness, but there will also be a certain pressure to endorse. Young candidates with uncertainty or misgivings will be looking for reassurance. Is Sophia ready for this?

She mouths something to me, something incomprehensible. *Grandmother what?*

Beyond Sophia, through the first doorway, past the small changing room and makeup mirror and studio doorway, is Richard. He sits on the edge of the leather couch, glasses off, leaning forward, another cameraman-reporter team across from him. I know he's not talking keys to the kingdom, but it's the same deliberate, controlled delivery.

The bus door opens, and Herman sidles up next to me, whispering, "Hey, you get a chance to talk to that candidate, the one with the grandmother story?"

"No, I think Sophia was trying to tell me about that."

"Sounds like it might be a good one."

The door opens again and another reporter boards the bus. He carries a steno pad and is followed by a still photographer, who's followed by another member of our team, who'd introduced himself this morning, saying, "My name's Les, but everybody calls me Vegas." Considering the black hair, Brylcreamed into a ducktail, it's fitting.

Vegas's official title is PA, for production assistant, and he'll serve as the trip gofer, fix-it man, whatever, though unlike a typical PA he's not a kid just out of college. This PA is pushing fifty—he's a guy who's been around the company forever and is full of stories about the old days.

Richard has finished up, is leading the other crew back toward us, creating their own pileup on the other side of the candidates and their cameraman. He takes in this media Mexican standoff and his shoulders rise. As he tells one of the Hooters girls—I'll let you guess which one—that she can run through auditioning for the news crew in the back, I'm heading for the door.

I hear Rich ask Herm for a word just as I push past Vegas, who, flashing his ever-present grin—like a barbecue champion who just can't help revealing the secret to what makes his ribs so tender—tries to stop me.

"Did you hear about the candidate with the grandmother . . . ?"

Outside, there's a tent that folds off the side of the bus. It's where the candidates first fill out their paperwork. Standing in front of the tent is Seamus, our security man for the entire trip. He's an ex-cop, one of New York's finest, now working the T&A beat. He looks like

Clint Eastwood reprising his Dirty Harry role as Harry Callahan, and the expression on his stony face, as I introduce myself, suggests that word just got back to him that I've been bad-mouthing his mother's Irish stew. He allows me entry into the tent nonetheless.

Of the dozen logo-emblazoned chairs, only three are filled. Two candidates are filling out their casting envelopes, while a print reporter interviews one of them. I take a seat, focus on the other one.

She's blonde, though blonde in the way that a painted stripe down the middle of a road is blonde, and looks a little like Drew Barrymore. But where the actress exudes a charm that is Betty Boop cutie-pie, with naughty-girl subtext, this blonde is missing the cutie-pie part.

The other reporter is firing away with questions, so I'd better get started. Only, when I ask for an interview, I'm surprised to hear my voice quaver.

"Sure," I hear her say, through the fireworks display of my inner thoughts: *Am I going to suffer a datinglike panic every time I try to talk to one of these women? Does my unease relate to putting them on the Playboy site without pay? Maybe it's that no one has actually defined what I'm supposed to be doing here.* "You can interview me."

"Great."

"But do I have to use my name? I don't like my name."

"What do you want to use?"

"Marilyn."

"So, Marilyn, how did you find out about the bus?"

"One of the girls where I strip heard about it."

Ah, yes.

"And how do your parents feel about it?"

That was a prepared question, one I cribbed from the other reporter, but given that Marilyn already strips for a living, I realize after uttering it that it's kind of lame. . . .

"I don't have parents. They're dead."

"That's terrible. I'm sorry," I say, feeling lousy, verging on responsible, like these lame interviewing skills may have been the cause. "Have you always wanted to be in *Playboy*?"

"Umm, well, I was going to do *Hustler*, but then someone told me that, like, if you've done *Hustler*, *Playboy* won't take you. Do you know what the deal is with that?"

"This, um, is my first day, so I don't know, but, um, yeah, one would guess that's a possibility, that if you do *Playboy*, *Hustler* would still take you, but not the other way around."

"Yeah, that's the way I figured it."

I'm out of interview questions already, but I can't help asking, out of my own curiosity . . .

"Marilyn, there must be someone you would go to if something happened."

"Oh, yeah. My brother. He's my best friend."

"And where's he?"

"I don't know. Some country. He's in the Navy, stationed on the other side of the world somewhere. Some country."

Lascivious aura, dead parents, all alone save for a brother lost in the ether, comfortable with going straight to a relatively harsh porn mag. And possessed of a fate-tempting name. Marilyn may be the name adopted by this century's greatest sex symbol, whose figure emblazons our bus, but Marilyn was also the name of another sexual legend, Marilyn Chambers, and it's difficult not to see whose footsteps this Marilyn is walking in.

I snap a couple pictures of the bus, just to do something, give myself a second to think. I still haven't figured out what to do with the material from my first interviewette, but as I puzzle over it, I see the crew from Playboy Video enter the tent and emerge with Marilyn.

The Playboy Video guys are going to join the bus at periodic intervals to shoot footage for a documentary on the Search, though, as anyone who's happened upon the Playboy Channel knows, Playboy

Video occupies a much more aggressive segment of the erotica/porn continuum.

The guys making up the video crew are based out of LA, as opposed to the rest of the company, who hail from Chicago, and the difference is distinct, with their sunglasses, baseball caps, and gum-chewing nonchalance about their work. As they head off away from the bus, I hear one of the video guys saying, "So, you ready to get naked for us?"

I'm thinking maybe things are better inside the bus, when Herm appears.

"Getting good stuff?" he asks, with a distinctly non-elfin smile on his face.

"A little slow," I offer, thinking of Marilyn. "We'll have to see."

"I talked to Richard, and he's kind of freaking out with so many people on the bus."

"Yeah."

"Well, he's not sure you're going to be able to be onboard. He thinks it might be better if you work out of the tent. . . ."

"You're kidding."

"It's stupid, don't worry about it, I'll take care of it, but for today, you're going to have to keep a low profile. Don't worry."

"For six months?"

"I know."

"Just me and Seamus?"

"I know."

"What about Vegas? It makes more sense for me to be in there than the PA."

"I know. Don't worry about it. Richard's just stressed. Trust me. Everything's going to be fine. We just need to start out slow."

I don't mean to be a baby. It's just, in my previous struggling-writer mode, I didn't have to deal with this kind of stuff, and if I did manage to enmesh myself in some schizophrenic disagreement with myself, there was always a ready starving-artist remedy: a nap.

*   *   *

"Excuse me, ladies?"

Five blow-dried heads turn in unison. I'm back in the tent, after giving myself a little personal time-out, during which I went up to my hotel room, checked for phone messages back in LA (none), powered up my laptop computer, opened the file on my bestseller, considered doing some writing, then thought about my daily Playboy deadline, shut down the computer, and returned to the bus.

"I'm the, um, Internet guy, for the Internet, and if I could just take your picture . . ."

I crouch down, raise camera to eye, see the viewfinder fill with decked-out hopefuls in a horseshoe seating arrangement. In the center, as I am about to press the shutter release, just making sure the composition is decent, I notice one of the candidates conferring with another.

"Excuse me," she says. "Is it okay if my friend and I aren't in it?"

"Of course, of course. If . . . you're kind of in the middle, if we could shift around . . ."

They've just taken up new seats, leaving me with three, when another candidate pipes up politely, also wanting out. And then another.

"Actually," I say before the fifth can say anything, "I just realized I need film."

Quickly I scurry to the far side of the bus, wondering if my brain is short-circuiting, mistranslating a seemingly harmless request for a photo, causing my tongue to say instead, *Would it be all right if I went down on you all?*

But I remind myself that I may be unusually sensitive to rejection, so try to buck up with some positive thinking: *Quit. Quit now. Walk away while you still have some dignity. Demand a ticket home, hop a plane. If nothing else, you'll have a legendary story, walking away from the greatest job ever, you inept loser.*

Vegas is squatting down in front of the storage lockers under the bus, where he's grabbing a couple Playboy Search 2000 T-shirts that are for VIPs. Seeing me pacing, Vegas calls out, "It's like we've died and gone to heaven only to find out it's ladies' night, huh?"

I'm struggling to come up with a suitable response when a voice calls, "Yo, Leif," and Seamus appears around the side of the bus. Seeing his granite features again, I instinctively think, *Don't hurt me!*, while hoping that at some point I will manage to feel something more like ease around this ex-cop.

"Dare you are," he says. "Rich's looking for you."

I experience a Laurel and Hardy moment as I try to board the bus at the same time our bus driver, Butch, the last of the Search team, is exiting. With goatee, near mullet, and proud belly, Butch is the extremely professional, unflappably jovial man behind the wheel. A stint in high school driving his school's only bus marked him as destined for this calling, and, as a true lover of travel, anytime he isn't driving, he will spend the duration of his stay actually seeing the sights of the cities we visit, rather than hanging out at the bus.

He tries to stop me on the stairway, but I brush him off politely.

"I know, thanks, but I've already heard. The grandmother story."

The I-teams have all disappeared, leaving the same three women I'd first seen this morning, along with Richard, Sophia, and James, the Playboy photographer for the first leg of the trip, sitting on the couches. With me at the top of the stairs, leaning against a pole, bracing for more bad news, they continue chatting, the subject being a bikini contest that is scheduled that night at a local Hooters. Last night's competition, it turns out, was at a different Hooters. The girls aren't sure if they will make this evening's event, since they're exhausted from staying up so late competing and then getting up so early for Playboy.

But they're encouraging my co-workers to attend, assuring them that they'll recruit a lot of cute girls to come down to the bus, that they'll probably be made celebrity judges, and that they're sure to be comped lots of free food.

As Sophia takes down bikini contest info, Richard stands up, shedding his momentary casualness, and with his clipped business voice asks the girls if they wouldn't mind staying for just a little longer. Though they must be faint with hunger, they flash sweeping smiles and nod enthusiastically.

"Well, buddy," Richard says, turning to me. "They're all yours. You want to use the photo studio, get some shots, whatever you need to get?"

I guess I smile, say something along the lines of, "Uhh-uh-huh," but the truth is, I'm both caught off guard by this benevolent gesture and, thanks to that chat with Herm on the airplane, totally unable to profit from it. Instead of sprinting back to the studio, telling the girls to strip off their clothes and initiate a boisterous pillow fight, I take a seat and say that I just need to interview them and perhaps get a picture outside the bus.

I don't know how many readers in their lifetime will be offered three smiling aspiring Playmates, along with access to a mobile photo studio, and have to take a pass. If it ever happens to you, be fore-warned: It's an empty, there-is-no-god-or-if-there-is-he-has-the-mind-of-a-Jack-in-the-box sensation.

"So, how'd you hear about the bus?" I hear myself saying, all the while thinking, *Is this all there is?*

Back outside, a woman in a tangerine-orange dress with hair in an up-do and a homely, friendly face a grandmother would surely love is posing for a reporter in front of the bus. I wait until they're done and then ask the candidate, nervous as ever, for a word.

"Are you the one with the grandmother story?"

Indeed she is, and launches immediately into the story she's been prompted to tell all day, about how her cute little old grandmother read about Playboy's visit in the newspaper and gave her grand-daughter a call and said, in her screechy grandmother voice, "You should go on down there, dearie, you're just as pretty as any of those gals Playboy has in their magazine."

"And . . . so that's what she said?"

"Yes, that's what she said." The granddaughter smiles.

"Did she say anything else?"

"Nope."

"And then you came down to the bus?"

"And then I came down to the bus."

There's the nightmare, right there in that grandmother story: the notion that I might spend six months roaming the country serving up this sort of softball propaganda. Phallus, the soap-opera-star-cum-reporter my friend Max and I conceived as the ideal man for this trip, would be all over the grandmother story, but for the moment I can't bring myself to play along.

"Okay, then, great. Thanks. You've been a big help."

At long last I'm surrounded by naked women. Unfortunately, they're all two-dimensional and fit in the palm of your hand. Just call me Gulliver. (I know, keep those wacky literary jokes coming.) Herm and I are back in the photo studio with James.

I don't know what I expected the Playboy photographer to look like, but James isn't it. He has curly black hair that is on the verge of ringlets, and a once-boyish face that's gone to middle age, a soft presence that is noticeably without edge. He sits on the couch, looking spent, can of soda in one hand, black marker in the other, flanked on both sides by casting envelopes.

Sophia steps back to tell James she's set up everything for the evening's bikini contest. He will be a judge and Hooters will let them make an announcement about the Playmate Search. She takes a seat next to James and he holds up a Polaroid to her. He takes the Polaroid back, face rapt, as though his mind has wandered off into solving a dazzling calculus equation.

"Nice chi-chi's, huh?"

"She's a little hottie."

"I want to give her a one, but her face is not real strong."

The grading system is rudimentary, with candidates receiving either a one, two, or three on their envelope. The point is to help "the committee" back at headquarters sort through what will be thousands and thousands of envelopes. Devoted professional that James is, he longs for an expansive scale, one that more accurately reflects the subtleties he sees. Sophia has no such trouble.

"Two," she says.

"You're right," he says, sounding relieved.

Given that the candidate in the photo is topless, this brings up an odd point. In the past, Playboy's searches have been for college girls, and since those auditions are held in hotels near campus, official spoken policy is that no nudity is involved, which is to be the policy of record on the trip, even though the auditions take place on a Playboy bus and behind closed doors.

I guess the policy is a vestige of the seventies and early eighties when Playboy's searches were routinely protested, but now, at the end of the nineties, isn't it an odd indication of our culture that even Playboy is denying nudity?

Herm and I sit on the floor, at James's feet amid a few envelopes of our own, the ones James has already graded. It turns out Herm neglected to mention a part of my job. James, it seems, takes, in addition to the Polaroids, digital images of some of the better candidates. It's a bit of a ruse for the media, the digital camera (and with it the implication that the bus is employing cutting-edge technology), because Playboy is sticking with their Polaroid tradition.

But Herm has plans for these images. He prefaced his explanation to me with, "I thought I told you," which always portends bad news, going on to say, "We're going to provide these digital casting images to the premium subscribers," leaving me wondering, *Premium subscribers?* He goes on to explain that the premium subscribers are the website's dues-paying members, which for some reason gives me an unsettled feeling. A little erotica is one thing, but who are the guys taking it to frequent-flyer status? These special paying customers are going to get a real behind-the-scenes glimpse of the Search—Playboy casting photos—while the Search is still in progress.

But to accomplish this, someone has to go through all the digital images James has downloaded to the computer and match them up with corresponding Polaroids out of the casting envelopes. Once a match is found, someone needs to attach the candidate's name to the digital image and make a note of whether she signed her release, giving Playboy full rights to use her image, free of charge, in any manner they choose. And that someone, Herm concludes, is me.

Given that we anticipate dealing with more than a hundred candidates a day, this will be no small process. Conceivably, one would have to go through a hundred envelopes to match one digital image, and there are digital images for more than thirty of the candidates. You do the math. It's like playing a game of Concentration, the Naked Lady Edition.

Under normal circumstances, I'm sure I'd be up for a rousing game of this sort, but given my uneasy feelings about the premium subscribers—and incidentally, you guys, if you're reading this know that I grow to love you!—and that Herman never told me about this part of the job, and that I've been getting no sleep, working with Herm late into the night to get all our technical glitches straightened out . . . well, that's really more than enough complications to take the fun out of Naked Lady Concentration.

This one on the screen is driving me crazy. Red hair, intimately placed dolphin tattoo, small breasts, large aureoles—I know I've seen her face, feel like I must have just looked at her envelope, but now I'll be damned if I can find it. I've almost gone through all our envelopes. I get to the last envelope with no success, when I remember . . .

The redhead. She was the first to back out of the group photo disaster. Her envelope must be among the ones James has yet to grade, and now I'm on a mission, must see something. Careful not to disturb James as he agonizes over the scoring, I start going through his envelopes until finally . . . red hair, dolphin, got it! I pull out the paperwork, her photocopied ID and Playboy release, find what I'm looking for, and victoriously mutter, "I knew it!"

It kills me, the irony of the candidates' reactions as they sign releases. I'm still having a hard time understanding the urge to pose in the first place, but am dumbfounded by candidates' cheerful willingness to sign legal releases that, among other things, give the premium subscribers access to their audition photos—yet that is one of the things Seamus explains to the candidates as they fill out their paperwork.

If these women have no problem with that, why, when I ask for a shot for the Internet—a shot that shows them clothed, wearing parkas, even—do they give me that look like I've just announced I'm with *Dirty Old Man Journal*?

Vegas has joined us in the back. He's working on the electronic board that controls the malfunctioning studio doors. James, meanwhile, is looking at a photo and cringing. "Bad boob job," he says, handing the photos to Sophia.

"Yeouch," she says, breaking into her melodic, scale-climbing laugh.

Vegas cranes his head away from the damaged wiring and in the direction of James. I'm wincing, watching his neck twisting, fearing the loud pop of his neck snapping as he struggles to look, though you'd never know it was uncomfortable from his grin.

"Just one comment," Richard says, flipping through a handful of Polaroids, shaking his head. "I think we need to work on the butt shots, pal."

James's jaw drops open, shoulders hunch forward protectively. "I'm not getting it?"

"You are—I'm just telling you what I know they're going to want at the home office. For their purposes, they really need it straight on, *wham,* okay, buddy?"

"Wellallright," James says, his Texan origins drawling out as his head drops back to the photo Sophia has just returned to him.

Herm and I, meanwhile, plod through the digital images. It doesn't take long for Herm to concede he's underestimated the time involved. He vows to get an assistant to join me on the road, thus freeing me for my dispatches.

"Hey, Rich," James says, wounded. "Isn't this it, didn't I get it here?"

"Yeah, that's it, buddy. That's great. Let's just make sure we get that every time."

"She was real nice," Vegas offers, screwdriver in hand, perhaps in an effort to lighten the mood. "Real nice. Her family was from Wyoming."

What's with this awe-shucks stuff? Is Vegas kidding? But as I bristle at his interest in the images, I'm forced to take a look at my own feelings about the Polaroids, which at the moment surround me.

I may have a suspicious ability to mime, and have written about my gay-seemingness and marginal hockey skills, but that's not to suggest I've been immune to the effects of *Playboy*. Right up there with the lingerie section in the Spiegel catalog, the *SI* swimsuit issue, and any woman's mag featuring an illustrated self-breast exam article, my employer has been a major force in the erotic image palette of my youth. I cringe to admit it, but after buying a new issue as a teen, I struggled to make it home without ogling the pages.

Hefner deserves a great deal of credit for providing young males what they most long to see, in that uncanny way the free market has of offering exactly what the buyer wants.

As I do my job, Naked Lady Concentration—a part of me trying to look just at the faces, not the bodies—I can't fully deny the nagging awareness of how little effect the pictures have on me. Sure, the Polaroids have that sketchy Polaroid feel—at one time the first choice of underground porn—but still, it's Playboy. Shouldn't I be feeling something other than numb?

The important thing is not to freak out. That's obvious. Freaking out would be about the least helpful thing I could do right now. To not freak out, it's critical I not think about certain things, things that might fall under the heading "Freakout Catalysts."

For instance, the time: twenty minutes to twelve. To think of the time is to realize I have until nine in the morning Chicago time to write two dispatches, covering respectively the bus kickoff party and Vancouver's Day One casting. Taking into account time zones, that gives me just over seven hours.

Another potential freakout catalyst: uncertainty over what exactly I'm supposed to write. Herm's "just have fun" was a blithe job description back in LA, when this job was hypothetical, but here in my hotel room it's just no help. Somehow I think *Marilyn is an aspiring whore who* . . . is not what they're looking for, but who knows, since nothing was ever said?

Finally, I must avoid dwelling on the innocent mix-up relating to my hiring. That whole thing where I was at Playboy being interviewed and they mentioned looking for a writer, and, caught up in the moment, I didn't contradict them, didn't suggest, *Oh, you're looking for a* writer, *well, the fact is I've got some pretty serious doubts about that and if I were you I'd keep looking.* These instances of miscommunication are so clear in hindsight.

I'm running. It's midnight and Vancouver is passing by. One minute I was rationally getting myself together, and then I was hyperventilating, and then I was running. And I hate running. Every time my foot hits pavement, all those bones coming together, I feel certain I don't have the normal amount of cartilage. But it's either run or take to the hotel ledge.

I'm heading down what appears to be a popular thoroughfare, full of shops, restaurants, and bars. Vancouver, you're an attractive city, so clean and striking, at times ornamental, Europe meets North America. And the people I weave through, strolling along, even at this late hour—*don't think time!*—again call to mind Europe, in their fashionable clothes, particularly shoes, these people are serious about shoes. . . .

Mastur . . .

That's it! That was the strange thing about that bus kickoff party, the way I felt around the Playmates, that funny feeling I couldn't quite put a finger on, that nagging I-know-you-from-someplace feeling seguing into a flash of embarrassment at "the highly compromised, totally unflattering position" associated with reading *Playboy.* It's a line I've already used in this book, but on the run is when it first occurs to me, is served up by my subconscious.

Which is why I started this run. Graham Greene posed writing dilemmas to his brain before going to sleep, confident the solution would be awaiting him in the morning, magically solved as he slept. For me, running can do it. I think it's the pain, the fact that I suffer when I run, am so focused on enduring that I'm no longer consciously obsessing on the problem.

Whatever. I have what I'm looking for, and it's a solution to two problems: The line not only gets the writing moving, gives me at least one chuckle for the first column, but, by making such a reference right from the start, provides a good test of how much freedom Playboy is going to allow. Might as well find out at the beginning what I've gotten myself into.

The panic is gone, having given way to euphoria, and in celebration I plant my left foot on the seat of a bus bench and take to the air, bounding up and over the handsome trash barrel next to the bench, clearing it by several feet, soaring a good six feet in the air. It's there in the air that I get my second epiphany.

Intrepid Reporter.

My handle, I think, returning to earth, resuming the run. That's what I'll call myself on the road, the character who sets out on a sojourn looking for Ms. Millennium. It's the ideal name for such a mercenary journalist—so perfect, perfectly stupid. But wait, no, that's not quite it: *Fearless Reporter.* That's stupid.

I'm flying now on this run, swinging off a store awning like a trapeze artist, an act of grace that goes unobserved. I'll be up all night tonight, that's true. But who cares? This simple high from coming up with an idea, out of nothing—this is what I live for, what every writer lives for, and is so opposite of a freakout.

I'm going in.

Sophia and Rich are outside the bus, Sophia with a print journalist toward the rear, Rich with a TV team shooting an interview in front. I've just emerged from the hotel, full of that sinking feeling you get when you send a letter off and are having second thoughts, wondering about the federal offense aspect of taking a crowbar to the mailbox. I wrote all last night, a total of four thousand words, then sent it off without reading it. But so tired—what did I write?

There's no time to worry. Things have picked up, thanks to all those features that ran last night on Vancouver's nightly news. ("Coming up, she says it was all her sweet little grandmother's idea . . .") Not only is Seamus's tent overflowing with candidates, but there are lots of curious noncandidates—families, flight attendants, packs of young guys. They mill around the outside of the bus, trying to peek in, posing for disposable camera shots. They're all kept at a distance by yellow police tape Seamus has strung around the monolithic coach.

No more welcome on the bus than the onlookers, I need to take advantage of Sophia's and Rich's distraction to get inside, find a story, and get out, because I need rest, badly.

I slip in the door unseen, but at the top of the stairs am blocked from proceeding. Vegas is on all fours, stocking the cupboard under the sink, filling it with cans of pork and beans and packs of Reese's peanut butter cups. Every second or so he cranes his head back, speaking to a woman seated up against the galley, her bronze legs bobbing near his head, within sniffing distance.

This is more like it. The bus is packed. Candidates line the couches, hip to hip, on both sides of the bus. Another woman stands by the entrance to the changing/makeup area, wrapped up in a white Playmate 2000 Search robe, ready to go on back. Barred as I am by Vegas, I rest a knee on the driver's seat, trying to remain as inconspicuous as possible, just peering around the edge, fly on the wall, hoping something will happen before I'm kicked out.

All the candidates are talking at once, in a way that speaks of nervous energy, and initially I can't make out what they're saying, hear it all as raw noise. Peering at the multitudes, I don't think there's much danger of the Search ending prematurely, don't believe we've found the Playmate of the Millennium on our second morning. You'd think that title would discourage even the self-confident—*I know I'm cute, but jeez, I'm not sure I'm Millennium material; Quarter Century, maybe, but Millennium?*—and yet, it's a full house.

My ears begin to make the adjustment, start to distinguish their chatter. Not surprisingly, the most popular topic of conversation is *Playboy*. They flip through recent issues, comparing photos, using words like *beautiful, stunning, sexy*. They discuss their favorite Playmates, arguing over their relative merits. They refer to having their own subscriptions. And they talk about what it would mean to be in *Playboy*, speaking with a kind of reverence.

That is, with the exception of the woman conversing with Vegas. The subject there appears to be self-tanners—how the heck you can apply them without getting your hands tan.

Rich has finished with the news guys, I see through the windshield, and still I'm without a dispatch topic. Fortunately, he goes for the cell phone, starts pacing, leaving me free to continue.

One story keeps popping up that, while not the answer to my writing needs, might explain some of the intensity of these women's devotion. Candidate after candidate tells the story, each a nearly exact duplicate of the other.

It happened at the age of ten. Maybe eleven. They were snooping around upstairs, the way kids will, and ended up looking under Mom and Dad's bathroom sink, when, voilà, they discovered a stack of magazines. They began flipping through, taking in the images, naked women. Beautiful, sexy naked women. And a wish was born—the candidates repeatedly profess this—to someday be like those women.

While I'm not a licensed psychiatrist, I do dabble, and I would have thought there'd be at least a hint of embarrassment in revealing such information, but the candidates aren't the slightest bit shameful. If nothing else, let this serve as a cue to all fathers with young daughters to put the book down and go rethink that not-so-clever hiding place.

Finally, James emerges from the studio and the bus goes silent. Elfin smile on his face, he extends to all a hearty welcome. He points out a portfolio of his own work, and while he talks, candidates pore over the sultry photos of naked women bathed in golden light and coo their appreciation. James has the demeanor of a particularly sensitive hairstylist and everything he says reassures—how glad he is that they all came out, how quick and painless this is going to be.

He asks if there are any questions. A candidate comments that James looks a lot like the guy playing the photographer in some made-for-TV movie about women wanting to be in *Playboy*. James blushes because, funnily enough, he was that guy. "Any more questions?"

"Do you have to have big boobs?"

"Why doesn't *Playboy* have more women of color?"

"What about short women?"

"I just had a baby and plan on losing ten pounds. Can I send more pictures when I do?"

"Is there a way to cover up tattoos?"

"Do neutrinos validate Einstein's theories by explaining the universe's missing mass?"

James does his best to keep up: no, look at Rachel Martinez; they're always looking; it's all about proportion; sure, just take down the address before you leave; you'd be surprised what we cover with makeup; and yes, Einstein's alleged blunder now appears to be yet another stroke of genius. Then he concludes by telling them a bit about what they'll be doing—just a quick couple shots, Polaroids, which they won't be allowed to see, because no one looks good on Polaroid.

From that point, the girls move on to changing rooms, where they slip on their bikinis and cover up with the plush Playmate 2000 Search robes, which they all jokingly ask to keep. They stop laughing when they're informed the robes are for sale, for a hundred and twenty-five dollars. Then it's a quick touch up in front of the makeup mirror, until the studio door magically opens and they're ushered in, to the place I—curses!—won't be seeing in action, the photo studio.

If the candidates seemed a tad *Playboy*-fanatical while waiting to go in, they're positively over-the-top when they emerge. I don't know what James is doing in there, but it is apparently good. Woman after woman strides up the narrow aisle, back toward the front of the bus, reassuring the others as she goes that they'll love it, that they'll only wish it weren't over so fast. Seeing those flushed smiles, there's no getting around the obvious analogy: It's as if they'd just participated in a rather exquisite bit of lovemaking. James, you devil.

Finally, as they reach the top of the stairs, each candidate receives a souvenir. It's a dog-tag-style necklace (though, understandably, we're supposed to call them bunny tags), except on the dog tag is the Search logo, a red silhouette of a reclining Marilyn Monroe as she first appeared in *Playboy*, along with the Search business card, which lists Search cities and dates. At the moment Vegas is doing the honors, handing over the plastic packets with great flourish. The candidates are thrilled to receive them, can't resist asking for two.

There's only one hiccup to the raging good cheer, a vexed-looking woman briskly making her way to the exit who says to no one in particular, "They didn't even ask to take a picture of my butt. It's like they don't even want to admit this is about tits and ass. Everyone's so nice and cheery, but this is Playboy. It's supposed to be about sex, isn't it?"

Given the preceding, it's a breath of fresh air. Someone else feels as if she's stumbled into something that is less Hugh Hefner's neighborhood than Mr. Rogers's.

*　　*　　*

Rich has finished up on the cell, so I make my exit, darting into the tent, where Seamus is speaking to the next wave. There are ten more aspirants, all with clipboards in their laps. They're filling out the envelopes, on the front of which is printed the application form and inside of which the candidates find a pink release form.

Seamus rattles off aspects of the Search that have to do with legal issues, about the release being optional, no one seeing their photographs other than the committee, and Playboy's not notifying them one way or the other for quite some time. It goes on and on, and, because of Seamus's Queens accent, sounds a little like a threat. One of the candidates, with mystified smile, says to her neighbor, "He sounds just like they do on *NYPD Blue.*"

Once he finishes, the girls go back to their applications, responding to questions about everything from career, to hobbies, to measurements. Surprisingly, measurements turn out to be the big quandary, with the majority of candidates having no clue. When they ask Seamus and me for help . . . well, ah . . . they're asking the wrong guys.

Luckily, Sophia materializes and, in a tone as rote as Seamus's speech, says, "For most of you, your hips will be the same as your bra size, and your waist will be the same, less ten inches. And if you're not sure of any of that, don't sweat it, because it's not a big deal. They're going to go on how your proportions look."

Another woman is fidgeting in her chair, brow furrowed. She clearly wants to ask something else. Sophia nudges, "And you, my dear?"

"Um . . ." She smiles. "Everyone else here brought a bathing suit."

"Well, a bra and pantie is fine."

She's still fidgeting.

"Honey," Sophia says, "it's all about what you're comfortable with. We just say two-piece bathing suit because that's what most of our ladies are most comfortable with, but if you prefer to go without anything, go for it, baby."

*   *   *

I guess this is it, my story for the day. Not the candidate without underwear, but all this, the environment . . . an introduction to the Search process, a bus tour for the readers. For photos, I've been shooting candidates' backs, or fronts when faces are obscured by hair, thus avoiding the painful matter of more candidate rejection.

I'm not thrilled with the topic, worry that it's boring, but I guess it's obligatory.

That night, while on a run, I do come up with a twist, though. While passing a construction site, I see the blinking lights, and decide to ask the web designer to include a blinking warning alerting the reader not be seduced by the virtual-reality nature of the dispatch bus tour. They should not mistakenly think they've journeyed to Vancouver for the day and hung out on the bus with beautiful aspiring Playmates. It only feels that way.

It's a little joke and, admittedly, not one that'll get me inducted into the Friars Club. But this much-touted Internet thing—I don't see how it's all that much better than the cutting-edge technology of my youth, the filmstrip. So I find myself intent on mocking our site, and along with it any of our visitors. And then, remembering a joke a candidate told me, I decide to make fun of our host country and its hockey obsession by including the joke in the dispatch:

Why do Canadians do it doggy-style? So they can both watch the game, ay?

Following yesterday's masturbation reference, it's hard not to suspect an unconscious plan . . . I'm really trying to get fired.

Vancouver, Day Three, and I'm covering men.

I shouldn't be surprised, should have foreseen this end as my own unique interpretation of working for Playboy. It's not that I'm writing about guys in *that* way—turn-ons, turn-offs, measurements. But still, I'm on the Playboy bus covering the less fair sex. Should've known.

Not that I had a choice. From the moment we opened for business, the bus has been surrounded by men. They're everywhere—husbands, boyfriends, friends, each claiming his own private space, arms crossed, staring down the beast, oblivious to the existence of the other guys.

With my welcome dispatch and virtual bus tour out of the way, I'm at a loss for obvious topics, particularly given the laundry list of material that's off limits. And as I wade out into the crowd, each guy nervously responds to my questions with a glowing appraisal of his girlfriend or wife. "She's the most beautiful woman in the world, whether or not she gets picked," and they'll "support her no matter what."

Even when I bait them, good-naturedly suggest that the bus's windowless, soundproof photo studio is "no sensory deprivation chamber," that their woman may emerge with an incriminating smile, they remain unshaken.

One guy actually sends to the bus a box filled with a dozen roses for a Day One candidate who appeared in the paper. The note reads simply, "Because your beauty made my day." Her name wasn't in the paper and he has no way of getting in touch with her. And he didn't include his name, so she has no way of contacting him. He did it, apparently, just to be nice.

In the face of such goodwill, I begin thinking of the piece I will file as the maybe-men-aren't-pigs dispatch.

Material for the day under control, I take the liberty of peeking into the bus, just to say hello, just for a second. It's bedlam inside. Twice as many women are packed onto the couches. They're sitting on each other's laps, occupying every conceivable position save hanging from the mirrored ceiling.

The buzz that was almost embarrassingly imperceptible on Day One has by Day Three built to a frenzy. I should have given my employer more credit for knowing how to create a sensation. Were I less obtuse, I also might have foreseen the explanation for the turnout that is whispered by one of the candidates: Waiting for the third day affords a better chance of losing that last pound or two.

The door swings open, causing me to jump, as Rich bounds up the steps, says a passing hello, and mutters something about needing to get James to pick it up—quit trying to make every woman's day. Back by the changing room, he meets Sophia, whispers to her, then bangs on the studio door and asks James for a word.

Whatever Rich said to her, Sophia looks none too happy about it as she steps into the bathroom and emerges with a foot-long aerosol can. Depressing the top, crop-dusting the chorus line as she goes, she walks the length of the bus, her face reddening. "Sometimes we get that not-so-fresh feeling, ladies. Nothing to be embarrassed about."

She stops when she reaches me and, trying to suppress a laugh, says, "Tell me this is going to be a funny anecdote when I'm living out in LA, a successful filmmaker, eating fruit salad off my pool boy's bronzed belly."

"Don't worry," I say, patting her back, "someday you'll truly regret this."

"F--k you."

I have this fleeting thought: *She* should be doing my job. Sophia, who studied film in school, is in her real life a freelance writer, does PR for Playboy to pay the bills, and in every exchange strikes me as more amusing, more interesting than myself. I haven't read her writing, but I wonder if she was considered, or if she could replace me if I don't make it.

I squelch that line of thought, ask instead, "How're things going?"

"Great, if James would move it along. Rich might start taking Polaroids in the hotel just to speed it up. Did you get to talk to James's potential Playmate?"

"Potential what?"

"Potential Playmate. Some little blonde hottie with a mouth like a blowup doll. You didn't see her? James was all hot and bothered, said he'd found his first Playmate of the trip."

I picture a candidate with an obscene plastic mouth, transplanted to the Mansion in M&M bikini, making personal appearances, dating a Tommy-Lee-like-rocker/human-tripod, and it hits me: *weird.* Seriously, *weird,* life-altering change. By the bus. There is actually something going on here.

And I missed her. Have let my readers down. Because I was interviewing men.

Eventually there's nothing left to do but take pictures of candidates. I'm terrified to do it, have had nothing other than bad experiences, but must have some token of feminine grace to feed in with the guy stories. This time, though, I approach the women as they step off the bus, opting to make my request while they're still aglow from their James encounter.

The supercomputer upstairs has also produced the line "I'm taking pictures for Playboy's website" as a substitute for "I'm taking shots for the Internet." My guess is that with all the media stories of illegal porn trafficking and celebrities' faces being morphed onto naked bodies, I wasn't helping my case with my previous gambit.

So I start to hear some yes's. I photograph the candidates standing in front of the door, red silhouette of Marilyn in the background, or in front of the bus, with bunny logo as backdrop. As I click away, I make for the first time the connection between the old expression "say cheese" and the contemporary slam "cheesy." As legitimate as the job is, I still can't shake a certain pervy feeling.

The feeling began back at the Mansion, taking pictures of Playmates in bikinis (though it has nothing to do with Playboy). There was a story a year ago that momentarily preoccupied local and national media—a lurid, horrible tale of the murder of a young "swimsuit model." They found her in the Angeles Crest Forest, where I go hiking. She was a former cheerleader and aspiring model, getting together with an amateur photographer so both could work on their portfolios. It's a struggle to shake that dark view of the amateur photographer/aspiring model relationship.

With this one candidate, Joan, there is a moment, though, when

I see possibility, a moment of heightened pulse. First off, call me an American, but I didn't realize that French Canadians really speak French, or what I mean is, I didn't understand that they speak it to the exclusion of English. Joan is from Quebec, actually drove all the way out, however far that is, for the audition, and barely speaks English. Which of course only adds to her adorableness.

She is the first candidate who looks like my own particular type. She has beautiful long sun-streaked hair, green eyes, stylized bookish glasses, a tiny chip at the corner of one of her front teeth, blue turtle-neck sweater, and smallish, god-given breasts. I'm inspired enough to ask her to step away from the bus over to this huge jade-green bush ten yards away, though even in this, stepping away from the bus, there's a painful moment of self-accusation.

"Say *fromage*!" The digital image in the preview screen, I must say, reveals her at her full darlingness. I show it to her, saying, "Beautiful, no?"

Sensing not complete hostility, I finally think to introduce myself, and am slightly disappointed to hear the three words that have haunted me since the seventies: "Like Leif Garrett," a Chinese-water-torture experience that, thanks to the accent, I'm able to ignore.

We exchange mini-bios while I dream of the life we will live together after the trip. We're going to be so happy, living on my once-lonely hill, Joan naked, me chasing. Naked, chasing, naked, chasing. But her long drive looms, and I can't think of anything to say to stall, which brings us to adieu, and the end of my dream.

I take minor solace in the statistical knowledge that each stop should yield at least one woman of my dreams.

Casting day over, Butch, Vegas, and Seamus packing up the tent and chairs, and Herm calls me into the bus and asks for a recap. He reviews the images as I report on the men-aren't-pigs concept.

"Leif," Herm says, stopping me. "We've got to talk."

"Okay," I say, mind racing—surprised, I must say, that it happened so quickly.

"I blame myself for this," Herm says. "Should have explained it in the beginning."

Was it the masturbation reference? Something I said about Hef? Mocking the Internet? The Canadian joke? Maybe even the men-aren't-pigs idea?

"The thing is, we can't have this," he says, holding the camera out to me.

He's displaying an image, an adorable family portrait, Dad and the kids waiting for Mom outside the Playboy bus.

"That's got to go."

"It does?" I ask, my brain not quite grasping what's being communicated.

"Sorry. Legal would never allow it."

"What are you talking about?"

"The kids. No children in any of the photos."

"Hey, thanks for making me feel so incredibly filthy."

"I'm sorry, but no kids. They can't have critics making the accusation, saying the magazine has kids on the site."

"But *they're* the freaks, the ones who'd look at these pictures and see something—"

"I know. I'm on your side."

I really can't believe it's just the third day and I've somehow gotten tangled up in kiddie porn.

On the Road

It moves.

That's the thought I have as we depart from Vancouver and head for Seattle. We've grown so used to thinking of the bus as our casting office that we're surprised it could be other than stationary.

Herman and I are in the back sprawled out with computers and casting envelopes. Evidently, the one place where the bus company cut corners is suspension. We cruise down the highway with the big sweeping undulations of a horse cantering across a field—except when we hit a pothole or other road irregularity, at which point there's a jarring crunch of metal and our equipment takes to the air.

I'm pretty sure this is a guaranteed way to get motion sickness, but what choice do we have? The way the trip is scheduled, there's no day off between these midweek city changes—finish casting on Wednesday in one city; start it all up again on Thursday in another—so Herman and I must tough it out, produce a dispatch while working occasionally in zero G's.

While we work, the rest of the crew enjoys their downtime. We can hear the sound of beers being cracked, a cork popping out of a bottle of wine. Someone is changing satellite channels, looking for something good on the huge TV. Glasses clink as the others toast "one down and twenty-some to go."

There's lots of honking, too, an urban soundtrack to the growing festivities, except we're a couple hours past rush hour and driving in what feels like free-flowing traffic.

"Hey! Hey!" Vegas screams. "Quick, get me a Polaroid. Hurry!"

Herman and I look toward the front, see Vegas struggling to open the window.

"Where's that Polaroid?"

Richard runs back for the camera as Vegas continues, now with wind rushing in, "Bee-ute-y-ful! Don't stop now, baby!"

Rich hands off the camera and Vegas grabs, shoots, flash pops, and then clicks off another. He triumphantly turns back to the bus, waving two Polaroids as they dry.

"Nice ones. I hope I got them."

Flashers. I finally get it. And the honking. We're in a huge black bus with our massive famous logo plastered on the side, not something these mild-mannered commuters see every day.

Polaroid camera out, Sophia and Richard start firing off shots of life on the inside. They pay a visit to the back, shoot Herman and me spread out all over the floor, clearly feeling sorry for ourselves, and return with the developed image, now with a caption they've penned in Sharpie: *How come nobody ever comes to our parties?*

It's a perfect sum-up, and even we have to laugh at ourselves, but Richard and Sophia are laughing especially hard, and seconds later they've pulled out the second Polaroid and are really going at it. They catch me, exhausted, with face down on the keyboard: *If I look close enough, I can almost see little naked women between the keys.* And Herman, in close-up, staring into the lens with eyes bugging out: *I once scored 6 million on Pacman!*

Vegas continues pounding his beer, multiple beers, while giving Butch grief about the lame satellite reception—since he can't even bring in Playboy's own cable channel—and the cars persist with their honking and baring of breasts. Sophia and Richard end up on the floor of the changing room, having laughed themselves into gasping-for-air fits that suggest they've been working too hard.

Meanwhile, Herman and I, though we're bouncing around like

exploding popcorn kernels, try to do our jobs, these jobs we're making up as we go along. Suddenly the bus seems so ludicrous, especially viewed as a means of travel, a crazy fun house way of transporting a half dozen people between cities. Herman and I look at each other, and we start laughing, taking it all in, and thinking how there's no way this situation was planned. Rather, that it just arose from a variety of plans, resulting in a great meaninglessness.

"What the f--k?" I ask, "Huh? Herm? Really, what the f--k?"

"I know." Herman snickers.

"You know? What's the point of this? All this? What is this?"

"I know."

Things have quieted down on the bus, with Herm and me back to Naked Lady Concentration, when the phone rings. Probably yet another hopeful from Vancouver, distraught to have missed the audition, but instead Sophia comes back, makes like a big sister, and says, "Oh, Fearless, it's a girl, and she wants to talk to that Internet guy. And she has zay French ak'son."

Joan.

I knew it. I don't mean to sound cocky, because that's the furthest thing from the truth, but with Joan, she was just so my type, and we're so different from the Playboy scene, and there was all that awkward silence. I just knew, would have almost placed a bet that the relationship would continue somehow . . . it was inevitable.

I have to say, as I walk toward the phone, I'm very psyched. She was such a doll, and I've always had a thing for women who speak French, and Quebec may be far away, but perhaps we can get together after Portland, when I'm home for a couple days. And with a paycheck, I could actually afford to fly her to LA.

It *is* her. I say hi, feeling warm all over.

She wants to know if I'm the guy, the Internet guy.

Yes, yes, I'm the guy, the Internet guy.

The Internet guy who took her picture?

It's a little painful that she doesn't remember my name, wasn't trying it out on the long drive back to Quebec—*Lef, Lef, Lef*—but yes, yes, the Internet guy who took her picture.

She doesn't understand why I took those pictures. Yes, she wants to know, the Internet, very bad, she's heard bad things about the Internet, girls whose pictures get on the Internet, very sick. Why did I do that, take her picture for the Internet? she wants to know.

"Whoa, Joan, hold on, whoa, take it easy," I tell her, sensing she's shaking as she speaks.

It's only for Playboy's website, I tell her. A story about the casting. And you were wearing a turtleneck and a coat, okay? Joan, okay? For Playboy. Nothing will happen. We don't do that, Joan, no cutting heads and putting them on bodies, yes? Just a nice picture, because you looked pretty, okay? It's simple. A compliment. No worries, Joan, okay?

She's relieved. She can't totally relax, because she was so worked up, but she's coming back down to earth, breathing more evenly.

"I just hear," she says, "Internet, Internet is bad, other model friends have bad experiences."

"Yes," I say, "I know, lots of girls have had bad experiences, lot of weird stuff out there on the Internet, and you're right to be concerned, to ask questions."

Okay. It's okay. She was just worried, wanted to know.

We're silent for a moment. She's still decompressing, and I'm having to calm down, too, having been totally caught up in it, feeling like I was defending my honor.

Joan, I'm not bad. Not sicko—je suis no perdu. *Can't you see that?*

Now that *that's* behind us, are we going to talk about the other thing, our connection?

"Okay," Joan says, "good-bye."

Or maybe not.

At last we arrive in Seattle, arrive late and are told how lucky we are that we didn't lose our rooms, on account of the big Shania Twain concert. We're all helping to bring luggage out to the lobby. I'm in the back, making sure I haven't missed any of my equipment, when Rich calls back, asks if I don't mind grabbing the used robes, bringing them out of the changing room so we can have them cleaned.

There are four of them, hanging next to four that are still in dry-cleaning bags. Taking them up in my arms, I notice where makeup has accumulated on the collar, and as I walk toward the front of the bus, I become aware of the cloud I walk in, the scent I'm breathing, the perfume of over three hundred women, all mingling together. I can only take it in small doses. But still, that's what I do, I breathe it in.

Seattle, Washington

The sky over Seattle is a lovely postcard blue and our glorious sun is blasting down full summer radiance, but judging by the parking lot where the bus is set up, it must've rained recently. Rained used condoms. They're scattered around the lot and in a neighboring alley, testament either to a freak meteorological occurrence or . . . what? Horny elves that come out at night? Am I the only one who looks at a discarded prophylactic and thinks, *There's a story in that condom?*

Rich is on the cell trying to arrange a new location. From gossip I've picked up, our trip may have gotten off ahead of schedule. Once Hef became enthusiastic about the concept, the project abruptly became a top priority. So to plan our route, and secure hotel accommodations, a freelancer was hired.

When I hear that word *freelancer,* I can't help suspecting something I'm no stranger to, *temp worker.* And looking around the parking lot, I imagine a temp from a service that doesn't discriminate against hiring primates. Surely some bored chimp picked this spot by throwing a dart at a map.

The problem is that candidates are unable to find us in this sketchy area, a fact that even from sixty feet away I can see is killing the construction workers five stories up on the steel structure looming over this location. They're all lined up on a beam, looking down at this nightmare/dream: Playboy bus parked under their site(!), but Playboy bus sans women(!).

It's also confusing to the two protestors picketing the bus. GOD HATES YOU FOR YOUR SIN, readeth one of their signs, but I think that's a bit strong. As I survey the scene, spent hypodermic needles and all, a more appropriate line comes to mind: GOD IS LOSING HIS PATIENCE WITH US.

With things so slow, the local news crews are sitting on the Playboy chairs outside with Seamus, waiting to do a story about the sexy fun down at the bus, as opposed to a story about what it's really like. Eyeing the news guys, thinking of Herm's prohibition against anything remotely sexy on my site, the full ridiculousness of my situation hits me.

The six o'clock news! These stories appear on the evening news, are in fact teasers to keep Mom and Pop and even the kids watching until the program's end ("Still to come: What's big, long, and black and causing local lovelies to flock to it . . . in their bathing suits?"). But turn to Playboy's own coverage of the Search, and hello parkas. It's galling.

"Hey, Fearless, there you are," Herm says, marching up to me in his manic way.

"Watch your step."

"Gross," he says, sidestepping a curdled rubber.

"I asked her to take it as a souvenir. Won't she be kicking herself when I'm famous."

"Are you feeling all right?"

"I think I caught something. I guess you better send me home."

"That's what I wanted to talk to you about. I got some e-mails this morning. . . ."

Go ahead, fire me. Do you hear me? Don't you think I've been asking for it, have realized that I must return to where I belong, back to writing my someday bestseller?

"It's good news. Fearless, we're a hit. My boss, my boss's boss, they're loving it."

My internal dialogue abruptly jumps the track. I don't get it. The jokes, the fun I've been making, the late-night rambling, none of which I've even reread, and my horrible photography . . .

"They love it, said the tone is just right. We're golden, Fearless. And then the mail. I've finally got the kinks out of your e-mail, and you've already got about fifty letters."

He pulls some crumpled papers from his pocket. Women asking for details on the Search, a guy wanting to know how to get his girl-friend off, another guy writing from a Middle Eastern nation where pornography is banned, asking me to send nude photos. But the overriding message is one of praise:

I've read every entry from your Kerouac meets Sinatra journal. The travel, the grind, the bikinis are all doing wonders to increase the gain knob on the pathos of our tiny little lives here in the dream factory that is Los Angeles. Very funny material. Keep on jiggling.

"Fearless, we're going to be huge."

It's strange. Befuddling, actually. The writer in me is wondering how this dashed-off, half-asleep stuff could make such an impression. . . . Are these people slow? Still, an instinctive law-of-the-jungle awareness begins to kick in. I sense an improvement of my station.

"Herm, that's great. Now there's something I wanted to talk to you about. . . ."

I'm in the photo studio, shooting the news guy shooting James shooting the candidate. All those steps removed put me deep in the corner, pressed tightly against the studio's carpet-covered wall. It's sad, but I can't remember the last time I was in more imminent danger of a rug burn.

James is demonstrating a pose. It's a simple one, hips turned out to the side, torso curved back, then arms up to head, as if playing with one's hair. Only James is a guy of middle age, dressed in form-less khakis and untucked shirt, with formless middle-aged body lurking underneath. I don't want to say he's without sex appeal; it's just that he's the antithesis of a sexy young woman. Picture your father casually trying to imitate a men's magazine pose. And yet James's face is a mask of conviction, his expression nearly religious, which reminds me he's mentioned having once been a seminary student.

I can't believe he's letting a news camera catch him like this, and yet I'm thrilled he is, because the photos I'm getting—James contorted into *Playboy* poses—are real images. Story-filled, funny, weird. Not to mention that I'm simultaneously managing to catch the candidate in her bikini.

With the candidate approximating the requested pose, James shifts to merely verbal coaching: "Hips out just a little . . . curvy, curvy, curvy . . . like that, now chin up, and tilting head just slightly . . . slight, slight, slight, too much, back . . . yes, now, looking gorgeous, you're going to hate me, but I just noticed you're not wearing heels, so up on tippy toes . . . tippy, tippy, tippy . . . yes, now hold that."

There's a flash of the Polaroid and then James says relax. The candidate, wearing only a small blue bikini, breaks into laughter as she returns to normal posture. "Oh, my god, I thought you were going to say, *Now if you'll just raise one leg up and put it behind your head!*"

We men join her laughter, with me crediting her for a plucky sense of humor under the circumstances. I take note of the news cameraman's zealous laughter and wonder if I, too, sound like that. James says, "I know, I know, I'm a tyrant. Unfortunately, if it's not uncomfortable, it's probably not right."

He continues talking, comparing the *Playboy* nude at the Millennium with nudes of the past, going so far as to refer to classic nudes we see in museums. In the latter, the woman is usually stretched out, reclining, while the contemporary *Playboy* shot now is the opposite. The muscles are engaged, suggesting the very active, extremely fit girl-next-door. The video camera's still rolling. I'm not sure this is going to make the nightly news's cut.

They run through two more poses, one on the couch, the other leaning on a small table. I continue taking pictures, trying to capture it all—a little James voguing, a little bikini, a little media coverage—while working on the rug burn. Amid all this claustrophobic activity, my mind manages to serve up yet another pearl: It's better in back. And just like that, my mission is to spend as much time in the studio as possible.

With three poses completed, James flips the switch that opens the door, allowing the news guy and me to exit so he and the candidate can be alone to take the real shots, presumably with less bikini. As I leave, though, James asks her if she wants to see and hands her the Polaroids, contrary to bus policy. Out of the corner of my eye I just catch the woman's gleeful smile as I hear her say, "Is that . . . I can't believe that's me."

I'm so pleased with the breakthrough, so sure the readership will be pleased with the historic moment when the Playboy Search 2000 daily dispatch first crossed the bikini line, that I take a demi-break, join my co-workers for dinner that night. Everyone but Vegas, who has to guard the bus until it's away from this unsavory location.

We all put away massive steaks and a few drinks and talk shop. It's going well, we conclude. The women are coming out in sufficient number that it seems we're getting one very strong candidate a day, someone who has a good chance of becoming a Playmate, if not Miss Millennium. In addition, there are three or four others who, if they can't make centerfold, would be good for some other area of the company.

On the way back to the hotel we decide to pay Vegas a visit, cheer him up. Rich punches the security code to open the door, but pauses at the sudden rustling coming from inside. Burglars?

Reaching the top of the stairs, we see Vegas sitting on the couch two feet away from a woman. She isn't young and has a fondness for gold jewelry, which, given her weathered appearance, calls to mind an industrious biker-bar barmaid who saved up her tips and bought the joint. The two appear to be posing for a portrait of an innocent couple watching television while guarding a bus. In a more accurate portrait, Vegas's hair would be combed, not quite so bed-head, and the buttons on the women's blouse wouldn't be mismatched

Vegas explains that she's a cousin or something, so we've merely come upon a family reunion, the first of a series of reunions Vegas will have as we travel the country. Still, as I rush off to begin a long night's work, I can't help feeling that things are going on behind my back, that I'm missing out on, at bare minimum, the world's greatest make-out vehicle.

The life of a Playboy photographer, one who was a seminary student, that's a story, right? That's a valid Seattle Day Two story, isn't it? It's merely a coincidence that this story accomplishes the collateral goals of getting me back in the studio and snapping more bathing suit shots.

James and I are on the couch. He begins his story back in the days of the telephone switchboard. His mother was an operator back then, working shoulder to shoulder with other young women at one of those endless switchboard consoles. Occasionally Mom would bring young James to work, from which he retains vivid memories of being passed up and down the rows, being cuddled, adored, fondled by an expanse of women.

He can't help thinking there might have been something in that female-centered upbringing that destined him for his work, inclined as he was to relate well to women. Obviously, time in the seminary added to the picture, imbuing him with a priest's-confessional trust-worthiness. It's clearly a simplification of the man, but nonetheless revelatory. A priest raised by women is exactly the aura he exudes and probably has as much to do with the smiles the candidates brandish upon exiting the studio as that I-can't-believe-it's-me reaction to the Polaroids.

He explains that becoming a Playboy photographer was an acci-dent. His specialty had been sports—football and auto racing. He shot women only on the side, as a hobby. But when one of his subjects took her portfolio to Playboy in Chicago, they not only liked her but wanted to know who her photographer was. Overnight, he went from men's sports to the world of shooting beautiful women.

"That must floor men," I say, "when you tell them what you do. Isn't Playboy photographer right up there with 'gynecologist to the stars'?"

"Well," James says, "you've seen what it's like. How do they react to you?"

"They tell me it's the greatest job in the world."

"Exactly."

"And is it?"

"Hard to say."

"But you enjoy it?"

"Well, this isn't what I normally do. These searches. If I'm shooting a layout, that's a straightforward assignment, just make the model look as gorgeous as possible in every shot."

"And here—make them look ugly?"

"Not that, never that, but realistic. I can get a good shot out of anyone. Any woman who comes on this bus, there's a pose, a way of presenting her to the camera where she's going to look good . . . though, once again, it may take lots of twisting and lifting and flexing to get there. But if that's all I do and the editors in Chicago have only *that* to judge from, and go to all the time and expense of flying someone to Chicago for test shots only to realize they're only going to get that one shot, not the eleven to fourteen pages they need, well, then I f----d up."

As he finishes, he brings thumb to mouth, absentmindedly sinks teeth into skin at the edge of his thumb. It's not easy to watch, this man weighed down by a terrible Catch-22: Put on this earth to make women beautiful, he's forced by circumstance to simultaneously give perspective, reveal his trick. It's as if a superhero were barred from using his or her powers to do good, were forced instead to use them for mediocrity.

*   *   *

It's late afternoon and I'm still working on the James story. I just finished interviewing a woman for the piece. She's an artist, was only picking up her car from the shop when she came around the corner and saw the bus. As to my question about James, about the experience, she says simply, "He made me feel beautiful. Call me old-fashioned, but that felt nice."

Then, as she's about to leave, she hands me her card, in case I just want to talk.

Moments later, a different candidate appears, actually returns to the bus to hand me a stick of fried meat. Turns out Taste of Seattle is right around the corner and she thought I might like to try alligator on a stick. She, too, hands me a card. About halfway through the alligator, James, who's been watching these last exchanges, says, "Let me tell you another story about this job."

There was a gorgeous woman. I would know who she is, but he won't divulge the name. She and James met through a mutual friend. James was impressed. Awesome eyes. The most gorgeous legs. Extraordinary chi-chi's. She mentioned wanting to get some shots done, both for her nascent acting career and possibly for submission to *Playboy*.

But James was wary. If he agreed to shoot every woman in LA who asked, he'd never have time for paid work. He did have an opening in his schedule, though, was between jobs, and she was really kind of amazing. So they worked over the next few days. It was all going great. She was wonderful in front of the camera. And they were really having fun.

He'd been doing this for more than twenty years, so he couldn't help but be guarded about these situations, but this one seemed different. After an early night of shooting, she suggested they go for dinner and a movie. He wanted to go, but was determined not to read anything into it. Then the movie was over and they were at her car, simply saying good night, and . . .

She kissed him. He didn't make the first move at all. And, wow, what a kiss! Still, he said something about being careful, about taking it slow. They agreed to hold off until they were finished working together, then proceed from there. Except that, once he'd given her the contact sheet, some prints, and all the negatives, and the romance could finally begin, she stopped returning his calls.

I resist making the joke, *Some people have different definitions of slow.*

Actually, I'm charmed, that this guy with a gift for making women look beautiful has told a story about his own search for love that in the end is a bit reminiscent of my drunken mime date. We appear to have more in common than I thought.

James is sulking at the memory of his dating story, but fortunately for his spirits a candidate shows up who requires no reality-check photographs. She's wickedly sexy and he can content himself with making her look amazing.

I'm back there with him, shooting shots of him shooting her, and my shots will go so well with my dispatch story, both in setting the mood and providing a little sexual pulse for my lonesome readers— she really is a beach-blanket sex kitten. I'm so pleased with the conclusion to the day's work that as James wraps up the breasts-covered portion of the shoot and it's my cue to leave, I suggest a photo of the two of them, photographer and model, sensitive James standing behind his siren, wrapping his arms around her tautest of stomachs.

So thrilled am I by my window into James's world and my own efforts at photography, I impulsively hand the digital off to James, saying, "Now one of me." As I step into James's place, the sex kitten spoons her warm high-performance body back into me and pulls my arms around. It's both majestic and pathetic—this recovering lonely guy glorying in the touching: *My god, it feels so good!*

Back out in the lounge, she and James finally emerge. James, looking especially pleased, passes around Polaroids to the rest of the crew. She is blushing, very happily, and James wants to share a secret, asks with a whisper if it's okay.

"You wouldn't think it to look at her, but she has a piercing in a very private place."

We all kind of murmur as Sophia wisecracks, "The one part of my body I'm especially careful not to let steel pass through." All of us chuckle, except for Vegas, who says, with all the finesse of a welder performing neurosurgery, "Can *we* see?"

I know what you want. Rather than wait for this story to get sexy or corrupt, you're hoping I depart from the Playboy Search and get back to my novel, because you, like everyone, love great rambling first novels.

I try to oblige. I'm back in my hotel room, where I decide to put off beginning the evening's dispatch. I've been lugging my own laptop on the trip, and I go so far as to push the power button and sit down before my familiar old screen. It's taking its time warming up, as it's wont to do, but before the desktop materializes . . . who am I kidding?

I don't want to write about the misadventures of a tortured misunderstood character who bears a strong similarity to me, I want to write about a tortured misunderstood character who happens to also be a Playboy photographer and former seminary student. It's not even a close call.

I click on quit. And I mean quit. I don't care what Burt or anyone else might say about returning to the novel later. It's over. I'm giving up. At this moment, that seems clear. Whatever *it* is, I didn't have it, but I *have* stumbled into something more fitting.

But before switching on the Playboy computer and getting to work, I check my personal e-mail and am rewarded with a note from a friend that goes a long way toward lifting my spirits. It starts off praising my dispatches, then digresses to a funny story about his recent midlife circumcision. He's been suffering the recurring problems that can plague the uncircumcised—those having to do with adhesion of skin to skin. They've been frequent enough that his doctor finally suggested he undergo the long-delayed rite of passage.

He writes that the procedure wasn't particularly painful, that the only time he experiences discomfort is during . . . erections. *Yeouch*.

Did I know that the average male experiences six to ten erections during the course of a night's sleep? he asks. Apparently it has to do with the body's need to ensure the extremity is receiving adequate blood supply. My friend can testify to the accuracy of the figure, because he's leaping out of bed with each one.

"It's kind of good news/bad news. On one hand, it's certainly nice to have affirmation of one's virility. On the other, there's a sadness in all that missed opportunity."

Day Three, Seattle, and I find myself once again out of story.

I've done the bus intro, men at the bus, news crews covering the bus, life of a Playboy photographer . . . and nothing. It's disappointing, because of how much I'm enjoying the process, writing about real people, not fictional characters.

I think of my old friend Burt, wonder what he would advise, and instantly the answer comes: Do nothing. So I do. I just sit back on the bus couch and wait, with faith, for something to happen.

A blonde woman sits down next to me. She smiles. I smile.

Actually, that's not accurate. The truth is, a redhead first sits down next to me. She wears white short-shorts and a see-through white blouse revealing a white bra underneath. Her hair is not just red but Ronald McDonald red, and with her screechy nail-on-chalkboard voice, she proudly announces that she's sixty-seven years old. She's here because she wants to keep her children and grandchildren on their toes, and she credits clogging with keeping her legs in shape.

Before she leaves, I stop her for a photo, wanting one from the waist down, the clogging-toned bare legs in their full glory. In the picture, it's hard to tell the age, and though Herm will try to spike the image, citing company policy about not isolating body parts ("We don't want to be accused of objectifying parts of the body"), I will send it to the designer, who will include it in the dispatch, inspiring the thought, *If only one reader mistakenly masturbates to that senior citizen's legs, my time here will not have been in vain.*

And then the blonde arrives, sits down next to me.

"What's up, girlfriend?" I ask.

Sophia, who's sitting across the aisle, laughs.

"You better watch the cheese factor," Sophia says, holding her arm out like it's the needle on a meter, the cheesy meter.

"What?"

"You're changing."

"Changing?"

"Cheesy."

"Jeez, I'm just trying to do my job."

Sophia holds her arm out again, ratchets up the cheesy meter.

"This all wasn't my idea."

"Okay, Fearless, calm down."

"I'm sorry, sweetheart, where were we?" I say to the blonde.

"Oh, my god," Sophia cries out.

The candidate, whose name is Mary, watches us patiently, sweetly, too nice to ask what is going on. She has long natural blonde hair, a broad infectious smile, sparkly dark blue eyes.

"So, my dear," I resume, "what brings you here?"

"Some of the guys I work with." She has a great voice, slightly hoarse, with a bit of a southern accent. "They signed me up, on the computer, on a dare, and I couldn't back down."

"Really?"

This might be good. Herm is hungry for these kinds of stories— confirmation that the website plays an increasingly important role in the company.

"Interesting. And where do you work?"

"Uh," she says, with the same pleasing rasp, "well, I'm, um, I work as an MP at a military correctional facility."

"Oh," I say, not quite comprehending. Then it comes to me. "You're a guard at an Army jail?"

"Yes."

"Male or female?"

"Male."

"May I see your envelope?"

She's not kidding, has written the same thing on her envelope under occupation, but still, my brain, the supercomputer, is having a hell of a time digesting this. It's like the plot of a bad porn movie— cheerleader becomes guard at a military prison. Inner computer still whirring, I make a deduction: Her voice is hoarse from yelling at the prisoners. *Mama mia.*

The key here is not to sound like a creep when I mention my work for the web. Don't give her the willies. Presumably, she could get in trouble with the military for dealing with Playboy—she has nothing to gain from talking to me—but I must get this story.

Real casual-like, I suggest that a story like hers might potentially be of interest to my readers. And she, the sunny vixen, says sure, even hitches her shoulders, like, *Oh, boy.*

"There's just one thing. Do you know . . . will there be a problem . . . how does . . ." I stumble because, much as I want this, I can't be responsible for her losing her job. "How does the Army feel about it?"

"We asked, and they said the position is, just don't appear in—or partially in—uniform in the shots and there won't be a problem. At least that's what they said."

So we talk. Mary is indeed an MP, *loves* being an MP, working in the prison, but what she'd really love to be is a drill sergeant. Since drill sergeants are, she says, the real hard-asses. They're the spit-spewing nightmares you see in movies who're responsible for training new recruits. She smiles engagingly as she imagines being one of those animals.

I stare at her, wanting to penetrate the soft exterior, wanting to know what sort of mayhem is going on in there. I ask what happens if she *does* appear in *Playboy.* Given the job and the way she looks, won't the men have an advantage over her?

"What do you mean?"

"Well, can't they get *Playboy*?"

"Oh, yes. They live for it."

"Well, wouldn't they consider that something they have over you, that they can see you naked whenever they want? Excuse me for saying this, but couldn't they get off to your image?"

"Aw, if I were to appear in *Playboy*, I think it would confirm their worst fears, that I'm as strong and confident and unafraid as they think. It would make them that much more scared of me."

The smile again, the twinkling eyes.

"Wow."

She laughs. But I can't let it go.

"But what about—what about the guys who . . . I can imagine in some men's minds, if you were to, I don't know, punish them, well, it wouldn't be much punishment, you know? They might enjoy it. Don't you think?"

She tells me that a military facility is different from a civilian one, totally different, and as a way of explaining what can happen in the military and how a woman's sexuality is not always the weak link civilians imagine, she tells me about a female drill sergeant she knows who, if she doesn't like how one of the men is behaving, gets in his face, inches away, and at the top of her lungs yells, "What the hell are you thinking, Private? Do you want to f--k me, is that what you're thinking? Private, is that it, do you want to f--k me? Answer me!"

"We just met," I mutter.

"And if he were to react in any way, if that private's lips even twitched, then that would be it, she'd be able to make him regret it, running, marching, cleaning, lots of things. And that's not even in the correctional facility."

There seem to be a feast of questions and issues here, relating to the sexes and power and eroticism, that are so knotted up, my senses are quickly overwhelmed. It's similar to the way all-you-can-eat buffets can make you feel full before you've had even a single serving. But it's time for Mary to go on back for her audition, and I'm left buzzing from the exchange.

Outside, when she's done, I pull her aside for a photo. With the red Marilyn silhouette beside her, I take her picture. Then, unsatisfied, I give her a bit of a James instruction. "Turn those hips out to the side, a little like Marilyn, yes, and then face forward." And as she does, I see the curves multiply and notice that in the act of arching up, her raised T-shirt reveals the slightest bare midriff.

"Umm . . ."

"What?" she asks, looking like something is wrong.

"Could you . . . your shirt, could you"—and here I'm thinking, please don't yell at me, don't yell, *Do you want to f--k me, Fearless?*— "pull it up just a little?"

The stomach is flat, creamy, toned, and the smile returns. As I put the camera away and we shake hands, I say thanks, though that doesn't begin to describe it.

I'm back in my room, running clothes on, about to head out for a jog, clear my head, get some ideas on how to kick off the MP dispatch . . . but there's something that won't let me head out the door, a certain nagging feeling.

I pace the room, staring at my bed, littered with casting envelopes and all they contain. What's bothering me has to do with the envelopes and what they represent: the women of the bus. But beyond that, I can't pin down the problem. Everything is going well, the higher-ups are letting me do what I want, the stories are getting better, the photos racier. True, the hope that I'd be able to work on the bestseller is gone, roadkill, but *that's* not it.

Somewhere in my thinking is that circumcision e-mail. Working for Playboy, being surrounded by the Polaroids, sharing tight spaces with bikini models—shouldn't I be feeling more arousal? Is it possible I'm physically endangering myself by not getting that critical blood flow?

Staring at the bed, unable to leave for my run, plagued by this nagging notion, I just . . . well, okay, I'm kind of kidding about the need for blood flow, but not really. It sounds totally idiotic, but it *is* possible I'm endangering myself.

So for the first time in my life, I force myself. In a sense—there in my hotel room, with envelopes from work sprawled out on the bed, and the photos of a particular military-inclined candidate in full view—I molest myself. I don't want to do it. I feel funny about it. I don't take the usual pleasure in it. Abandoned by my libido, I must resort to persistent CPR-like mechanics. But it has to be done. We're talking about the health and well-being of a vital human organ.

When it's over, and I'm forcing myself not to sleep but to go take that run after all, a part of me senses a line has been crossed with regard to work and personal life. Another part is just thinking, *You complete weirdo.*

Portland, Oregon

So, I'm in the shower last night," Sophia says, pausing to sip coffee.

We're in Portland, Day One, last city of the trip's first leg.

"Soph, in the shower?" Vegas pipes up, taking advantage of Sophia's tactical error of pausing. "With those beautiful yabbos?"

The joke has already been established—not in a harassing way, more as a way of paying homage—that we're rambling around the country in search of the country's two greatest breasts, when in fact they might well be with us the whole time.

"Easy, Vegas. You'll be happy to know that's where this is headed. So I'm in the shower, tired and zoning out a bit, when it hits me that I'm doing something without thinking about it. I'm up on toes, legs crossed, looking back over my shoulder, then I'm flat-footed, crossing arms under—Vegas, this is for you—the yabbos, giving them just that bit of support, doing the look, gazing at them fondly . . . and that's when it hits me. . . ."

"They're works of art?"

"That I'm doing the poses. I'm doing the *Playboy* poses. I've actually caught myself, without thinking about it, running through the *Playboy* poses, considering how I would look."

Incredulous, Sophia takes another sip from her coffee. When neither Rich, James, Vegas, Seamus, nor I respond, she looks up.

"You guys? Do you have any idea how disturbing that is? For *me*, to be checking myself out like that, in only our third city? Do you see how that would make me feel?"

Vegas, appearing to come out of a trance, finally speaks. "I bet you looked amazing." Rich, James, Seamus, and I continue not getting it. Pretending, I like to think.

We've been open for business for two hours now and not a single candidate has shown up. For the optimists on the bus who were struggling to believe Seattle's crack alley was a fluke, Portland's bus location offers no solace. The vehicle is stationed in that great suburban life-free zone, an office park out by the airport.

The problem, and the reason I mention it (aside from my own urban bias), is that it's next to impossible to find—middle of nowhere, all the buildings by design visually indistinguishable. Drive-by business is out. However many hundreds of thousands of dollars went into our rolling PR campaign are totally wasted here. Once again, an unavoidable thought floats by: *Get me the head of the monkey who planned this thing.*

Across from me, two past-their-prime on-camera guys swap grisly stories about covering crime scenes in the eighties. One of the guys worked in Baltimore, the other in Cleveland, and they keep saying, "You think that's bad . . ." and then launch into a more vivid account of mutilated human remains. Mercifully, their Grand Guignol is interrupted by a beautiful head poking through the doorway—a face that calls to mind one of *Playboy*'s most popular Playmates of all times—eighties siren and Leif lust object Shannon Tweed.

"Anyone home?"

"I modeled a little, growing up, much as you can model in Portland, but even that ended kind of prematurely," she says to Rich. The two of them are in the back studio squared off while I squat down on my knees, holding the microphone out to capture digital audio for the website.

"Prematurely?" Rich responds.

She, Emma, casts exquisite eyes down for a second. "Or 'too-maturely,' I guess."

Rich looks on, like, Me not getting it, so that now the well-defined face flushes pink.

"You're supposed to be really thin. . . ."

And? We're still not . . .

". . . not womanly . . ."

Not womanly? . . .

". . . and I kept filling out . . ."

"Gotcha," Rich says. "Sorry."

Yes, gotcha. Too womanly to model. Her form too much like a woman's to represent women: the damn prejudice of the modeling industry. When will it stop!

But you know what this means, of course. They're real. They're real! Rich and I call on our professionalism not to yell out, "Yippee!"

"You're the first person I've met in the cemetery plot brokering business," I suggest.

Emma brokers funeral plots, most often to senior citizens, though I don't totally get the brokering aspect. But it's some company she and her boyfriend started.

"I'm not surprised," she says.

We loiter outside the studio door, she in Playboy robe, standing eye to eye with me and flashing a solar-flare smile. Another candidate arrived while Rich was interviewing Emma and is now in the back studio, so I'm capitalizing on the downtime until the door opens.

"You must do well. I mean, up against the competition . . . if I were seventy-something . . . I can't even imagine what you must look like . . . through a seventy-year-old's eyes . . ."

She isn't totally following this halting ramble, so I don't make the nerdy comparison to the suicide palaces in Kurt Vonnegut's stories with their tall blonde suicide attendants. We can hear them finishing up inside. *Wrap it up, get the picture.*

". . . I just . . . if it were between buying from you or some cigar-chomping comb-over guy . . . I know where I'm going to buy my plot."

"Oh . . . no, we sell by phone. It's a telemarketing business."

"Oh, I see. Well . . ."

The phone? You look like you do and you don't incorporate it into your business? Are you crazy? Or really innocent? Or stupid?

"I think you're about to go in," I say, hearing movement on the other side of the door. "Um, do you mind . . . can I take a picture of you for Playboy's website?"

"Of course! Right here?"

"Yeah, that would be great. Just put your hands on your hips, twist out . . ."

Emma reaches for the robe—to cinch it up tighter, I assume—and I look down to make sure the camera is on, ready to go. I look up to see her robe parted, hands on hips at underwear and . . . breasts, exposed breasts—unleashed, really—red-alert shocking, full C-plus cup, no D, standing so out and up, I can't believe they're real.

"No!" I say, not full exclamation, really, but loud, startling, as I reach for her robe, scaring her. "Actually, for the website . . ."—I'm closing the robe—"we can't use, for the website . . . closed robe is fine. Okay? Great. Yeah, just like that. Pretty smile. Very nice. Okay, good luck. 'Bye."

Emma is still in back, has been for what must be coming up on half an hour. Which is a lot of Polaroids. I'm still catching my breath. Honestly, it's a shock—that out-of-time, not-making-connections sensation we get after a physical trauma or deeply disturbing news.

My racing pulse derives not just from Emma's proximity, but how horribly I handled her exposure. Why *not*, for example, just take the robe-open photo, even though I couldn't use it? I might have avoided making her feel uncomfortable, then taken a second picture with the robe closed. Anything would have been better than yelping like I did.

"Ooh, she's pretty," says a woman next to me, holding open an issue of *Playboy* to her friend. "Isn't she pretty?"

"Yeah, she looks like what's-her-name, um, Ashley, don't you think?"

"Totally. Sexy girl."

Out the window, I notice a brand-spanking-new Lexus that wasn't there before. The new arrivals are both underwhelming: absence of "good bone structure," traces of battles with acne, legs are a little formless, shoulders a tad chunky. I'd still describe them as attractive, but time won't be kind. In a split second I've dismissed them as dispatch material. Was I always like this?

"Those nipples don't know that each other exists," one of the women says.

Sneaking a look, I see that it's true. The model on the page has nipples that appear cockeyed.

"Can't they fix those in the computer?" asks the other.

I'm starting to think I've underestimated these two and they could provide material for my dispatch. But after Emma, I can't get up the interest, would rather puzzle over that encounter.

It reminds me of conversations I had before the trip began. Friends wanted me to level with them: "It's just a publicity thing, right?" Not sure what they were driving at, I'd respond that, from what I had seen, Playboy was taking the Search seriously. "But come on," my friends would insist, "any woman that hot, you're not going to find her out in Iowa waiting tables. She's already going to be out here in LA, with an agent, lawyer, and astrologer."

Essentially, they were asking if Hefner's mythical girl-next-door—the perfectly figured sweet spirit who is magically unspoiled by the attention her appearance has brought her—still exists. For decades the concept was a critical variable in the formula that enabled the magazine to seem part of the mainstream while riding the frontiers of sex, and, memo to my friends, apparently she does exist, and is selling funeral plots.

"Oooooh," one of the two candidates groans, flipping the page again.

"It's like she never heard of wax!"

They flip another page, which features drastically contrasting pubic grooming.

"That's jarring, don't you think?" one asks, flipping back to the previous page, and then forward. "It makes me dizzy."

Okay, I like these girls. Without asking, I pick up their envelopes.

"So, you're both aestheticians?" I ask, mentally calculating the price of that new Lexus parked out there to be over forty grand.

They look up from the magazine. Molly, closest to me, with wavy hair piled high on her head, smiles. Hester, sitting on the other side of Molly, looks less certain. Neither responds. I ask them about Portland, and they point out that I'm not *in* Portland.

"Where am I?"

"You're nowhere," Hester says.

"But we're staying downtown."

"Well, has anyone mentioned strip clubs yet?"

"We just got here."

"Well . . ." Hester starts.

" . . . they will," Molly finishes.

"Two hundred and thirty-six. Most in the country per capita and that's about all there is."

"But not you two, because you're aestheticians."

"Yeah, right," Molly adds.

I'd already heard of this phenomenon in Vancouver and Seattle. Aesthetician—a person licensed to work in a beauty parlor?—was a code way of saying, *I'm a stripper, and I've heard that Playboy doesn't like strippers, or doesn't like people saying they're strippers, so I'm calling myself an aesthetician.*

"If you want to have fun, you could come for dinner Thursday. Molly is an amazing cook."

"Well, I like to cook. That's what I love to do. Cook huge meals and tell anyone who wants to come over to my house."

"You should come," Hester says. "It's a beautiful house, with like a restaurant kitchen."

"You're totally welcome. Thursday's going to be good. I'm making chocolate soufflé."

They both make "Mmmmm" sounds.

"Lots of wine, soufflé, we'll introduce you to some cute girls. It'll be fu-uh-un."

According to the hobbies section of Hester's envelope, she's also really into quilting, is taking French, and someday hopes to move to France.

Just as I'm entertaining the invitation, Emma finally emerges, giving us all one last modest brilliant smile as she leaves. Hester and Molly exchange sotto voce exclamations of, "She's beautiful," before Sophia beckons the two friends to come back.

As they walk off, it occurs to me. Molly, damn it, you aesthetician/stripper, you've not only appropriated my intended life, but the intended life of every struggling artist with bourgeois dreams: nice car, homeowner, big kitchen, open-door policy, friends, cooking, wine, cute girls, French lessons, inevitable move to France. Just substitute boxing at the Y for quilting.

It's quiet again on the bus. Rich, James, and Sophia are bemoaning their efforts with a recent arrival, a rare African-American candidate. We were all thrilled when she came in—athletic, curvy body, beautiful brown skin, big brown eyes, great face—but James couldn't get a satisfactory image of her, couldn't get her to relax. Rich took her back to the hotel, with Sophia along as a chaperone, in hopes of changing the setting, giving her more time, in a vain attempt to chase away her anxiety.

"It's amazing how you never can tell," Rich says.

James just nods, chewing the edge of his thumb, looking discouraged.

"She couldn't let go," Rich continues. "Great body, beautiful face, but the moment the camera flashed, she was all tense and blank. I tried everything."

"He did," Sophia seconds. "Too bad. Such a cutie."

"This isn't going to sound real PC," Rich says. "And I make no judgment on the cultural merits of stripping, but man, a girl like that, you kind of wish you could have her strip for a while. Three months. There's just something about what they learn, working men over for money, sucking it out of them, that you can't explain. You can't teach. You know?"

James and Sophia nod in agreement. I join in. Yes, things only a stripper knows.

"It's like . . . what we need is a stripper camp. That's it. Summer comes around and off they go to stripper camp for three months. They'd have classes in working the brass pole, mastering the who's-your-daddy expression."

"Touching yourself," Sophia offers. "Bringing hands up thighs, over stomach, and then, for the merit badge, working your breasts."

"They could make their own G-strings in crafts," James suggests.

"And sailing," I add. "Lots and lots of sailing."

The others look at me, somewhat—I fear—accusingly.

"What? You don't want them to burn out, do you?"

It's late in the day and I need to get serious. The dispatch needs work. With reader mail demanding more on James, I've been working on a sequel to the Playboy photographer story, which means I need to get more shots of James at work back in the studio. . . . What? I do.

Fortunately, we're all getting so chummy, James is happy to have me along, even suggests the candidates it would work well with: three friends, three hyped-up giggly young women who insist on coming back together, much as this is frowned upon. But it's late in the day and, while they're certainly cute, they don't look like contenders, so James humors them.

The door isn't even shut when the girls, practically jumping up and down, start in.

"Can we get naked, now?"

"Gol," James says. "Just hold on a second. Now who wants to go first?"

"Me," the tallest of the three says, stepping forward. "So I can get naked?"

"No. We usually start off with bathing suit."

"I want to be naked."

"Well . . ." James laughs, then fires off a Polaroid of the woman, without even posing her. "Okay, have it your way."

The bra and panties are off. Like that, before James can kick me out. And the hands go to the breasts. Which seems ridiculous, trying to cover up . . . and, wait, why is she looking around as she covers her breasts?

"It's up there, behind you," James says.

And she turns in the indicated direction, toward, it turns out, the air-conditioning vent, which she arches up to, hands tugging on— *ah-ha!* not covering breasts—nipples, which when she turns back around are erect, thus changing her breasts' shape, giving them a firmer presence.

This bit of preparation proves too much for the friends, who defiantly slip out of their bras and panties, start in on their own nipples, while doing a bit of jumping around, proclaiming, as they do, their nudity, as in, *We're naked! We're naked!* Merely writing these words, describing this scene, it's impossible not to anticipate reactions, either that I made it up or that I've chosen a nonrepresentative scene based on my sweeping agenda to paint all women as simply dying to get naked for a Playboy photographer.

But I don't really care what people think, am too struck by the moment. Not only am I shocked at their comfort, but there's something else. As I try to get pictures for the dispatch—shots of James taking pictures, with the candidate in the background, ideally her breasts covered by James's arm or the camera—I'm again fixated on my own reaction.

A room full of naked girls. Shouldn't I be feeling something now? No matter how inhibiting the work environment—no matter how effective a brake it can be on the libido—shouldn't my walls of restraint be crumbling in the face of these three joyous nipple-tweaking candidates hopping around like a trio of nudist lottery winners? Incredibly, ice still runs through my system—must I take myself by force again?

"What do *you* drive?" he asks, breaking the long silence. We're throttling along the highway, bodies pressed deep into seats that belong to a black seven-series BMW. Tinted windows.

"Oh, same. BMW. Little older model," I respond. Mine is fifteen years older, heavily rusted, and not something I bought but a sympathy gift from a friend who heard about my mime date.

The black silhouette of forest flickers past. We float over a highway that is desolate, except for our convoy of top-of-the-line, all-the-options BMWs.

"I thought this place was close by," I say.

"This place? No, not this place."

When Vegas and Rich had asked if I wanted to go to the strip club, I'd just assumed it was the place by the hotel where they'd gone the previous night. So, I thought, go for one drink, blow off a little steam, then come back and work. But this trek, I'll be stuck out all night.

"It's worth the drive. Classy. One of the top three. You just wait. You're going to see some hot chicks. But shit, with your job, maybe they won't seem that great. And it's a Tuesday night, some of the hottest girls only work Thursday, Friday, Saturday."

"Oh."

The guy driving me is baby-faced, wears a tight short-sleeve shirt, revealing biceps that remind me of my thigh. He's mentioned that he and his friends, drivers of the other BMWs, own a health club in town, but that's all I know. I don't know his name, how we know them, or why exactly they're driving us.

"But f--k, we've got two hundred and thirty-eight clubs in Portland, did you know that?"

"I heard two hundred and thirty-six."

"Whatever. Most in the country."

"And that's per capita?"

"Buyer's market. These girls, say the word, and they're yours at the end of the night."

"Really?"

"Oh, yeah. They'll stay the night, or until you tell them to take off. And most of 'em you don't even have to pay, though it's probably a good idea, not much, but give 'em twenty."

Stuff like this is going on all the time, isn't it? While I string together one courting disaster after another, with months and months of isolation in between, the rest of you all are waiting for me to go home, and then it's everyone in the hot tub.

"Well, not you. You hand out a few of those cards from the bus and you're good to go."

I'm an inadequate male. The job is wasted on me. The Playboy Search cards, listing all of our tour dates, are prime mating currency. And I've been completely blind to it.

"Oh, and shrimp cocktail. This place has killer shrimp cocktail."

"Good to have you out, Fearless."

Rich and I clink longnecks.

"Good to be out," I respond, sounding insincere, though I mean it. I'm starting to feel that Rich and I could be friends, that beneath our different objectives, we share some worldviews. But at the moment I'm distracted, looking out over a room of naked women.

We arrived at the club and were immediately led to a table with a RESERVED sign. There was much staring as we settled in our seats. One couldn't help but wonder if word of our arrival had preceded us. Or was it that Vegas had forgotten to take off—or, possibly, had forgotten to not put back on after showering—his Playboy Search 2000 crew shirt?

Sitting next to Rich, looking out over the room—predictable smoky glass, brass, white Christmas-style lights bordering stage and ceiling—I understand the term *cathouse*. The way the girls work the room, descend on men slumped back in chairs, it's like peeking through the fence of the neighborhood cat lady, cans of food scattered around yard, the cats pouncing, feeding. The truth is, I've barely been in a strip club before. Certainly never sober.

The BMW guys we came with have made themselves at home, are kicking back and taking long moist pulls off their cocks . . . I mean cigars, as they look out over the room, then setting cock . . . sorry, cigar down and raising up plump pink-hued shrimp to lips.

Vegas, too, appears comfortable, nestled in his own chair in a side room, where this large stripper straddles his legs and loses her clothes. She must be six feet tall, has a mannish face, thick brown hair piled high on head, poochie belly, and the broad expansive ass of a classical painter's dreams. Peering through the smoke, it's like looking back in time, into the private room of some Tombstone saloon, where Miss Kitty is doing her thing, as Vegas, sporting a prosperous belly, ever-present good-buddy smile, keeps one hand on his six-shooter.

"Vegas seems to have found a friend."

Rich rolls his eyes. "He likes the big girls."

"Hi," says a voice, and we look up to see this tall, lovely figure of a woman.

"That's all right, darlin," Rich says, "I'm not looking for a dance."

"But," she says, fingers going to straps of full-length gown, "your friend paid for it." Back in the side room, Vegas, his dancer gone, raises his hand, giving us the thumbs-up. But just as the dancer's hands are poised to drop the long gown, Rich, smiling, shakes his head with impressive subtlety, letting her know she can keep the dance and the money.

"I've got to hand it to you," I say over the music. "This whole thing, it's a little like riding wild horses?"

"Yeah, you've got to let them run a little."

"We're going to be fried after six months, huh?"

"That's if things go well."

As if on cue, Vegas appears. "Boy, oh, boy," he gushes, "I went to stand up, but had to wait it out. That little lady gave me a tingle."

I try to mind my own business, nursing my beer, taking in the sights, geekily amusing myself with jokes I imagine using in response to periodic requests for a dance.

I haven't had a good lap dance since the day my dad kicked my mom out of the house.

You're not going to charge me extra if I cry?

Sweetheart, you're nice, what are you on?

I'm distracted from my routine by the waitress returning with another three orders of shrimp cocktail. These guys love shrimp cocktail. And for a gentlemen's club on a country road a half hour outside of Portland, they look pretty impressive. But there's something else, something my BMW buddy slips her, after which she looks over at us, breaks into a smile. Before I figure it out, though . . .

"Hello, excuse me?" a nearby voice is saying.

As I look back from the shrimp guys, she stands before me, with wavy black hair and brown skin, but light eyes, greenish hazel.

"What's a girl have to do to get your attention, stick my kootchie in your face?"

"I'm sorry?" I say, thinking, *Your parents sent me, and they want you to know they love you, and want you to come home—now, how about that dance?*

"Courtesy of your friend. Just relax."

I hear giggling, Vegas, in the pause between songs. I try to do the Rich head shake, but her eyes close as she listens to the music. The dress falls. My hands suddenly seem . . . where to put them? Or really, where to look? Her breasts are small, pretty, nipples brown. When her eyes open, I smile at her, as in, *Very nice, thanks for letting me look.*

The bottom falls, complicating matters, because with face and breasts, I can kind of take it in all at once. But face, breasts, and rest of body—I would have to break eye contact, which is rude, and has me wanting to apologize.

And the hands, really, what to do with the hands, because aren't they supposed to be reaching out and touching? That's certainly what they're thinking. The immobilization confuses them.

She turns around, presenting shapely ass, but . . . *oh, my* . . . bends over at the waist, ass parting to reveal it all, the whole business, albeit inverted, the star-shaped asshole, then her womanliness, neatly shaved, dark labia, separating slightly, demurely, not at all gaping, just hinting at the inner world, tight entrance to the vagina, inner labia, clitoris . . . and her face, looking up at me, inverted through her legs . . . !

Is this something I'm supposed to know how to do? Was it the subject of some talk I never had? Were this woman and I in a sexual situation, I would feel comfortable, am a great fan of this mystical region, particularly the awesome self-lubricating feature and smoothest of all textures. But as a spectator, am I supposed to think she's enjoying this, isn't tuning out, trying to remember if she paid the water bill? And why are vaginas, which are such an essential fact of human life, so visually unfamiliar to us, to the point that in the seventies women were encouraged by various books to get out the mirror and take a good look at the vagina? Performance artist Karen Finley got into the spirit of it all, invited her audiences to have a look, which led to her getting in trouble with the NEA. And isn't the vagina, or absence thereof, one of the distinguishing features of *Playboy*? It's that line they don't cross, the simple parting of legs, as demonstrated by my friend here to music—and what so many candidates refer to on the bus when explaining why *Playboy* is the only magazine they'd ever pose for, saying they'd never "spread." And why am I *thinking* so much right now? That's the biggest question, why I am not going with it. Because I'm pretty sure, from the looks of my neighbors, that I'm the only one going through intellectual meltdown at the moment.

Clearly, the candidates aren't the only ones who could use stripper camp.

"Ohmygod, yes, I just love it, I love it so much," she says.

It's Shalimar, owner of the vagina, though she tells me to call her Myra, now back in her dress and sitting next to me, responding to my request that she tell me about a passion. She's off to the races, rhapsodizing, delirious with joy.

"Just talking about it, I can't wait for tomorrow. I probably won't even be able to sleep."

The *it* in question is golf. Myra loves to play golf. She only picked it up a year ago, and still isn't great, but who cares, as long as she can play, which she does every morning. She's at the course by six A.M., which means she rarely gets more than three hours of sleep, often less. But she doesn't care about sleep, just wants to find a threesome to join and get on the tee. And at her course, it's often three Japanese guys.

The image of her on the course with three proper Japanese gentlemen who know nothing about her nocturnal activities is a good one. Her story is that she started working here at seventeen as a cocktail waitress, quickly bringing in the majority of revenue for her family. And then, after a couple years, she finally got up the courage one night, after a couple drinks.

"But wasn't it awkward, Myra? I mean, especially that part, you know? Bending over? For a stranger, presenting like that. It's so personal."

Myra laughs at this, or at me. "It is, but that first time, I don't know how to describe it, it was unreal . . . I wouldn't trade that first time for anything."

"Seriously?"

"You want to know the weird thing? It was the first time any man had seen me naked!"

"You'd been having sex with the lights off?"

"No, no." Myra laughs again, a nice laugh. "I was a virgin, such a good girl."

"Wow, if only there were some way to let your customers know."

"I know."

"I'm sure you'd make premium tips."

"But, you know, I'm not one anymore, a virgin."

Myra is up onstage, had to respond to her name being repeatedly called, leaving me again to the troubled terrain of my thoughts. These girls, the Myras, Mollys, and Hesters—you know what? I like them. They're just likable.

It may be lust, however deeply buried. Or it could be the artist/sex worker connection. Like Hemingway and his prostitutes, or all the painters and their courtesan/models—the kindred connection between sex workers and artists, both existing on the fringe of accepted society, both convinced for different reasons the reality of civilization doesn't match up with its idea of itself. Something like that.

Or maybe it's less fancy, more like this: I just like the new model. These women I've been meeting are all about eight to ten years my junior and, judged by their sexuality, humor, and optimism in the face of less-than-rosy prospects, well, they seem beyond the things I'm still dealing with.

Which sets me off on the girl-next-door business. Looking out over this gentlemen's club setting, a place crawling with seemingly uninhibited young women, the obvious connection hits me. The girl-next-door who is comfortable with overtly displaying her sexuality is often a girl-next-door of middle to lower class who is pretty and probably won't be going to college and yet wants something more than just getting married or a boring secretarial job.

It's my guess that there's always been a much greater supply of these women than spots in *Playboy* magazine. Strip clubs simply took the supply and copied the *Playboy* model. Where as Hefner transformed the conventional "stag" magazine into a men's magazine, strip clubs morphed into gentelemen's clubs. Odd, then, that the women working the gentlemen's clubs are supposedly barred from being considered girl-next-door—at least as *Playboy* defines it.

My brain is reeling from so much thinking, and I'm realizing I should find a way to get back to the hotel and dash off a dispatch, when I see my BMW pal making his way back to the table, weaving in a way that tells me he's not a safe candidate for a ride home.

"Did you get some shrimp?" he asks.

"No, it looked good, but I guess they ran out."

"That's f----d up," he says, taking stogie from mouth. "Saw you talking with that chick."

"Yeah . . ."

"Brown-skin."

"Noticeably."

"So," he says, "did you seal the deal? You taking her back to the hotel?"

"Yeah, we'll see."

Having exhausted all possible conversation, there's a moment of awkward silence, during which a dancer steps before us, asks if we want a dance. BMW buddy takes a long puff and then, as he exhales, pulls a card from his shirt pocket, the same thing I noticed him doing earlier. I now recognize it as a Playmate 2000 Search business card, with our phone number and tour dates.

"These boys are from Playboy," he says. "We think you've got a really good look."

I'm over at the bar, alone, wondering if I should fork up the fifty bucks a cab will cost to take me back into the city. I can't keep doing this, not getting any sleep and expecting I'll always come up with material. What if I get home and make the mistake of sitting down on the bed and the next thing I know I'm waking up at nine in the morning and there's no dispatch?

"Hey, I've been looking for you."

"Myra." *You're back.*

We hop up on stools, lean in again. I ask if her dance was prosperous and she shrugs. Not in the mood, she says. Just wants to go home and sleep. She asks why I left my friends and I correct her—they're not my friends, or the muscle guys aren't. I don't even know their names.

"They're here all the time. I don't even think they're old enough to drink legally."

Under twenty-one? Jesus. "So the girls here know they're not from Playboy?"

"Absolutely. Or they should. But the way they're handing out those cards, who knows? Some of these girls aren't real smart."

"I don't have anything to do with picking," I respond. "I'm writing about it. I don't have any say . . . about as much as the muscle guys. The guy in the Playboy shirt—he's not the one, either. It's the other one, with the goatee, in the glasses. He's the man."

"Leif, please. Something tells me Playboy's Miss Millennium is not going to be an African-American, Jewish, and a stripper."

Fair enough. You know, I'm well aware of the party line that every woman in this place was at one time or another the young and unwilling subject of a train pulled by a drunken melange of uncles, stepfathers, and high school guidance counselors, but I can't help thinking Myra is A-okay.

"Myra, I've got to get out of here. I'm going to be up all night with work."

"That's cool. Let me score you a ride. A couple girls are getting off soon."

It occurs to me—*something Suites*—I don't even remember the name of our hotel. "I don't even know the name of our hotel."

She smiles. "Well, you're in luck, because every girl in this place does."

She's so sweet, so helpful, and I've taken so much of her time, and, I'm thinking I need to make it up to her somehow. As we hop off the stools, I hold out a twenty, feeling sheepish. But she just pushes it away.

"Don't be stupid. I don't want your money."

*   *   *

"Are you going to run today?" Sophia asks.

"Too tired. I was up until four-thirty."

"Don't you at least want to put your shorts on?"

"No."

Sophia has seen me running, informed me that the running does good things for my legs.

"You suck," she concludes.

She's joking, but even if she weren't, I'd be pleased to be on the receiving end of these comments. A woman working on this bus, it seems only fair she should get to vent.

"Are you psyched to be going home?" she asks, referring to the brief respite we're allowed as the bus makes its way down the Southwest.

"Excited but worried."

"About what?"

"That I'll start riding the city bus all day, you know, to feel comfortable, and I'll bring a camera, and I'll ask women about their genital piercings, just to keep sharp."

"Honey, this job is messing you up big time," she says. "Ladies, can anyone explain to Leif and me the point of genital piercings?"

One of the candidates raises her head, looks around to see if anyone else is going to respond.

"Yes?" I ask.

"Well . . . it killed getting it done, but after, I was wet for two days."

"Okay, then," Sophia responds, "I guess we have a winner."

Another candidate nods. "Ever since I got mine, I can get off while driving the car."

"Ma'am," I say, mimicking Seamus's cop voice, "do you know why I pulled you over?"

The candidates give this a collective laugh.

"But seriously," I continue, "how do we know you're not doing it at this very moment? And what if everyone did it? What would happen to this country? Everyone sitting all day long, hands free, supposedly working? These labial rings are an anathema to a thriving economy. Employers are going to have to affix genital sensors, ensure you're not getting off on company time. Mental note for business venture: office chairs with built-in monitoring apparatus."

"Easy, cheesy," Sophia says, laughing.

"Is it my fault I kill on the bus, the bus is my muse, these are my people?"

"Why don't you go put your shorts on?"

I'm about to give Sophia a good talking-to about harassment, but her expression stops me. She's leaning out into the aisle, looking toward the back of the bus, slowly mouthing the words, "Ohmygod!" I look, expecting to see smoke, bus fire, but it's something even more riveting. I, too, make the stunned ohmygod expression as I gaze upon that ass.

The ass is in the changing area and because the ass owner chooses to keep her legs straight as she leans in and applies make-up, her butt, minimally covered in a yellow T-back bikini bottom, is pushed out into the open doorway. In fact, it's framed by the doorway, like, you know, that stuff that's framed and hung in museums—art. I think, *I must record its teachings. Then we will construct idols. We will spread its word and people will come to worship.*

A quick aside about this particular body-part obsession. As Jennifer Lopez would attest, we're at once obsessed with the behind and simultaneously intent on denying the obsession. But isn't it natural to be floored on occasion? And come on, it's not like our culture is the first. Need I mention it: bustles? The Victorians were all about booty, to the point that they built grand fake butts into their clothes. Now that's obsessed.

The ass disappears and seconds later the owner emerges. She carries her purse, Prada, and, rather than don the robe, carries it over her arm. She lays it on the couch, then daintily sits down. She crosses her legs, draws a perfectly manicured hand through expertly bobbed hair that has been expensively dyed blonde with frosted highlights. Gold bangles jangle. There's also a gold necklace and diamond earrings. And just when she's established the aura of the prima donna, she turns to the rest of us, smiles brightly, asks how we're all doing on this lovely day.

Someone should open a window, because the entire bus has become too warm, the air uncomfortably still, and not a person on board is unaware why. I'm not exaggerating. No one is unaffected. Watching her sitting there, waiting patiently, smiling away, I feel like I'm watching a lioness lying in the shade, absentmindedly swishing her tail back and forth.

Rich appears moments later, extends his hand to the woman, Nicole, and invites her back. Spotting the look in my eyes, he uses the expression "us," as in "Come back with us," as in *Grab your camera, Fearless.*

Richard asks Nicole to stand in front of the screen. She walks delicately toward it, in a way that makes me want to offer my hand for support. But then, as Richard, with camera held halfway to face, begins explaining what he's looking for, her smile drops and her eyes fix on the camera lens—so distinctly that Richard stops speaking, raises the camera to his face, and fires off a shot. The room floods for a split second with white light. And we're off.

With lips parted, eyes locked, the look on her face is, what? Lust? An implication that life is about sex and only sex? I'm struggling to put words to it, but the experience is ineffable. I cannot take my eyes off her. I have to remind myself to take pictures.

Rich needs no such reminder—and this is the part he leaves out when he tells this story to my embarrassment throughout the rest of the trip. As he blasts away, tossing undeveloped Polaroids to the ground, he assumes an unusual crouch position. For yoga types—*hello, California!*—it's a little Warrior One, left foot forward, only left foot is rotated forty-five degrees to the right.

Rich kind of lunges at Nicole. And as he says things like, "Okay,

great, now..." but before he finishes, Nicole makes an adjustment—cocking one leg out, or bringing arms together to enhance
cleavage, or raising hands to hair as torso rotates, or (my personal
favorite) thrusting hands in waist of T-back and quickly wrapping
them so she is bound by the bottom of her swimsuit, which she seems
to be in act of ripping off.

With Nicole in perpetual motion, under bombardment from
flash, I can feel my heart beating, not only in my chest, but in the
neck, temple, and hands. Not in a bad, headachy way, but in the
manner of life affirmation. She raises arms toward neck and, though
I don't see it, undoes the bow in her top, whisks top off, while
covering breasts, then uncovering, then turning around to give us the
opportunity to get coverage of the butt.

It's in this setting that something happens, something embarrassing. I'd much rather skip over it, assume it's not as bad as I'm
thinking. Allow me this false hope, knowing the truth is about to
come out.

Nicole once again dressed, we talk with her in the studio. James
has come back from his break, and Sophia has joined us, is marveling
at the Polaroids. We're all complimenting Nicole, when someone
points out her envelope. Under occupation it says, "Featured
Dancer."

"I know," Nicole says. "I heard that Playboy doesn't like to use
strippers. All the girls said to lie, but I thought if I put 'Featured
Dancer' that might make a difference."

As in, *I thought if I alluded to the fact I'm a local phenomenon, the
kind of performer whom word has spread about, whom men come from
all over the state to see, that might make a difference.*

We all react in silence to Nicole's suggestion. I have no idea if
Playboy does have a policy—in fact am inclined to doubt it—but
nonetheless, if it were true, Nicole's logic wouldn't hold up. Being
particularly gifted at stripping wouldn't change things.

"That's not better? Should I've put something else?"

We collectively shrug shoulders. Who can say? But we do suddenly grow curious about her full range of activities. Does she, for instance, work anywhere else? Does she have any hobbies that have begun to verge on a career? Besides working out?

"I'm taking a class."

"So," someone says, "you're a student."

"It's just ceramics."

"So, you were saying you're a student."

"Should I do the envelope over?"

"Are you asking for another envelope?"

"Um . . . yes?"

Of her own free will, the young scholar fills out a fresh envelope, and then, with girl-next-door smile and jangling jewelry, tells us to have a great day, and is gone. We watch the finishing-school walk across the parking lot, witness her gracefully slide into a convertible BMW, hiking her long skirt a few inches as she does. As she hits the ignition, punches the gas, and squeals, ever so daintily, out of the lot, her license plate is briefly visible. The plate reads: KANDI.

We're back to lounging, all recovering from Kandi. Were any of us smokers, surely we'd be lighting up. I'm trying to bring my heart rate down, trying to remember my name. Unbelievable. I'm content to bask in the afterglow of those heightened feelings, not to mention a bit relieved that Rich has chosen not to take this chance to talk to me about what happened inside.

"So," Rich says, rejoining us, "you should have seen Fearless in there."

Here it comes. F--k this. I hate being embarrassed.

"What did he do?" Sophia asks, sitting up.

Rich takes a seat, rubs his hands together. Jesus, he's really warming up for this one.

"Well, we're doing our thing, going through the poses, and Kandi knows what to do—let's just say she's a prime candidate for director of stripper camp—and everything's going fine, when all of a sudden . . ." Rich pauses, letting out an actual hoot of pleasure.

"What, Rich, what'd he do?"

I want to be somewhere far away. Is the *Mir* space station still vacant and aloft?

Not to stall, but I wish I were more up to the task of portraying Rich here. While everyone's personality is fractured, part sane, part crazy, Rich's parts are as distinct as anyone I know. There is the corporate machine who made me so uncomfortable when we first met in Chicago, the Rich who goes before local news cameras every day reciting party lines, but there's also this other Rich. Rich as he is now, telling this story, is funny, wickedly funny, make-you-gasp funny, shock-you funny. I just wish I could capture his humor better. . . . Okay, I'm stalling.

"Fearless, who's been totally silent, all of sudden"—and here Rich's face changes, the voice dropping down to a decent impersonation of Bill Murray in Caddyshack—"he goes, Fearless goes, 'Oh, yeah! That's it, that's the stuff. Just like that. Nice.' "

Everyone but me is laughing. Laughing hard. Maybe you had to be there, had to be a little punch-drunk, but this comes off as hilarious. They're crying with laughter.

"That isn't accurate," I plead. "He's exaggerating."

The truth is, I did speak up, did contribute maybe a word or two. Just enough, I thought, to fit in, to justify myself with the camera, things like Rich was saying.

"I'm looking back," Rich continues, "hoping, hoping he doesn't go, *Who's your daddy?*"

Again, exaggeration. As I said, I was trying to fit in. And, okay, maybe it did sound like it was slipping out, but I'm new to this and, watching, there was something incredible about it.

"And I'm giving him this look, like, *Shut the f--k up, Fearless, I'm trying to work,* but he just keeps going, 'Oh, yeah, more of that, yeah, baby.' "

I never said "Yeah, baby."

*   *   *

It's after two A.M. I'm in my hotel room, surrounded by laptops and diskettes and cables and silence. While some of my co-workers are out who knows where—at a strip club or judging a T-shirt contest, this nightly routine that's part recruiting, part chance to blow off steam from the bus's surprising decorum—I'm as usual sleep-deprived and hunched over the computer.

And I'm writing about it all, writing an apologia to my readers, which I plan on running with the last day of Portland's dispatch. I don't know how it happened, but I have become my father in this job. Not that my pop ever worked a job like this. But the work ethic. Aside from being at the strip club, it's been all work, crazy hours. These hotel rooms, up alone at all hours, typing frantically, a couple thousand words a day, six days a week.

Never again. That's what I'm telling the readership. I promised them a great voyeur experience. Somehow I got suckered into respon-sibility. I should be ashamed. I beg for patience, the understanding that on the next leg of the trip I'll be a new man—reckless, hedo-nistic, someone they'll be proud of—when I'm startled by pounding on the door.

"Kandi?"

I don't say that. Actually, I'm pretty sure it's some boyfriend I've offended, come to hurl me around the room, break the computer over my head, so I'm not quick to rise. But the knocking continues, sounds like a boyfriend with multiple arms, an octopus boyfriend beating on the door.

Through the eyehole I see multiple sets of eyes, all trying to peek back in at me, but they look familiar, so I open the door. The crew, except for Butch and Seamus, are standing before me, all rocking back and forth, like they're riding a ship in a storm. There are lipstick marks on Sophia, kiss prints on cheek, forehead, neck.

Ohmygod, I missed it, they're saying. It was unbelievable. She was . . . unbelievable. They couldn't believe it. And Sophia had never had a lap dance before. And she couldn't get over the ass and

Vegas says that Sophia got a tingle. And Sophia says she may have gotten a tingle, but why not, because she rocks. That girl rocks. She just totally took control and was so sexy and funny and not like anyone else in the whole place. And I really should have been there.

I try to shush them, telling them they're going to get me in trouble.

But wait, wait, I have to listen. It was Kandi. They're talking about Kandi. And she really was brilliant, like, amazing, you had to see it. She said she prefers dancing for women, because they're nervous, and polite, and usually a little surprised to enjoy it. And yes, yes, that's where the kiss marks came from. And Sophia's ankle, she didn't know it was so sensitive before.

And I'm right back in the bus studio, my chest again thumping, senses reeling. Gone is the tranquil self-possession I'd been enjoying in the hotel room, the sense of purpose, the monklike work ethic, the chuckling over work well done. It will take me hours to come down from this.

"You guys have to get out of here. I'll never get to sleep now. I can't hear about Kandi. Don't you understand? Please go."

They don't care. They don't want to stop talking about Kandi. She was so brilliant. I tell them I'm sorry, but have to slam the door in their faces.

The country is on fire, one of those days that supports the view that the globe is indeed warming. In Portland, the AC units that cool the bus and tent are failing. As with other Day Threes, things are hectic, and many of the candidates, in deference to the heat, exit the bus with clothes thrown over their shoulders, wearing only bikinis and heels.

This image—one young woman after another stepping out of black bus in scant coverage, striding across the searing asphalt, wiping brow and looking for keys, all with apparent self-confidence—I can't help imagining our candidates spending the day like this, trucking around town in such skimpy covering, with a demeanor that asks: *You got a problem with it?*

Slumped on the couch, eyes closed, I've got my material for the day. It includes our first candidate with a prosthetic leg, Helen. It was a birth defect, which led to her being a poster child throughout her youth. She says she loved being the center of attention. She also loves leading a very physical life—gymnastics, dancing, and bikini contests.

Unfortunately, those activities all take their toll, wearing down the skin and bone that remain, so that over the years she's repeatedly gone into the hospital to have more of the bone removed, the skin reconfigured. Her big problem is that she's exhausted the bone below the knee. Doctors have warned that she's close to losing the joint, which will drastically alter her mobility, and with it her ability to do the things she loves

Of course, she's always wanted to be in *Playboy,* ever since discovering Dad's copies in the bathroom. She only wishes she'd worn her high heels to the audition instead of her stupid running shoes. "High heels are to a woman like cotton candy is to a kid," she says.

"Why didn't you wear your heels?"

"We couldn't get the foot off my leg. It's a new leg and they put the foot on too tight. I have different feet at different angles for different shoes. My boyfriend tried. I tried. I just about broke my hand trying. My boyfriend looked at me and said, 'I don't want to see you crying,' and I said, 'Baby, I don't want to go to this audition not wearing heels.'"

It's worth pointing out, as this first part of the trip comes to a close, how subjective is the version of life on the bus I've presented here and in the dispatches. Later in the Search, interviewing a candidate who really, seriously looks a lot like Barbie, the doll—and who will eventually become a Playmate—I ask her something about her desires. Hers is a simple vision: She sees a house. A big house. One of those big houses high up on a cliff over Malibu.

Yes, and . . . ?

She just wants to live there. That's it. She wants to live in this big beautiful castle high up over the ocean. She has no idea how she'll end up there, in the Malibu Barbie house, but that's it. In talking to her, I recognize my tunnel vision, realize that versions of her are passing me by every day, neglected, in my prejudice, in favor of candidates with missing legs, or grandchildren, or drill-sergeant ambitions.

Here on the couch, thinking about heading home, I can't believe how fried I am after only nine days. It feels good, having risen to the challenge and not freaked out. If only . . . if only there'd been *something*, a little romantic interaction, just a glimmer, enough to refresh my memory of the life I once knew before this return to virginity.

At least I seem to have stumbled for a moment into the semblance of a career. And isn't that what people focus on when love isn't within reach? It's going to be tough, though. Somehow I don't thrill to the prospect of returning to my lonely lair up on the hill over Echo Park.

That smell. Someone has just taken a seat next to me and, eyes closed, I call it: "Aveda."

Aveda is a line of hair and beauty products now widely known, but when I was in high school and deep in the throes of first love, it was a little-known Minnesota company. To know Aveda's products back then was almost to be part of a secret society.

"Good nose," the voice says.

I open my eyes. The woman is friendly looking, but beyond that I barely notice her, so mired am I in lugubriousness. She has brown hair, no visible makeup, a tan skirt, tank top.

"I work at a day spa. I'm an aesthetician."

And I'm a Chippendale dancer.

But she goes on to tell me about her spa. It's located in a log cabin on the outskirts of town, situated next to a creek. It's a really cool place to work, and I should come and check it out. She gives facials, but is going to school for massage, is almost certified. People are always telling her how amazing she's made them feel, and she loves that.

Funny what a little passion will do. The mention of the log cabin and her glowing commentary on her work actually pushes me up to a sitting position.

"Let me take your picture," I say, uncharacteristically direct.

"Okay," she says, laughing. "Now?"

No, I say, we'll wait until they put her in a robe. She asks what we've been doing at night. I tell her about my isolation, staying up all night, my runs. I leave out the strip club. She in turn tells me about Portland nightlife, mentioning one club she thinks I'd like.

There's something about her face. I can't help staring. It's a bit asymmetrical, but in a stealthful way, so you feel like you're discovering her beauty, that you're the first to see it.

"What are you going to do when you leave here?" I ask. "Go home?"

"Go home, check my messages."

"Are you a message person, are you the type of person whom friends call?"

"I'll have a few."

"Playboy gave me this pager, but it never goes off. I can barely justify a regular phone."

"I'm sure it's not that bad."

"No, it's not a sympathy thing, I have lots of friends, I'm just not the type people call . . . but who'll be on your machine?" *Do you have a boyfriend?*

"My sister, friends."

"So what do you think you'll do tonight?" *I want to ask you out.*

"Probably do something with my sister, go to the club I was talking about."

I glance over my shoulder at Richard and Sophia—they're sitting on the other side, toward the front of the bus, laughing about something, doubled over in tears—then turn back to the candidate, whose name, according to her passport, is Eve. Speaking in the hushed voice of a conspirator, I say, "I'm not supposed to . . . I don't . . . I'm not sure I'm supposed to do this."

Eve sneaks a look over my shoulder, seems to appreciate my situation.

"Maybe you could call me at the hotel when you're going? We could meet there?"

"Great."

We're both smiling at each other, a bit nervously.

"Let's get you in a robe, hon," Sophia calls out, causing Eve and me to both start.

We meet in the changing area. She's in her robe and we stand facing each other. I hadn't noticed her height when we were sitting down—she's almost my size, just shy of six feet tall. We grin at each other, in this little space, which would all be pleasant, if I weren't aware that this rising nervousness is the exact thing that tends to shut off my brain, leaving me nothing to say. I decide to get out of here quickly so she doesn't get spooked.

"What do you want me to do?" she asks.

"What do you have on under there?"

"Not much."

My heart thumps against my chest like it's trying to get out. It turns out she was here the day before. She'd only come to hold a friend's hand and hadn't thought much of it, but to her surprise, James was interested, which made her think it might make sense to actually take a shower and look nice. That's why she's here, hadn't resorted to the pretense of a bathing suit. So much for me "discovering" her beauty.

"Actually, just stand there. You look cute just like that."

"Smiling or no?"

"No smile."

I take the photo, capture her ignoring my direction, flashing the beautiful smile.

"That's great," I say, voice again hushed. "We'll talk on your way out."

I return to the waiting area, fighting to play it cool, affect the mild-mannered persona of a guy just doing his job. Fortunately, nobody's paying attention, so I can take my seat, pretend to go over the photos in my camera.

The only problem is, I start to listen to my co-workers' conversation. And I don't know how it's come up or whose point it is, but they're talking about Hefner and his feelings for the candidates once they actually become strong contenders, likely Playmates. The word is, Hef's very protective, that he tends to pull the Playmates into a tight-knit family that we can't be a part of.

Eve is in the studio for a long time and when she finally emerges I'm waiting to give her a bunny tag. We tell each other it was nice to meet, engaging in uncomfortable playacting. Sotto voce, I confide my last name and hotel, and she says, "Around ten o'clock." And that's it. Were I not feeling in need of a hit of oxygen, I'd actually describe my behavior as smooth.

James comes out, his eyes and mouth comically wide open, a stack of Polaroids in hand.

"That girl is ho-o-ot," he says, a boyish crooked smile breaking out on his face. "I'm telling you. Darn. Awesome legs, rocking natural chi-chi's. I think we've got a Playmate here."

My stomach drops: Eve = Playmate = Hef's tight-knit family.

The Polaroids are passed around, with "Wow" and "Mercy" the primary reactions. The stack is coming to me, prompting a moment of indecision as I wonder just what the gentleman's code of conduct says about viewing stacks of Polaroids showing one's upcoming date naked.

They're remarkable. It has to do with the angle at which James has shot her, but Eve is a giant, with long, strong, perfect legs, round hips, narrow waist, and extremely full breasts of the sort people no longer believe can be real. It's the body of a woman who could take off in a spaceship with a payload of drone males and colonize a new world.

How did I get myself into this mess?

There's something about being in an upscale metropolitan hotel at night. My room is softly lit and reflected back at me in a sweeping wall of windows. Out beyond, Portland at night looms. Being multiple floors up, the reflection/view combination has me floating among the city lights, as close as one can come to life among stars. It's beautiful, and romantic, and would only be improved upon were I not alone.

Which I am. Alone, that is. I'm trying to work—casting envelopes scattered all over the queen-size bed—but am doing more pacing than anything. The phone sits silent, refusing to ring. It refused to ring at nine, nine-thirty, ten, ten-thirty, and all points in between. Now, at ten to eleven, it seems clear that it *isn't* going to ring, because even if Eve were to decide she wants to call, she'd be embarrassed to have waited this late. It's equally clear that if the phone does ring, I'm not going to pick it up, because it would be embarrassing to be alone in a hotel room this late on a Wednesday night—Mr. Big Playboy Guy.

That leaves the awkward question of what to do with myself. It's awkward because the only place I can think to go is the club Eve mentioned, and there's a chance she'll be there. I'm guessing it's a small chance, given that she's blowing me off and would want to avoid running into me. But still . . .

The phone rings, scaring the shit out of me. It's lame that I'm here alone this late, isn't it? Don't I have anything better to do? She's going to know I'm desperate, which kills the whole thing. I clear my throat. *Shake it off, Leif. Dude, be cool. Answer the phone as a normal person.*

It's crowded. I hear that right away. And it's Eve. We exchange hellos.

"So," she says out of nowhere. "We're here."

"Cool," I choke out, hearing *we're* and remembering her mentioning doing something with her sister.

"I'm with . . . my boyfriend and a good friend of ours. I told them about you and we'd all like you to join us, if you feel like it."

It takes my nerve-wracked mind only a moment to look up *boyfriend* in my internal dictionary and discover that it is indeed the word I thought it was, one that lists no synonyms such as, *see also, sister. God, I can't get a f----g break.* How could I so totally misread this woman? How will I ever tell people I was on the bus trip, met ten thousand women, and never managed to have sex? With those kinds of numbers, you figure there might at least be *accidental* penetration—fly becoming unzipped, candidate in changing area, losing balance and falling onto my penis. . . .

"I know what it's like to be in a hotel room in a strange city and not know anyone."

The thing I can't figure—and don't have a lot of time to wrestle with—is, which is worse: sitting in my hotel room after this chain of events or cabbing it to the bar and hanging with the boyfriend? They're equally repellent options, but the sound of Eve's voice and her apparent empathy . . .

"Are you sure I should come?"

"Yes, we'd love you to come," she responds, and promptly tells me how to direct the cabdriver to this joint. Which is how it's settled, with me not really deciding, but heading for the door, wondering not if I'm about to feel humiliated, but rather *how* humiliated.

I see them the moment I walk in the door. Through the crowd, by the windows. I try to walk suavely, heroically toward their table, but the message doesn't make it to my legs, which instead take me to the bar. The bartender immediately offers to make me a drink, for which I could kiss her. As she turns to pour my Jack Daniel's with a splash of Coke, I see out of the corner of my eye that Eve is on her way over. For a half second, I contemplate turning around and sprinting out the door.

"Hey," Eve says, "we're on the other side."

"I know. I saw you."

I've never seen uncut diamonds, but I'm guessing they're rough, surprisingly rocklike, and that their transformation at the hand of a diamond cutter must be miraculous. Eve's appearance brings this to mind. Not that she was a rock before, but the metamorphosis is something.

She wears a long, charcoal gray straight skirt. Her top is also gray, but a shade lighter. I don't know what to call it. It's strapless and form-fitting, like wool that has been stretched over a hat form. It's basically a tube top, but a tube top from the forties, giving her the appearance of a classy vamp, a modern femme fatale. And her hair is twisted up, held by a lacquered chopstick, formal but messy. It's possible to look equally good, or as good, with different qualities. But not better. Wars have been fought over women like this.

My friend the bartender brings me the drink, and I take a big slug, one hand on the bar to steady myself.

"Are you going to join us?" Eve says, a bit puzzled by my desperate thirst-quenching.

I take another gulp, making sure to act like this is normal, like, *In my country, it's tradition that when we enter a drinking establishment, we always stop at the bar and chug down a mixed drink, especially when we see the party we're joining only ten yards away.*

Eve stares at me, head slightly cocked, puzzled puppy, and then grabs my hand and leads me on.

Stiff Jack and Coke aside, I'm feeling a little tense as I sit down. Actually, I'm wondering what's taking the waitress so long to come over and suggest another round. The boyfriend, Jared, let's immediately establish, is big. He's Cro-Magnon big, with heavy brow, strapping arms. There is not a moment's confusion about who could kick whose ass.

He wears one of those Kangaroo hats backward and bobs his head slightly, not to the bar's music, but to an internal hip-hop soundtrack. Were I forced to make a snap judgment, I'd have to say he seems like the type of guy who, born mildly retarded, was abandoned by his family in the inner city to be raised by a pack of urban wolves.

The waitress finally arrives and is in the process of taking our drink order when she lets out a terrible scream—"Ohmygod!"—and goes running out of the restaurant. In testament to the level of tension at our table, no one comments.

I sit next to Eve, across from Jared and his friend Dave. Given Eve's arresting appearance, I don't feel comfortable giving her more than a sliver of my peripheral vision. So I'm looking at Jared and Dave and manage not to say, *I'd like to make babies with your woman.*

Dave breaks the standoff, asking, "So what's the deal with this job—you travel around the country looking at naked women in the back of a bus?" Pleased to have a pitch I can swing at, I launch into a few 2000 Search anecdotes—tales that inevitably lead to the statement: *That's the greatest job in the world.*

Issue of Playboy raised, Eve has a question. She knows I'm only along for the ride, that I just do the column, but is curious if I have any sense of how she did. My first response is a pang of hurt, the apparent confirmation of my dark fear, that this is why I was invited out.

Simultaneously, though, I'm thinking, *Eve, are you kidding, do they not have mirrors in Portland, do you not know that if there were any justice in the world they'd change the magazine's name from* Playboy *to* Eve? I'm also thinking, or rather *wondering* how Eve will like life in Echo Park as my personal sex—the word *slave* has a negative connotation—companion. Sex companion.

My response is guarded. I don't share James's comment about having found a Playmate in Eve. My hedging is based mostly on my own fleeting knowledge of promises made at auditions that don't always pan out. Instead, I stick with deductions based on what is apparent. They asked her to come back. They worked extra with her. Both Rich and James got involved. These are all positive signs.

Eve is thrilled. It would just mean so much for her to get in *Playboy,* which is the first disappointing thing about this woman. She seems to have everything going for her. I don't get it. Why would someone like her care?

It's not, she says, about affirmation. "I mean, I realize I'm pretty." But there's something else. It would just mean something, something tied in to her sexuality, and freedom, and parents, and cutting ties.

She's not sure how to put it into words, just that it would be "freeing."

How big a factor lust is in my thinking, I can't say. You hear Playmates or celebrities making these statements about the freedom of posing and you want to gag, draw their attention to the other incidentals—money, fame, vanity. But the way Eve speaks, struggles to put her finger on it, it's at least one of the more honest, most explicable statements I've yet heard on the subject.

The conversation continues, leaving *Playboy*, moving off into life and dreams. And as I register what's happening, that Eve and I have shifted to impassioned, flirtatious conversation, I feel the need to pull back, literally—shift my chair toward the table, break the connection with this woman, ask the guys what they do for a living, how much they can bench.

But just as my hands take hold of the seat, a funny thing occurs: I ask myself *why*. Yes, why should I try to win these guys over? Why not indulge instead in an honest display of emotion, reveal the obvious, that I'm interested in Eve? Why abide by the chivalrous code that you don't go after someone's girlfriend when the guy has shown no indication of being worthy?

So, we talk and I'm feeling it, that freedom Eve alluded to, the freedom of breaking a personal shackle. I mean, how dumb have I been all of these years, worrying that guys I'll never see again will like me? And in the midst of this sprawling conversation, Eve looks over at Jared, still puffing a cigar, rocking his head, looking menacing. "To Jared, that's all there is to life. He thinks it's all penis size and f-----g."

I can't help but wince, noting as I do that my adversary's implied ace in the hole is, for me, a bit of an Achille's heel. I mean, don't think I've inspired a great deal of locker room insecurity. But that flash of fear is outweighed by the confirmation that my sensors weren't entirely off, that she's not *that* into this guy. It seems a payoff, a reward of sorts, for that Hemingway moment, showing my cards.

Seconds later, the missing waitress returns. "Sorry about that," she says breathlessly. "My dog ran away a month ago, and just now, when

I was at your table, I saw him peek in the doorway. I don't know how he found me. I just started working here. It's kind of a miracle."

My heart is pounding like it's trying to tell me something. And so are my head, feet, and every other inch of my body, thanks to the sound system in the club we've relocated to. The club is densely packed with attractive, smiling men. If I hadn't already been suspicious of the relationship between Jared and Dave, hadn't detected in Dave's fawning proximity a certain adoration for his big buddy, the fact that the two immediately mount a stage platform at the front of the club, whip off their shirts, and started reenacting the dance sequence from *Cruising* would have certainly raised an eyebrow.

Jared's funkin' up a sweat over his powerful torso as a sea of dancing men approvingly look on. And the fact is, the guy can dance, especially for a big man. It's strange, though. I would have pegged Jared as the type to roll members of this gay crowd in a dark alley, and here he's doing something else entirely, leading them on.

Eve says we should go for drinks. She picks an opening in the crowd and dives in, looking over her shoulder at the stage. As the crowd swallows us up, she takes my hand. There's a lot of staring as we pass through. The men, particularly the drag queens, look Eve over from head to toe, with a gaze that seems part confession, *If I were to make an exception, she'd be it.*

When we're finally at the bar, though the thirsty gyrating men are four deep, a bartender picks Eve out. Two beers arrive, along with two tequila shots, which Eve and I quaff down with a gusto that would please a cowboy but hint that neither of us is, at present, perfectly centered. She again takes my hand and leads me back, not to the stage and her boys, but to the center of the dance floor, the crowd's dense epicenter.

"We live together," she says, "My appendix burst. I nearly died, didn't have insurance, couldn't work for a while. He paid for everything."

Ah-ha! I think as we continue holding hands, sneak looks toward the stage, which is obscured by a towering drag queen with full-on tropical fruit Carmen Miranda hat. Carmen smiles at me in that way people smile admiringly at couples who strike them as enviable. *Yes, I want to say, we're exactly the attractive, sexy, happy couple we appear to be. Isn't life uncomplicated?*

"I owe him a lot of money," she says, pausing to take a sip from her drink, without for a moment breaking eye contact. "He has this thing about giving me his credit card, just when I'm feeling shitty, and telling me to go shopping, or his mom . . . they, his parents, have a lot of money . . . she'll ask me to come with her, and I admit it, I like to shop. It's stupid, I know."

My heart is really straining now, tugging at the reins. There was already chemistry, lust, drama in the mix, but now the damsel-in-distress angle, a woman needing to be saved—sadly, I'm not beyond responding to such signals. *She can come on the road with me, order room service all day until I come home at night, and then . . .*

"I know I've got to get away from him."

I hear sirens. Whistles. It's in the music. Carmen has danced away, revealing that the platform is now devoid of Jared and Dave. . . .

"Yeah," I shout in her ear, feeling like I should say something, while thinking of Jared and our contrasting arsenals: he—manly, brash, moneyed, sexually confident; me—artsy, introverted, a Playboy employee, a sexual fixer-upper. "I was surprised. I didn't get it."

"He thinks we're engaged."

We're holding hands, and still locking eyes, and my sense of violating the Code is particularly acute at this last admission. I'm pondering whether targeting someone's fiancée is different than going after a girlfriend. And I'm wondering if we're about to kiss, followed by a movie moment—you know, hand tapping me on shoulder, me sucker-turning to it, huge fist rapidly approaching, lights going out . . . coming to as Carmen Miranda bestows mouth-to-mouth.

"Did you see my pictures?"

Polaroids, with their inimitable contraband quality: Eve, slumped down on couch, divine legs, from low angle, resembling parallel lines heading off to infinity . . . sheer underwear pulled tight . . . flawless stomach, stretching up to miraculously natural, feed-a-village earth mother breasts. But the New Me is incomplete, because I can only scrunch up a didn't-hear-you face and say, "I'm sorry?"

She asks again, looking deep into my eyes.

Yes, I saw them, and while I was embarrassed, being a shy guy, there was a part of me that wanted to cry at how beautiful your body is. But at the same time, there was that fear, intimidation, Eve looking in those pictures like a mountain and me imagining myself in miniature, in lederhosen, struggling to scale . . .

"No," I say. Then, cringing at what I'm saying, "I guess I should have."

There's a shift in the crowd and suddenly Jared appears, still the badass but now covered in sweat. He assumes a posture that tries to say he just happened on us, but his eyes suggest otherwise.

"They're closing," he says. "Let's get out of here."

There's talk of hitting an after-hours spot, but Dave needs to go to bed, so we drop him at his car. He gives me his card, though we hardly spoke. He *does* seem incredibly nice, particularly fond of Eve. While this is going on, though, Jared and Eve must have talked, because when I get in the car, she tells me that there's been a change. Jared is going to drop us off at the after-hours place and then we'll both have to cab it at the end of the night, if I don't mind.

I manage to not yell out something inappropriate like, *Hooray!* I envision Eve and me back in my hotel room, in this unbelievable, soul-melding session under the covers. If the whole trip is going to be like this, I really *am* gong to have to track down god and personally thank him/her.

Jared, whose furrowed brow is visible in the rearview mirror, is bumming. The big man is sullen, hurting. I feel bad for the guy and for a second think I should say, *No, I should be calling it a night, too,* but then the New Me kicks in again with, *Too f-----g bad, yo, 'cause when the two gangstas go into the jungle, only one comes out.* The New Me insists on creating new clichés.

Though the car is shaking with hip-hop, things seem strangely quiet. Eve sneaks a look over at Jared. And what I see in her face gives me a sinking don't-put-the-condom-on-yet feeling. Jared pretends not to notice her, continues staring ahead, and it's then that I recognize what that sneaky lug is up to—he's stealing a page from *my* playbook. He's trying to look sensitive, to feign feelings. *The sneaky motherfu . . .*

"Are you sure you don't want to come out?" Eve asks.

Of course he doesn't. He just shakes his head resolutely. And then—the cunning bastard—he turns to face her head-on, with his jaw set, looking tough, but then, if you look closely, it might just be those eyes are a little watery. Just a touch, the hint of tears. Of all the nerve!

We pull into the parking lot. A line is rapidly forming as we hop out. I tell Jared it was nice to meet him, thank him for showing me the city, careful as I do not to twist my thanks, give them a gloating quality, because I really don't bear him any ill will.

Now, Eve, if you'll just say good night and swing that door shut. Her hand is poised . . . door ready to swing on its hinge. *C'mon, Eve, you can do it.* Instead, she walks over to me.

"Hang on for just one second. Sorry. I've got to talk to him."

"No problem," I say, while thinking, *NOOOOOOOOO!*

They're in the car. I'm standing in no-man's-land between the ever-lengthening line and the car. Jared continues facing forward, Eve is turned to face his profile. The talking isn't animated, but the way he's not turning, hanging tough, well, the physical politics really, really suck.

Finally, the door opens. Eve gets out, but doesn't close the door, which is, of course, not good.

"I'm sorry," she says, shaking her head. "It just . . . we talked . . . I have to go back."

At this moment, with her fumbling for words and not standing up straight, she's the antithesis of the woman who was talking about what being in *Playboy* would mean. She's a goddess fallen to earth. I'm crushed, and more than a little embarrassed. But seeing her beaten down is the worst part.

"You could still check it out. It's a fun place," she says hollowly. "Or we'll drive you to your hotel. Whatever you want."

As was the case at the night's beginning, there's a moment when I'm calculating the less humiliating option. I say, "No, let's just call it a night," and head for the car. I could have salvaged some pride, opted for the club, but slinking back into the car, I'm hit by an unexpectedly good feeling. My actions have been an admission that it was all about Eve. I've revealed myself, shown I was battling for her. I just happened to lose.

Several uncomfortable minutes later, Jared pulls up to the hotel and I thank him. Eve gets out with me and we share a big hug. I kiss her on the cheek. And then, still holding each other, we face off, break into smiles. I don't think Jared can see our heads from his angle—we're in his blind spot. We could actually kiss here, which is what the smile is about, I think. I'm imagining planting one on her and then running for the sanctuary of the hotel lobby.

At the same time, there's an aspect of this that isn't particularly funny. The part that has to do with me returning to the room alone, sleeping alone, suspecting that the trip will pass this way. What it really came down to is the one moment when I blinked, fell short of the New Me. *Did you see my pictures?* That, for me, was the failing. Not owning up, not saying what was in my mind, not meeting life's challenge.

"Someday," Eve says as we separate, "you should write about women who can't . . . can't get themselves to leave men who they know aren't good for them."

Los Angeles, California III

And then I woke up.

Or so it would seem. I'm back from the road. Back at a favorite old drinking haunt, the French joint where I once took my mime date, now standing among a crowd of my pals, like the old days, two weeks ago, as if I'd never left.

Perhaps I never did, merely nodded off mid-drink, long enough to register a particularly vivid dream. I might suspect such were it not for all the attention being focused on me, as if it were my birthday, which it isn't.

"Don't believe a word he says," I overhear my friend Estella telling another friend. "I know for a fact he's been working the drive-up window at his neighborhood Jack in the Box for the last two weeks. Couldn't make the rent, too proud to tell his friends, so he made it all up."

Meanwhile, another female pal whom I'm talking to stops me midsentence. "No offense, but with your job, I feel like you're staring at my chest and judging me. It's creeping me out."

Later, I happen to mention that my computer is in the trunk of my car, and suddenly I'm out with a couple male friends, hunched over the open trunk—as if conducting a drug deal—showing them photos from the road, to their disbelief. One of my best buddies, Wayne, is there. Wide-eyed, he keeps saying, "That's *not* your job.

That is *not* your job." And then he vows to join me at some point on the road.

Another friend politely asks if I've, you know, gotten lucky. I explain how chaotic it all is, mention my uncertainty over what's permissible, but refer to Eve, allude to a bright future.

Back inside, someone's friend who used to dance with the London Ballet insists on showing me her legs, hiking her skirt in the process, revealing the instruments of her livelihood, joking about my taking pictures of her naked. And then not joking.

For those who haven't had the pleasure, life in LA pursuing one's dreams means—for a substantial chunk of the populace—doing nothing ninety percent of the time. It's all about waiting for something to happen, to the extent that when something does happen to one of us, the report of the happening provides temporary sustenance for everyone else.

Such is my mini-celebrity status that drinks are bought for me throughout the night. Soon I'm so swept up in the adulation, and sufficiently well lubricated, that I dare to offer a former girlfriend bra size advice:

"The thing is, it's the wrong size, okay? This B-business, it's craziness. I think I always thought, the way you were kind of shoehorning yourself in, but I didn't have the . . . vocabulary to talk about it. You're not a B. Not at all. B-plus, maybe, more likely C-minus. It's not something to be embarrassed about. It's incredibly common, bra missizing. Nobody really talks about it . . . and the sizing system is all wrong, isn't comprehensive enough. . . ."

By the time I notice her face—equal parts bemused and concerned—it's way too late to suggest I'm kidding. My only option, I feel, is to see it through to the end.

"Laugh if you want, but that doesn't change the reality that I'm right and you'd be a lot more comfortable if you took the time to locate a bra maker that makes a larger B or a smaller C and then stick with that bra. That's it. I've said my piece. What you do now is up to you."

I know what she's going to say before she says it. Yes, I know the job is changing me, that in a million years the old Leif would never be talking like this. And I also know what she'll say beyond that: that she's glad I'm enjoying myself and earning some money at what I want to do, but what about the novel? Is this all worth giving up on the bestseller?

"Do you . . ." she begins, apparently feeling awkward spitting it out, "I mean, you're not driving tonight, are you?"

Were I not totally convinced Burt is on my side, I'd be a little uneasy at how hard he's laughing right now.

"Fearless Reporter," he chokes. "Well, I'll never spoil your secret."

Yes. Ha, ha. That's a good one. I'm laughing along with him. Because I did come up with the name, intended the joke. Only, I'm not sure I appreciated what an outright joke it is.

"Fearless Reporter." The laughter continues. "Paging Dr. Freud, paging Dr. Freud."

My shrink manages to collect himself, dry his eyes. I've been giving him the skinny on the trip, an encapsulated version of the foregoing. And we talk about all the characters I'm meeting, and how I seem to have gotten over my chronic napping issue, and the unique nature of the writing job, and how it's exactly what I was after.

Having finished listening to my update, Burt is ready to make a pronouncement: "This job of yours has saved you a lot of money, not to mention a lot of time spent in that chair."

"Yeah, if you'd only told me happiness is so easy," I say. "Dependent on just a few ingredients—exposure to thousands of women, getting paid to write whatever I want, traveling around the country in a million-dollar bus—I would have opted for it years ago."

Now we're both laughing.

"The only thing," I say, not knowing where I'm going, but knowing, like a good patient, that something is there, "is . . ."

"What? Don't edit. Spit it out."

"I just, I think, being back in my place, the treehouse, I think of the years that've gone by, the world down below, me going in circles . . . and . . ."

"Yes?"

It's the way they look at you. Therapists, these students of faces, know the moment you're vulnerable and they pounce, give you this particularly understanding, compassionate look, and the tears start welling up. . . .

"And . . . it's . . ."—and they're streaming now, those cool slippery trails, the odd misfit tear making its salty way into my mouth—"it . . . it's f----g depressing, thinking of that, f----g bleak, and I'm just worried, that's it, I'm worried, or scared, whatever . . . I don't want to go back to that. When this is over, I don't want to give it all up, end up back there, cut off like that. . . ."

"You won't."

"I'm not so sure."

"Trust me. You won't. You've come too far."

I grab a tissue, wipe my face dry, now feeling like laughing, the rush that follows a good cry. "But what if you're wrong, what if all this other advice has just been lucky guesses?"

Ha, ha, ha.

I must have been speaking fast, must have blurted all that out, because Burt isn't reaching for the appointment book and sneaking a look at the clock. I see we have fifteen minutes left. Given my usual halting, qualification-after-qualification manner of speaking, that uncensored fluidity must've revealed more to Burt than anything I actually said.

"I was thinking . . . the other day . . ." I begin, no idea where this is going, "I was in my car, at an intersection, waiting for the light to turn yellow . . . this woman was in the crosswalk, catching the afternoon light. Big brown eyes, and a short skirt, high heels, a lot going on as she walked. There was a truck, to my left, beat-to-shit pickup filled with gardening equipment, and in the cab four men, wearing straw cowboy hats, brown skin darkened by sheen of dirt and sweat, like a workingman's Mount Rushmore. Enormous smiles, as they watched her pass. She looked lost in thought, but then something brought her out of it, and she looked to the side, to the truck, where the four did something amazing. . . ."

"Yes?" Burt prompts.

"They just kept looking, kept smiling, as she walked off. . . ."

"Have you thought of hanging out at construction sites?"

"It wasn't that. They weren't whistling. But they also weren't hiding. And they were right. She looked great, in that light. It was beauty, and those guys celebrated it."

"And you?"

"Pretended to change the radio station."

"And why do you think that is?"

"Because I'm an idiot."

"Well, there's that."

"And that gets me back to the bus. . . ."

I tell Burt about Vegas. How he's like those guys. On the bus, he's a kid in a candy store, loves the proximity to women, loves looking at their pictures, asking questions, getting in their space. There's an innocence about it, about his obliviousness. He's like a kid in that he doesn't know any better, doesn't even know what boundaries are, what the word *inappropriate* means.

Or does he? It's hard not to wonder if deep down he knows more than he lets on.

"He's my anti-doppelgänger—with his cluelessness about propriety. I'm excruciatingly conscious of my every look, thought, word, and deed. And while I fantasize about being like those gardeners, able to look at a woman with appreciation, the thought that I might be a Vegas makes my skin crawl. So I'm stuck, and I'm sick of it, and I feel like I'm the only one."

There's so much I'm not saying, now that we're getting into this, so many other confused, paradoxical feelings I have about my sex. It's everything:

Going for runs in the evening, the way women walking alone will hear the rapidly approaching footsteps and whip their heads around, their faces filled for a moment with terror.

Or growing up with a sister, watching her dating emotionally arrested guys, stupid guys, mean guys, dangerous guys—guys who have more than earned a good roughing up, but are so pathetic and doomed I can't bring myself to do it.

Or women friends who, at some point in their life, usually college, have had a sexual experience involving too much alcohol and something less than consent. Or less fuzzy stories, full-on rape—good friend dragged into an alley. . . close to being killed.

Even bathroom graffiti—who writes it? It's not me and it's not you, but who is it? Who walking among us feels compelled midshit to scribble out that thought about women being whores or all loving it in the ass? And in the same vein, those moronic letters I get from readers: "I want pussy" and "Send me porn." Who *are* these men?

Had Burt and I time to get into all of this, I know what his question would be. He'd turn it on me, ask what this list of offenses has to do with me: Why should I feel this guilt on behalf of other men? I'm not like that, so why not just go ahead and smile when I see a beautiful woman? A good question.

"I wonder if you ever considered going to a prostitute."

What? Is he just testing me, assessing my desperation? "For sex?"

"No, for investment advice. Yes, for sex."

"Ouch."

I already kind of know Burt's theory on this, his quaint septuagenarian's view that as a general rule people place too much emphasis on sex, make it too big a deal. But a prostitute? Pay for sex? I've never had a problem with women. Have been *pursued* by women, smart, sexy, highly desirable women.

Okay, maybe since moving to LA, where the penniless, overly self-deprecating, nice-guy struggling writer figure lacks the cachet it does in other parts of the country, things have been on the decline, but . . . paying! Just exactly how pathetic does my therapist think I am?

At last, Burt is moving for the appointment book.

"This is an important area. Can we meet again before you leave?"

"I'm getting on a plane tomorrow." But so what? *Suggest a phone session, dummy. You know there's more. What about Eve, not admitting looking at her pictures? And the deeper doubts, about sexual potency, particularly when in the presence of others, a condition you've christened situational impotence.*

Don't you think after all these years it might be time to bring this up?

"Well, when you get back. . . . It's going to be fine. I can't tell you how thrilled I am about this job. This is the payoff, when things like this happen."

"Yeah, just in the nick of time."

We're standing up now, coming together for our hug. We hug. Two men hugging, an act that after years still makes me a little tense.

"Okay, now go out there and live. And don't think so much."

Right. Live. Don't think so much. And—as my neurotic mind can't helpfully suggest—prostitutes. He was kidding about that, right?

A rooster crows, but, thanks to the acoustics of the valley down below, sounds much closer, like he's in my yard, a ventriloquist rooster. Up above, a hawk soars motionless, riding a thermal updraft. I'm sitting on my balcony, which, perched as my place is at the edge of the hill, gives the perspective that I, too, am aloft. Given how rotten the balcony's wood is, there's always the chance that I'll actually take flight, however briefly.

I have a million-dollar view from a condemnable home. My landlord has asked me not to use the balcony until he fixes it, along with the severely cracked foundation, but I can't oblige. This is where I work. Countless hours were spent here working on the bestseller and, with a day off, I could be taking advantage, getting back to it. While I do have my laptop open, am typing away, I guess we all know that's not what I'm doing. Even the hawk sees through me.

I'm typing in my journal. This period of time right after therapy can be especially productive. The session is over, but the mind still spins, has been woken up. Ensuing thoughts tend to be of the more revelatory variety. And after this last session, I'm flashing back to a summer during college.

I was attending a summer session in upstate New York, was supposed to be taking classes so I could tack on a second major to my BS in business administration, but on a prescient whim I'd also signed up for a photography class with a renowned instructor—the sort of teacher who's a favorite to generations of students.

He must have been in his sixties, perhaps seventy, but his agile mind made him seem decades younger. As a lifelong bachelor who lived with his mother and was said to have been close with famously controversial photographer Robert Mapplethorpe, he also may have been homosexual.

This teacher had a small cabin on a ridge in the low-lying hills of the Catskills. There he'd bring small groups of favored students for wine, cheese, and mind-expanding conversations in front of the fire. Oh, and saunas.

The sauna was homemade, a compartment built around the fireplace's chimney. It was the size of a phone booth, only big enough for two occupants—rather cozy, especially for the guy who ended up in there with our teacher. And one night, toward the end of the summer, I arrived to learn that everyone else had bowed out. I would be the only one.

The wine was barely uncorked when my teacher asked to take my portrait. While I wasn't thrilled about the idea, the shots he wanted were just of my face. I was fully clothed and, thanks to the coolness of the night, even wearing a sweater, so I said sure.

After he finished a roll of film, he mentioned another project he had in mind. He was working on a series of images, philosophy-related, something about Heidegger's theories of being and time. He and another photographer friend were exchanging interpretations through the mail. To illustrate his theories, my teacher suggested—this being Heidegger—I'd need to be naked.

"Hmm," I responded, instantly concluding there was a limit to which I'd go for art. "I'll think about it, but I'm guessing no." He merely smiled, eyes twinkling, in a way that suggested this response was absolutely fine with him.

Then, postsauna—I wanted to decline the sauna, but couldn't devise an excuse—as we were staring into the fire, both squatting down, arms wrapped around knees, talking about the photo series I was working on, he suggested a massage. Right there on the sheepskin rug. As with the sauna, I didn't know what to say. I kept thinking, *Don't be rude.*

It was probably a good massage. He applied authentic massage oil, just like a masseur, but my body, laying face down, was never able to get much beyond living rigor mortis. The fact is, I'm on the uptight side, even struggle to be comfortable naked around girlfriends, so relaxation under the circumstances wasn't in the cards.

"I think that if everyone gave and received a massage a day, war would be less common," he said as he rolled me over.

Panic began to set in. Having my chest worked on, my stomach rubbed, my thighs kneaded, without so much as a fig leaf for cover, and knowing, were I to open my eyes, his eyes would be looking into mine—*help!*

As my instructor ran out of surface, he said something about the end of the line. I began sitting up, feeling guilty about being so uptight, but glad the experience was over. At that moment my teacher, with a graceful flourish of his hand, brought his index finger down on—*ohmygod*—my penis! He gave the end a little tap, made a sound like "*Boink,*" and concluded, "all done."

Unf--kingreal! Was that a pass? Had I been harassed? Would I have to start appreciating Bette Davis?

Or was he kidding, playing with me, making light of my tension?

Or something different, a philosophical riddle I should have understood?

It's easy to ridicule people who naively blunder into absurd situations, unless you've been there yourself, on the sheepskin rug, getting your johnson *boinked*. Having undergone the experience, my internal alarms tend to go off when, for example, I witness three women getting naked for a photographer. I'm concerned that they should be more careful, more on their guard, even in just signing releases. And—to bring it close to home, as Burt would surely have me do—that I not be confused with one of the bad guys.

Actually, there's one other mental gem from the sheepskin encounter. It's a true classic from the errant-thought department, was there among the welter of confused feelings: *Even here, I wish it were, um, bigger, particularly at rest, because, it just seems like,* boink? *Come on, that's not the sound effect of the well hung.*

Albuquerque, New Mexico

◆

Never having been to a bikini contest in my life—never, incidentally, ever *thinking* I'd go—I hadn't imagined there could be both bad and good bikini contests. But as my current assistant and I cab down an unlit two-lane highway, through desolate terrain that is greater Albuquerque, it hits me that the bikini contest in my head may not be the same one we're headed to see.

Somehow I hadn't known about Albuquerque's gang problem until the cabdriver—with a foreboding "Good luck getting a ride back"—drops us off. The bar is a little rectangular cinder-block structure on top of a small rocky rise. There are two squad cars in front of the building, and at the entrance two enormous bouncers. One passes a metal detection wand over my body. The other frisks me—my first physical intimacy on the road.

Vegas is in what is intended to be the VIP area, right in front of the dance floor. It has been so designated by taking one of those long brightly colored plastic cords with the beer flags hanging down and wrapping it around a series of stools as a means of roping off an area around two tables.

"Seventy-two bucks," Vegas's hoarse voice cackles as we approach. "They're competing for seventy-two bucks tonight. I got a hundred if we do it in my hotel room."

This was Vegas's idea. Rich, Sophia, and James are still on hiatus.

Day One, Albuquerque, had been brutally slow, so it seemed sensible to do some recruiting. But seventy-two dollars? It's a squalid sum. Something tells me Miss Millennium isn't in the house.

When the competition finally gets under way, there're only three competitors, two Latinos and a dyed-blonde gringa. The one I'm drawn to is one of the two Latinos. Rather than a bikini, she wears tight black jeans and a black sleeveless jeans top. The top is short, though, so a decent amount of her ample flesh spills out. And she carries a squirt bottle of pale yellow substance that I guess is cooking oil, though darker minds might suggest urine.

Vegas, meanwhile, can't take his eyes off the blonde. She isn't particularly pretty, has a sharp nose, small eyes, and a general worn-down look. But I know him well enough to realize that with the dyed-blonde hair, large fake boobs, and strong bikini body, he's powerless to see a face.

"That chick's hot," he says, upending another brew, as my own stomach sinks. On his shirt he's wearing a HELLO, MY NAME IS . . . sticker, slapped on at an odd angle. But instead of his name, someone's written a more ominous word: J U d g E. This could be trouble.

The contestant in the jeans is brilliant. Understandably, one might have anticipated a theatrical removal of clothes, a crafty appeal to the power of revealed flesh, a literal showing of bikini in compliance with the "bikini contest" theme. One would have been wrong. She's competing in a bikini contest wearing denim.

I'm already screaming myself hoarse—her biggest and only fan—when she starts in with the oil. Raising it high before the crowd, still strutting, Ms. Jeans upends the bottle, gives it a good squeeze, and sends that golden oil streaming down on herself, where it's promptly wicked by the heavy fabric and succeeds merely in darkening already dark material. Pointless. Nonetheless, she goes through the motions a contestant would go through were she actually in a bikini, and as the oil streams down she rubs her hands over her jeans.

I bang on the table. I whistle through my fingers. I yell with what's left of my voice. I don't care if I'm the only one who gets her. Including the contestant herself.

The crowd favorite is number two. She's busty, though not at all huge, and very much real, in the sense that her bikini top rides distinctly lower than it would if she were sporting augmentation. The bottom to her suit, instead of being cut high on the thighs, is a pair of little shorts—a tactically wise move, considering her substantial hips and booty. And as for working the crowd, she does little more than walk back and forth a couple times, hands on hips, a don't-mess-with-me expression on her face. The boys love it, achieving with their applause the decibel level of a crowd several times their size.

The blonde is last. Clearly a veteran of the bikini wars, she hits the dance floor with smile firmly affixed, dancing around with sufficient energy to get her bust bouncing as much as silicone will allow. Periodically, her smile transforms to a wide-mouthed "Wow," as if the crowd were going crazy, which it isn't. They barely acknowledge her, beyond hissing and whispering, *"Puta."*

Vegas, in confirmation of my worst fears, gazes on reverently. He watches with every ounce of concentration, clearly moved, to the point that he's oblivious to the rest of the crowd—like a parent watching his child portray a tree in a play, unable to imagine he's watching anything other than theatrical genius.

"I think it might be time to call a cab," I say to my assistant, who couldn't agree more. "Use the Playboy thing, offer a twenty-dollar tip, just get someone out here."

The MC has each of the girls step forward again, giving the crowd a last chance to weigh in. Again, I'm alone in worshiping the girl in jeans, the room explodes for girl number two, and Vegas is in thrall to number three. The MC heads to the VIP area. I wonder if there's time to run for the cops, who're still stationed outside, or if I should get ready to take cover under the table.

After a brief consultation with Vegas, none of which I can hear, the MC heads back to center floor, face clearly betraying surprise.

"Ladies and gentlemen, this is unexpected. The judge from Playboy calls it a tie."

I breathe out, loosen my grip on the table as the chorus of "Bull-shit" rings out across the bar. I see scowling faces twisted in confusion and dismay.

A showdown commences, girls number two and three battling it out for the seventy-two big ones. This time it's even more lopsided, the catcalling less whispered, more mean, and Vegas still beams. When the MC finally comes over, he daringly hands the mike to Vegas, relinquishing any chance of censoring the verdict.

"Any sign of that cab?"

"Not yet, but the guy had heard about us being in town . . ." my assistant says.

"Dis . . . dis was real tough," Vegas says. "Extremely difficult."

At least a couple members of the audience break into laughter.

"The guy said they'd definitely come out here. He said, 'Be careful until we get there.' "

Once again, it's too late to get the cops. *Vegas, don't do it.*

"It's a shame in dis sort of thing that one person has to lose."

See beyond the hair color, beyond the boob job, to the real possibility of mayhem.

"And really, let's say no one is a loser. Not by a long shot. So the winner is . . ."

It's that moment in Russian roulette. . . .

"Two. Number two."

When the roaring finally dies down, long after Two has claimed the seventy-two crumpled bucks fresh from the register and Vegas has been surrounded by short, stocky men with shaved heads, all patting him on the back and holding out beers for him, we hear the blaring of a horn, see our escape out the window. As we race out, it's impossible not to think, *It's good to be back.*

I'm in the back of the bus with a living angel. She has long, very straight sun-streaked blonde hair, parted on the side, held back with a barrette, freshly cleansed Dove-girl blushing skin, and a lovely serious smile. It's a face that is as sweetly beautiful as any you've ever seen.

Raj, the current photographer, is loading film into the Polaroid. He doesn't look up, absently suggests, "Toss your robe on the couch." Which she does. In fact, she folds it, lays it down, then takes her place before the screen, hands clasped behind her back, naked but for the black pumps.

"Oh . . . okay," Raj says when he looks up. "They did tell you you can wear something for this? It's whatever's comfortable, so you're fine, great, but just to be sure . . ."

Raj, by the way, rivals James in the sensitivity department, particularly with his aversion to breast augmentation. Several women in Albuquerque mention their imminent operations, asking if they can send additional photos to Playboy of their new appearance, and Raj, a dimunitive man of Indian descent, his face distorted à la Munch's *The Shriek,* groans, "But no, no. They're perfect already. Please."

I know, I know what you're thinking, *Yeah, the Playboy photographer was trying to talk women out of boob jobs?* But that's what happened, repeatedly.

Getting back to the current, very naked candidate: Her white cheeks do not color, no more than the light pink they already are. She merely shakes her head, chin up, indicating she is fine, waiting. She has no tan line, with the body the same ivorylike coloring as the face, a marvel to the rest of us, who look like death when pale. Against the white, her nipples, like her lips, are crimson. And for those who pine for a bygone era when beauty was equated with carrying extra pounds, know that her thighs and butt are fuller than we're used to seeing.

"Do you know when this would happen, if I were to be picked?"

"I don't know," says Raj, "but the search is going on for another four and a half months, so not until after that. Is there a problem?"

"I didn't know if I should write it on my envelope. I'm four months pregnant, so it would have to either be now or sometime after the birth."

"Well, we'll just note that," Raj says, picking up the envelope, which neither of us had yet looked at. "And it looks from this like you just had a child?"

"Yes, she's just five months old. Turns out I got pregnant on the first possible cycle."

She still stands naked, arms still clasped behind her back.

"Well, you look amazing. Seriously," Raj says, as I nod.

"Thanks. I've actually got three others. All girls. This'll be my fifth."

"And one child with cerebral palsy? That must be difficult. This is quite an application," he continues, handing it off to me. "We're very glad that you came down to the bus."

I scan through familiar terrain—married, mother, 35C, from Colorado (meaning she drove hours to get here)—until I come to the final section. The hobbies, special skills, additional comments section. She's written: *I volunteer as a pediatric AIDS worker, which I consider a great honor.*

"Can I see?"

It's Vegas, who's been sitting on the couch this whole time, ostensibly working on the laptop computer, though I'm pretty sure he doesn't even know where the power button is. Why is *he* here? I keep thinking there must be some reason he needs to be in the studio every time a woman is naked back here. I have vague visions: a scandal, the cover of *USA Today*, my having to get a lawyer, being doomed to live out my life in a Kato Kaelin-esque fame limbo—all because of Vegas.

Incidentally, there's a perfectly innocent explanation for the fact that I keep ending up in the back taking pictures of candidates without their clothes on when we all know I'm not allowed to have any nudity on my website. See, the studio's digital camera broke down this morning, so it just made sense, Raj and I agreed, that we should work together. That way, we have pictures for the premium subscribers without candidates having to go through poses twice, and I don't have to give up my camera. That's why I'm in the back so much.

Day Three is coming to a close. I'm back in my room, staring up at the wagon-wheel chandelier, contemplating the parade of candidates Albuquerque has thrown at us: The old-fashioned burlesque dancer who, in her act, lights parts of her body, saying, "There's not a part of my body I can't burn." The candidate, just divorced, who drove three hours with her son, mother, and grandmother. The ninety-something former-Ziegfeld girl candidate. The professional motorcycle racer. And last but not least, the candidate who spent the day in jail.

Her name was Carmen and she was speeding—hauling ass, apparently—in an effort to make her morning audition time, when she was pulled over and dragged to the police station. Dressed up for Playboy—makeup, tight clothes—she was tossed in a holding cell, with a mix of offenders divided between those who wanted to get close to her ("There were girls in my cell who *liked me,* but I'm sorry, I don't go that way") and those who wanted to beat her up.

She endured six hours of hard time before her sister heard her phone message, bolted from work, gathered bail money, and took care of the paperwork to bust Carmen out. And yet, Carmen's first request, upon attaining her freedom, was to ask her sister to take her down to the bus to see if it wasn't too late. That is, after she took a shower.

I took her picture in front of the bus—and it was a good one. I'd asked her if she wouldn't mind crossing her arms in back, suggestive of cuffs. The crossed arms, combined with the twisting she must do to face the camera, nicely enhanced the visible contours, in a way that James would surely have appreciated. Topping it off, Carmen had flashed a sweet *Mona-Lisa*-of-the-slammer smile.

When I'd asked her why—why it was worth spending a day in jail—she said, "Because it's dead here." It's the same line candidate after candidate has uttered on the road. It reminds me of a conversation I had with one of the Playmates at the kickoff party. Explaining her life, she said, "I lived in Omaha working forty hours a week doing data entry, now I'm in Los Angeles at the Mansion. It seemed like a no-brainer."

It all makes me think of the circus. Way, way back, before the Internet, and video games, and really affordable cocaine, the big top was the diversion of choice, and the expression "to run away with the circus" meant something. When they picked up stakes and headed on, tagging along was a means of escaping, seeing the world. Today it would be running away with the band.

It suddenly—and, you might add, finally—strikes me: We're alike, the candidates and me. When I was a kid, I wanted to be a clown. Desperately. At eight I had the makeup, the costume, the application to Clown College in Clearwater, Florida. Books occupied a similar space in my childhood. There, too, life was more fun, more surprising—more big top than suburbia.

Laying here in my Wild West bedroom, having become a student of these candidates, it seems such a funny realization, that we have this shared desire for something different.

"Get out here."

Must have nodded off, after all that thinking, but I'm holding the phone to my ear. "Leif, are you there?" Raj asks. "I'm telling you, there's something about her, past lives or something, your kind of girl."

By the time I make it across our hotel's sprawling parking lot to the distant corner where the management has permitted us to park the bus, it's too late. She's already back in her clothes. Raj introduces me, not by the Fearless title, but by my name.

"Like the Viking?"

It's a small thing, her making that connection, but a good sign and has me feeling an immediate bond with this candidate, Daisy, and wanting to take her picture. So she changes for me, back into her nonflashy, very functional two-piece, gray with blue trim. But the body is a riot: foal-like legs, narrow hips, and full breasts that have an air of the new car about them—not that they were just purchased or have that smell, but rather, only recently developed. It's the improbable Barbie body that men are accused of expecting women to have.

"I know, it's not much to you professional pervs, but in this cow town, I'm kind of the shit."

Since the bus is empty, I might as well take advantage, shoot some pictures of her out here, against the black background of leather couches. But I've never posed someone lying down, so it becomes something of a test. Raj hangs back as I maneuver Daisy onto her stomach, propped up on elbows, legs raised, and ankles crossed. As I study her through the lens, I can't help but notice that the cleavage is impressively enhanced by elbows and gravity.

I ask Raj for a critique and he pronounces it quite good, says it's very close, only suggests that I ask her to cheat her butt up a little. Which I do, and though she says, "That's real comfortable," you can see the curves multiply, achieving the flex James spoke of.

Her eyes—slow, languid, blinking—are gorgeous. There's something about them so dazzling that they remind me, each time the lids rise, that eyes really do reveal a world within. And the feeling she radiates with those eyes is a strong sense of herself, of not trying to work the camera, of being indifferent to its opinion of her. Or am I just saying I really, really like her ass?

We talk as I take these shots, me loosing a volley of questions. She was at the pet store in the mall looking at the little doggies, thinking about buying one, and her aunt—who raised her—called her pager. The aunt had seen the news and said, "From the looks on TV, the competition's not real stiff." And as to what brought her by, she said, "Haven't you looked around? If I can even get a trip to LA, then hell, yeah, I'm thrilled."

I have Daisy stretch out on her side, ask her to cheat her hip up and twist slightly, her torso coming a little forward. More curves.

"You like your job?" she asks.

"It's growing on me."

"Taking pictures of these loose women all day?"

"You're being too hard on yourself."

The eyes again close and open softly.

"Do you limit how many you sleep with in a day, or do you avoid restricting yourself?"

It's great just to be out of the bus's confining photo studio with its gray-carpeted walls. Against the black of the couch, Daisy pops out. And, with Raj back in the studio, I'm alone with a willing model. The situation feels so ripe for so much more. Yet my lack of knowledge and my self-consciousness acts like a governor on what this could be. The impotence of it all.

"And what's your husband going to say about this posing?"

"Yeah, right. Not married now, nor, if I can help it, will I ever be."

"Let me guess, you have a boyfriend, and he's the greatest."

"I have a boyfriend and he's kind of a dick."

Sadly, I'm out of poses and Daisy has to rush off to school. She's in college, works as a greeter at the Wal-Mart, and is on her way to medical school.

That night, after a solo dinner at a bar—the candidates weren't kidding, it really *is* dead here—I review my Daisy images. She reminds me of the Sphynx, propped on elbows, poker-faced, the knowing youngster. And instead of covering up my feelings, I let the Fearless Reporter go off in the dispatch, really wax on about her desirability. Since nothing's going to happen—Playboy can't object to fantasy—it feels like the first time I have some real freedom.

Daisy, I write in open embrace of my predicament, *we'll always never have Paris.*

Austin, Texas

———————————————◆———————————————

I'm just stepping out of the hotdog-mobile. They gave me a tour, the hotdog-mobile crew. The promotional vehicle of one of this nation's premiere processed meat companies, the giant hotdog on wheels is on its own search, touring the nation, casting their next national commercial advertising campaign, which will feature one lucky child singing their famous hotdog song. And we're staying at the same hotel. Using the same parking lot. Giant pink weiner and black Playboy bunny bus. What are the chances?

As I bid the hotdog crew adieu—and incidentally, the mobile weiner is much smaller inside than it looks, and a mess, not at all in the same league as our bus—I'm wondering if it's not a sign, running into the hotdog. I'm torn between interpreting it as an omen and letting go, concluding that sometimes a hotdog-mobile is just a hotdog-mobile, when I'm stopped in my tracks.

"Oh, wow," she—curling-iron-curled brown hair, short skirt, pretty legs, small B-cup—says. "You're the guy, the Fearless Reporter. You look just like your picture. I've read every word of the coverage. That bikini contest in Albuquerque was so funny. What's that hotdog doing here?"

This is a first. Recognition from a candidate. It takes me a second to remember when I put a picture of myself on the site. I guess it was when we were back in Portland and I was writing about James.

There was that shot of me with my hands around that candidate's waist, with the caption below that read, *I've got a mentor.*

I escort my fan onto the bus for her appointment. It's Day One in Austin and things are slow, enough so that I was touring a hotdog. The low turnout is a surprise. Austin is one of a handful of platinum Playboy towns—municipalities that possess the critical combination of a bounty of attractive women and a pro-Playboy stance. Texas in general is supposed to be the Playboy promised land.

Rich, who is back with the bus, is off trying to solve the Austin dearth. But Sophia is on board, and with our lone candidate in the back studio, we're free to catch up. She complains that living on the road screws up her sense of time so badly that, back home, it took her the entire break to readjust. And then she comes back to the bus, making her feel disoriented again. But she wants to know about me.

I take her through some shots stored on my computer, while catching her up on the bus: the we're-on-a-road-to-nowhere vibe of Albuquerque, the nudity overload, and my breakthrough of posing Daisy. Sophia laughs, saying she has to get this on video for the movie she's been meaning to shoot of the bus. She's had her video camera along since the beginning, but rarely has time to use it. I'm not sure it's such a good idea, getting me on tape.

"Fearless," Sophia says, taking a closer look at the computer. "These photos are hot. This Daisy, what a babe. Sexy, sexy photos."

"You don't think I'm going to hell?"

"Honey, relax. You're not in hell. You're just on fire."

Back in my room, late at night, I take a break from scraping together a dispatch to check my e-mail. My heart stutters for a moment when I see it come up on-screen. It's a note from Daisy. The first candidate to have written me, she declares: *My dear Viking, I hate Paris anyway.*

She hates Paris? For a second I don't get it . . . and then I do. It's an allusion to my line about us never having Paris. I'd written a whole passage about lusting after these unavailable women, and

Daisy has apparently read it, read those thoughts. It suddenly occurs to me: *Holy shit, people are reading this stuff!*

Of course, it's *obvious* people are reading it. I've received hundreds of e-mails from readers. But the process has been weird: all those nights in hotel rooms, the rest of the world sleeping, my never printing out the copy, but rather just sending impulses over the phone line—it has felt more like just keeping a journal.

Reading and rereading Daisy's note, it begins to hit me that people are traipsing along with me, seeing me as a character in a book. They're clicking on these dispatches with their morning coffee, reading the current installment.

But it's real, I'm not a character. This is my life.

There's something about a dozen attractive women dressed up for a night on the town. It's a synergistic thing—the result is a sexual wattage greater than the sum of its parts. As the bus heads down Austin's main drag with a load of gussied-up candidates, the men on board are all climbing the walls. It's actually physically uncomfortable. Enough with the pretense, would you girls please get your clothes off and commence with the orgy?

Day Two's casting had proved to be another bust, so Rich was forced to take the drastic measure of corralling all the cute women to audition the last two days—the twelve on board—and take them out to create a buzz about Playboy's being in town.

We barrel along, Sophia playing DJ; Vegas, bartender; and Collin—the cameraman from Playboy Video who's rejoined us for the day—taping as the candidates lean out the window, waving and blowing kisses to stunned males.

The bus pulls up at our destination, which appears to be, from what I can see through the window, your typical softly lit cajun-influenced jazz supper club. The bus hasn't even pulled to a complete stop when the men start gathering, many out of breath, having just caught up with the Pied Piper.

"Girls! Girls!" Seamus shouts over the music. "Shut those windows now!"

The girls oblige, leaning back in and sliding tinted windows shut, all still smiling brightly, buzzing on wine and adoration, showing no signs of being affected by Seamus's angry tone.

"Rich, man," Seamus says. "It's a friggin' zoo. I'm supposed to control this?"

Rich steps closer to the windows, peeks out. Glassy-eyed male heads keep appearing on the other side of the windows, as if mounted on pogo sticks.

"We should be all right," he says with some uncertainty. "We'll get the club's bouncer to help us clear a path first, then we'll bring the girls out."

I've got men on my back. They're pressing enough so that if I were to step aside, four or five would fall to the sidewalk. I have my arms stretched out, serving as the blocking back between Vegas and the club's security monolith, which makes shooting my photos a special challenge. But I whip out my camera just as the door swings open.

Collin slips out first, camera on shoulder, his small floodlight illuminating the bus door, as the first of the girls hits the bottom stair. She's one of the prettiest, a shorter Cindy Crawford, wearing a full-length slinky shimmery baby-blue dress. As the guys begin to surge, and I have to sink down into a squat and drive back with my thighs, I get a shot of her lips blossoming into a smile.

It happens eleven more times. Eleven more candidates step off the bus and meet a surge of love. I fight back the scrum, take photos. It's funny, isn't it? These are local girls, largely no different from women who are already in the club, or from the girls these guys were chatting up before they gave chase. And yet with this context—Playboy, the bus, the concentration of cute women all dressed up—these girls-next-door have been transformed into Playmates.

Inside, the honorary Playmates are grouped at small tables in the far corner, in a roped-off VIP section. The club takes its security seriously, and with the girls in the corner, Seamus has a much easier job keeping guys away. Meanwhile, Rich and Sophia are in conference, she appealing to him to at least buy these girls drinks in exchange for coming out. But Rich doesn't like it, fears a budgetary blowup.

"Rich, come on, they've given up their night for us. We've got to do *something*."

Outside, men are tapping on the restaurant's window.

"Hey, Seamus, please, get those guys to move back—and keep the candidates away from windows," Rich says. He turns quickly back to Sophia. "We told them they were going to have to pay."

He wants to end the night, pack up and go home, before I've managed to get my dispatch.

"Rich," I say, butting in. "If it helps, I think the website would be okay with picking up part of the tab."

Rich considers this. For all I know, the bar tab will be coming out of my own pocket, but the night must go on.

"Thanks, buddy. Okay, we'll buy a couple rounds, but that's it. No food."

Still, nothing happens. The girls have their drinks, but segregated in the corner in a subdued jazz place without the magic of the bus or adoration of panting males, the night is going flat.

My co-workers aren't helping. While Seamus stands guard, the rest have taken a booth together apart from the girls and, between sneaking looks at their watches, have the hangdog look of a group of employees trapped at a work function. *What the f--k?* Would they really rather be back at the hotel watching cable?

Think, think. Look at them, forlorn, staring into drinks, the power of that sexual wattage radiating out into the night. Imagine what the readers would think if they saw. . . .

And that's it, the readers. Something about getting back to them straightens me up.

"Seamus," I say, holding out the camera, "do me a favor here."

I slip between the young Cindy Crawford and another candidate, this one vaguely Hispanic, equally soft and lovely, and ask, "Would you two mind very much if we took a picture together?" and before I finish they're already sitting up, a sparkle back in their eyes, leaning in to me, their different perfumes commingling. "Only, it's for my readers, and if you can play it up a little, you know, like . . . like you want to . . ."

And here, for a split second, I see my co-workers shooting me dirty looks, as if they can't believe the cheeseball lengths I'm going to. *Well, kiss my ass, you guys.* . . .

"Yeah, like you want to, um . . ."

"F--k you?" says little Cindy.

"F--k me, exactly."

Their lips bookend my cheeks, so moist, cool yet hot . . . someone's hand grabs my hair—*Ay, caramba.* There's a flash, with Seamus saying with a laugh, "You son of a bitch."

"Hey, what about us?" a voice calls out from a table of four candidates. "We want a chance."

"No," says another candidate from a table of three, "over here."

The clamor escalates, all the candidates asking to pose. It's inescapable: I'm on to something.

Time passes like it must for toddlers playing in those pens that are filled with colored plastic balls. You know, those fast-food-restaurant rumpus-room things, where the kids jump into the balls, swim around in them, and sometimes get sucked under and need to be rescued? In my case it's not plastic I swim in but rather lips and breasts and moisturized legs. Like an ecstatic tyke, I throw myself into the piles of girls, over and over, never questioning, just enjoying.

Partly in response to the photos, partly in response to the round of shots I buy, the night begins to accelerate. A few civilian suitors break through Seamus's line of defense. Collin breaks away from the grumblers and starts chatting up a couple candidates. And he's followed quickly by Bruce, a freelance writer doing a piece on the bus.

Bruce writes for several of the leading men's magazines, usually about sex. It's the sort of career I might be headed for after the bus. Passing the table where he sits, I can't help hearing one of his two tablemates—a busty blonde with hair piled high, looking vaguely like Dolly Parton's fresh-faced niece—saying something that piques my curiosity. I hear "baby-sitter and fresh sheets." Of course, a normal person would pass by such a conversation without giving it a second thought, but not someone who's developing a mental divining rod for the salacious.

"Yeah," she says, as I slip into a seat, pretending to be working on my camera, "we're not gay, not really even bi, at least I wouldn't call it that . . . but it's nice, every so often, maybe once a month, to get together, have fun, make each other feel good, in a safe situation. . . ."

Bruce responds, expounding on this trend toward female bisexuality over the last ten years, sharing research he's surveyed, and contrasting male and female bisexuality, all of which is of great interest to his tablemates.

"Nice going, Fearless," Rich says. He's propped up against Sophia in the booth. They look toward the tables, shaking their heads at the display, candidates no longer nicely seated, now up around their tables, dancing provocatively in this low-lit club, some with men they've just met, others with each other. "Yeah, Leif," Sophia says, taking my camera from me, "thanks in advance for the bags I'll be sporting under my eyes tomorrow morning."

She works the camera, starts reviewing images. Her sour expression begins to recede, teeters on the edge of a smile, and finally gives way as she spots a shot of me sitting with a candidate in my lap, the bunny tag hung around the girl's neck wedged at that moment between my teeth.

"Vintage dispatch, Fearless," she says, laughing. "Your readers will be sick with jealousy."

"Like anyone with a natural gift, I'm not sure I deserve praise," I respond, finishing off my third—or is it my fifth?—Jack and Coke.

Rich has also taken a look. Pensive, he sets the camera down, takes off his glasses, and gives his face and eyes a good rub.

"Remember at the beginning those shots he was taking of women outside the bus?"

"All those shots of girls in their jackets," Sophia adds.

Yes, yes. I know, I know.

"And then there was Kandi," Sophia recalls, laughing. " 'Oh, yeah, that's the stuff, that's hot.' "

That woman worked the camera like a cheetah mauling a zebra; what was I supposed to do?

"I'm just saying, Fearless, you're fast on your way to being the guy who has the hardest time when this is over," Rich says, replacing the glasses. "It's just a slippery slope, you know?"

I hear him, though it's a struggle. Whether from the Jack and Cokes, or the high of getting those pictures, or the sense that I'm missing out on the action, I have to force every word to linger in my head. And that begs the question: How am I going to be able to write tonight?

"Come upstairs with us, Leif," says a young female voice. "We want to dance."

It's little Cindy, in the long blue dress, with her friend.

I look back to Rich and Sophia, with an expression that must be full of childlike pleading, because Sophia laughs, says, "Go dance." I stand up and take little Cindy's hand, only to hear, as we walk off, with me waving, Rich add, "He's playing with fire."

Upstairs, on the dance floor in front of an Austin swing band, I dance with Little Cindy and friend, me working both of them, twirling with right and left hand, like an old-fashioned Vaudeville guy spinning plates on sticks. Am I really pulling this off, suavely dancing with these two beauties? Or is this one of those situations where you're drunk and it's only in your head that it looks good? Either way, the girls seem to be having fun.

And then, with no warning, just when it's getting amazing, we're filing out.

Sophia, I think, appears. Or maybe it's one of the fresh-sheets women. Things are getting foggy, but we're making our way through the crowd, heading toward the bus, having received the information that the bus is pulling out. Immediately. For some reason Rich is pissed.

The bus is bouncing along through Austin, retracing our route back to the hotel. We're in the back, with the door closed, whooping it up out of Rich's sight, ignoring whatever he's dealing with. Collin, Sophia, me, and the candidates, playing music, dancing, falling, wrestling. One of the fresh-sheets-and-babysitter candidates straddles me. She's posing for what I've envisioned as the ideal last shot of the night: me on my back receiving CPR from vixen candidate.

The crowd mills around outside the bus in front of the hotel, like a crowd that spills outside a club after it closes—diehards not finished having fun. Rich curtly thanks everyone, saying the night is over almost in a legal way, but no one disperses.

Time to start downloading these images from the camera, get them to Chicago, and figure out what the hell to write, I'm thinking, as I say, "Lots of fun to meet you two," to fresh-sheets-and-babysitter, "thanks so much for all your help."

We're standing off to the side, a little away from the others. Coffee, this is going to take a lot of coffee. And staying up all night. As long as I don't pass out. The key is not passing out.

"You're coming home with us."

It's not an idle possibility, passing out.

"You're coming home with us," the Dolly niece lookalike is saying, while her friend, glacial blue eyes twinkling, nods in agreement.

I'm going home with them? It just doesn't make any sense . . . what she's saying . . . I'm already home, am staying at the hotel . . . *fresh sheets, babysitter*—holy . . . this is it . . . the statistical inevitability, candid offer of casual sex . . . and not just the two of us, but the three of us, as in threesome, as in the summa cum laude of male fantasy scenarios. . . .

"That is absolutely the nicest offer I've ever had—"

"Good," one says, while the other is on the verge of pouncing. "Let's get out of here."

Candles, warm bath, fresh sheets, tangled bodies, making contact with body parts and not even being sure where they're coming from . . . but, but, but . . . Rich is only about five yards away. Can he see what's going on, recognize the telltale signs of a man being propositioned with a threesome? I blink my eyes, make sure they're not bugging out.

"The only thing is . . ."

This can't possibly be wrong, can it? That keys-to-the-kingdom speech, this couldn't be something I'm supposed to decline? What kind of sick job would put a man in such a position?

"The thing is, I actually have a lot of work, my night, it's really just beginning."

"So, don't do it."

A deceptively simple solution. But failing to do a dispatch, being fired for going home with two candidates—it's a good story, perhaps the ultimate cocktail party tale, but should I?

"This stuff has to go up, there are people in Chicago, their job is to work with this stuff . . . if I don't give them anything . . ." I can't believe I am even hesitating.

The crowd's thinning. We're becoming increasingly obvious. I swear, Rich is eyeing us.

"How about this?" they suggest. "There's a gentlemen's club across the street. Why don't we go over there, we'll buy you a couple lap dances, and you can think about it?"

"I guess we . . . Wait a second, if I get the lap dances . . . you're trying to trick me."

We laugh at this, but I'm thinking, weighing it all, the risk to the job, the situational impotency. And yet, how can I say that word that is the opposite of yes? There just has to be a way. . . .

"How about this?" I say, new vision coming into focus. "How about if I bring my computer over and set up in the bedroom? It's perfect, I can do my work while you two . . . you'll do, you know. I can incorporate that into what I'm writing, tie this all together, which makes for a much easier dispatch. I'll finish my work, then join in. It's perfect."

I must say—the two of them, writing about it as it happens, gradually sobering up, finally stepping into the scene, making the shift from voyeur chronicler to participant—it's a f-----g good idea.

Fresh-sheets-and-babysitter stare for a beat, looking at me like I'm speaking Chinese.

"No, not that way."

"But it'll be great, and very sexy for you, having all the readers out there."

"No."

We're staring at each other. They're waiting for a response.

"If I can't bring my work . . . I hate to do this"—my insides are a psychological tsunami—"but I'm going to have to say I can't."

"Well, if you change your mind, we'll be across the street."

We hug—soft, warm, inviting—and I stumble back to my room. I manage to dump photos into the computer, send them to Chicago. Accompanying them is a single blurb, something about the photos hopefully explaining why their Fearless Reporter was in no shape to write a dispatch, but that he hopes the readers will understand, see that he's living up to his pledge.

Exhausted, I fall into bed, wondering for a second if it's not too late, the gentlemen's club. But I'm already losing consciousness. . . .

"Please, Rich, be fair. Be human. You've got to give me another shot."

It's Raj, groveling to Rich outside the bus.

"Nope. Sorry, pal."

Turns out he lost his wallet last night. Instead of accompanying us on our drunken excursion, he spent the evening canceling credit cards.

"We can take it out again tonight. It'll be fun. Why not?"

"No, buddy, that was a onetime deal."

Sophia stands next to them, videotaping the exchange.

"Rich, just one more time."

"No can do. Last night was Hale-Bopp. Once in a lifetime."

I stumble past, thinking Raj is lucky. *Leif, you miserable, sorry excuse for a man, a threesome—a threesome with complimentary lap dances. Are you completely devoid of gray matter?*

"Hey, Fearless," Sophia says, blocking my path to the bus, zooming her camera in on my face. "Looking a little jaundiced. Anything you'd like to get off your chest?"

"No comment."

"Leif?! Now I'm curious."

"I'm not well. I've got to sit down."

The first thing I see when I enter the bus is this big dude in expensive leather jacket and dark shades taking up the space of three women, which is odd, given the prohibition against male non-employees violating the bus's sanctity. According to Sophia, he was once a famous football player, a larger-than-life, showboat type. He's really our first celeb on the bus, thus a natural story for the day.

I ask him about his girlfriend, the pretty young thing emerging from the changing room.

"Her? Girlfriend? Come on! At that age, you just play. They's playthings. She's my plaything. One of them."

A collective shiver overtakes the rest of us.

"Come on, baby, come here and let me see you."

She shuffles over, rolling her eyes, looking none too comfortable.

"Yeah, baby. Why don't you open that thing up? Show me the squirrel."

In the immortal words of Ed McMahon: *Hi-yo!*

"Be good," the plaything responds.

"Don't be that way, child, show me some squirrel. You know you got it."

Must he make it so hard to write a sunny story about the nice athlete we met on the bus?

"Squirrel, baby, show it. Why you being this way?"

Another candidate, just joining us after touching up her makeup, asks, "A tattoo?"

"Yeah, right, a tattoo. Heh-heh. What about you? You might have one, too. Open that robe, let's see if you've got some squirrel."

There's uncomfortable laughter . . . recognition.

Still, I keep looking for a story, and for a moment it seems I'm on to something. Our guest of honor starts talking about all the public speaking he does, about his personal battle with drugs and alcohol. This is *something*, the human side to a conflicted character. We're on our way to a dispatch.

Except he mentions the great pay he gets for working behind the podium. And the more he talks, the more he explains the money to be made profiting off drug and alcohol abuse—as opposed to, say, working for free with the sorts of kids who may have been nudged closer to such a life by the flashy life he led as a pro—the more depressed I become. No story here—at least, not for the site.

Outside, I'm about to head to my hotel room for a good cry, but Sophia blocks my way.

"Not so fast," she says. "Don't you think it's time you contributed to my film?"

"Can we do this later? I need a moment alone."

"Work got you down? Get it off your chest, you'll feel better."

"Not after Rich sees it."

"No one's going to see it, at least until the Search ends."

"No."

"Okay, then, no more using me in your dispatches."

She's got me there. Sophia has become a fixture of the dispatches, with extensive coverage given to her growing appreciation of certain candidates, beginning with Kandi, as well as our efforts—mostly joking—to trick her into exposing the glories beneath her shirt.

"Sophia, if you show this to *anyone* . . ."

The confession pours forth in a torrent. Starting back in Portland and my quasi-date with Eve, then the e-mail flirtation with Daisy, and finally last night's botched threesome. All the while I'm spitting it out, emphasizing the personal vs. professional quandary, glossing over—omitting—references to certain alleged sexual issues, Sophia is laughing, in silence, not wanting to screw up the sound. Mime laughing.

And then, just as I'm throwing up my hands, literally, in frustration, not knowing what the hell I'm to do, a hand comes at me into the camera's frame, presenting an ecru business card with home number. And with that, and a wave, she's gone, a woman I spoke to on the bus only for a moment. I'd commented on her hair.

"Did you see that?" I ask Sophia, but don't need to, since she's holding her hand over her mouth. "Did she overhear me? Was she listening? She wasn't? That was just coincidence? Okay, you see what I'm saying? What am I supposed to do?"

"Hey, Fearless, can I have a word with you when you're done?"

It's Rich, stepping out of the bus, and I must go ghostwhite. *Was he listening?*

We pull two of the folding chairs off to the side. Rich begins, says he wants to "keep the communication open." He can't get into great detail, but wants me to know that the issue has been discussed. And this situation won't occur again. So-and-so's duties are being stripped to the core, and the person is to have zero contact with the problem area.

What's this about, you ask? Well, remember a certain person's extensive back-of-the-bus loitering back in Albuquerque and my premonitions of my own Katofication in *USA Today*? I may have taken steps, uttered a few off-hand remarks to Sophia about what was happening in Rich's absence, knowing they'd travel from her ears to his. I may have done that.

Rich assures me it's now under control. Still, I can't resist venting a bit, recalling some of the past situations, the awkwardness. He understands, appreciates my candor, stresses again that what I'm describing is exactly the sort of thing that won't happen in the future. So I say "Okay" and he says "Okay" and we nod, the ways guys do when they've addressed a serious matter. But something still isn't right, so I keep talking.

"It's just that, well, here's a separate question—what's the deal with the crew and candidates?" I blurt out. "Because, well, I'm just not sure, and I don't think I've done anything wrong, but it's a little confusing, you know? This situation? It's kind of tricky to know what—"

"Oh, no, *noooo*," Rich says, cutting me off. "I've got no problem with socializing. Well, except, obviously, for certain people. But I've no problem with you socializing. At times it's part of the job, and others . . . well, we're on the road for long periods—you especially. It can't be that we don't interact. That would be ridiculous."

"Well, okay, it's just, I . . ." What the hell *am* I saying? "I just wanted to ask, make sure." I now feel like a goof, wanting it to be over. "I wasn't sure, didn't want to, you know . . ."

"Absolutely."

"Great, okay."

Okay, what?

Herm, from his perch in Playboy's Chicago headquarters, assures me that the site's readership is growing by leaps and bounds, that management is thrilled. He's even hired me to cover a party at the Mansion during the upcoming mid-Search break. But still, there's been no confirmation regarding my contract extension for the second half. And New Orleans, which we're now en route to, is the last city of the first half.

This may be the last stop for the Fearless Reporter. I try to be philosophical about the possibility that the end may be nigh. Rich's warning about the slippery slope of this job, this world . . . well, let's just say it's getting difficult to remember what the hell my novel was about. And if this is going to be it, there's little point to erring on the side of caution.

Late that night we arrive in New Orleans. I immediately head out into the Quarter. Walking along the old streets, past beautiful sagging facades, stopping at a diner, scarfing down a shrimp po'boy, then, heading farther in, finding a tiny ancient bar, with a drunk at work at the piano and a patron actually reading with a penlight (reading!)—it feels right, ending things in New Orleans.

Back at our grand hotel, I decide to check e-mail before the long night's work. There are twenty-four in all—readers reacting to that mess I drunkenly posted in Austin. I start opening the files. Long strings of exclamations leap off the screen. They hate me! I make their life look miserable! They'll do anything to join me: clean the bus toilets, carry my bags!

One of the more literate of the bunch: *You have got to be kidding me. Sucking on the necklace? Unbef-----glievable. Just as really rich people sometimes seem like randomly chosen Homo sapiens who have been selected to experience enormous pleasure, so you seem like a representative male, sent to coddle and smooch and flirt for the bunch of us. You dog. You're a dog and a half. Has it occurred to you that given Newton's theory that every action has an equal and opposite reaction, you may be required to spend a few decades shivering in a wet basement to satisfy the cosmic economy?*

New Orleans, Louisiana

◆

Everyone tells me I'm a guy trapped in a girl's body."

In baseball, when a player is on a hitting streak, he sometimes has the sense of knowing what the pitcher is going to throw before he throws it. Thursday morning, on the bus, working on my computer, these two extremely attractive sisters, Ashley and Brett, are among our first candidates, and having only heard the above, I'm ready to jump on it.

"That's so weird," I say. "Everyone tells me I'm a girl trapped in a guy's body."

Everyone on the bus looks over, the line hitting one of those quiet moments.

"Actually, that's wrong," I continue, all eyes on me. "No one tells me that. I've just known it." More quiet. "How else do you explain the vaginal discharge?"

Ashley's back in the studio. Brett isn't here to try out, has come only for moral support, and, unlike so many of the moral supporters who quickly acquiesce, Brett is having none of it. She flips through a *Playboy* as I look on. The body in which she is trapped is a good one, that of a lithe runway model. She has beautiful long obsidian-black hair, which looks all the more striking because of an imperfection in her right eye, a small crimson amorphous shape amid the white. The guy part comes out in her speech, the surprising, hoarse, Cajun-influenced voice of singing sensation Harry Connick Jr.

"What is this?" female Harry Connick says in exaggerated disgust. "What's happened to *Playboy*? I used to like their pictures, but what is this?"

Brett has the *Playboy* Newsstand Special open to a layout with a businesswoman theme. In it, a brunette has her hair up in a bun, has a cell phone pressed to her ear, is standing next to her desk, wearing tailored suit jacket and blouse, but instead of pants or skirt, merely garter belt and nylons. Her free, nonphone hand appears to be headed in the direction of her sex organ.

"What are you talking about?" I respond. "This goes on all the time. You young ladies, you career types, are frequently making your business calls pantsless and on the verge of playing with yourselves."

Brett looks at me.

"It's true, they've done studies."

"Get the f--k out of here," she suggests, or, more accurately, rasps. "I'm talking about that. Right there. You see that?"

She taps her finger emphatically on the picture, right on the spot, as if she were reading the model's mind.

"That's *nasty.* Okay? The magazine didn't use to be like this. The pictures used to be nice. That shit is nasty. Come on!"

What Brett is referring to—how to write this delicately?—is that the model is very exposed, down there. More to the point, she is very, what, *labially pronounced,* is that the term? In LA, many a specialist might even identify the model in this picture as a candidate for the booming vaginal rejuvenation trade.

"Hmmm . . ." I say. "She looks pretty to me. I think you have a sick mind."

Again she stops up short.

"You don't think that looks trashy?"

"Trashy? You should have seen what they wanted her to do. I was at that shoot, and the photographer had this big German shepherd and wanted her to—"

"You lie."

Our knees our touching as we say this, eyes locked on each other.

"And then I was the one who said, 'Hold on just a second. I think we're in danger of crossing over into the realm of questionable taste,' and that totally stopped everyone for a second, even the dog, and everyone, you know, took a time-out."

"Really? Who the f--k are you? Don't you work for this company?"

"I'm not an employee, exactly."

I can't help but notice that all the self-questioning inner monologue—so prevalent in exchanges with past candidates—is absent from my mind.

"You probably already have plans," Brett says, "but I waitress at stupid McTeeanay's and have to compete in a bikini contest tomorrow night. You should come."

With that all settled, I'm free to work on the day's dispatch and, again, as if on cue . . .

She has long henna-hued hair, with natural waves running through it, a style that must have been the thing way back in the Garden of Eden. I can't help joking with my co-workers about her age—"Okay, Blockbuster video card for ID? Sure, why not?"— because she looks maybe sixteen, with her waif-thin figure and sweet-kid face. She has faint eyebrows, like the framed *Playboy* cover on the wall of Kim Basinger, before she got fame and eyebrows.

Across the street, there's an abandoned old red boxcar, surrounded by weeds, and it's there that I take pictures of Vivian. She's awkward, not sure what to do, and though the hair blazes in the sun, the pictures are weak. We're not establishing a connection, and I'm wondering what I'm doing wrong. Maybe she's like the girl in Portland, the sort of person who looks good but can't photograph well.

Over my shoulder, the French Quarter looms, like the edge of a forest. It's a shame, being in New Orleans and settling for a boxcar as a location. I should ask Vivian if she has the time to go explore, but I don't say anything and it's probably this indecision that's killing our photos, keeping my mind off the work. But after Brett, I'm fresh out of aplomb.

Two hours later, though, Vivian is walking back toward the bus, dressed head to toe in a new outfit, and weighed down with three shopping bags full of additional purchases. She wears black Capri pants and a closely tailored white blouse, which look expensive. This day is verging on hallucinatory: Did Vivian do all this for me?

"Don't you look great."

"I should never go shopping. Once I start, I can't stop. I just spent six hundred dollars."

I've rarely spent that much money clothes shopping in a year, much less a day.

"What's going on?" I ask, hoping she has free time, because I'm going to ask.

"The guys from Video wanted to film me giving them a tour of the Quarter."

That's too bad.

Playboy Video—Collin the cameraman, Vince the director, and a sound guy they've hired locally—I now see, are waiting in their white minivan rental. I give Vivian a hand as she climbs in. As Vince immediately begins peppering her with questions about New Orleans, Collin leans out the passenger window and beckons me closer.

"How'd it go, Dick?" he asks, using his pet name for me.

"Huh?"

"You shot her earlier, didn't you? What's she like? Is she going to get crazy for us?"

I'm still not used to the reality that in asking something like that he's soliciting a professional opinion. I shrug.

"We had four others this morning," he says. "It was tough to get them to keep their clothes on."

"Really?" I can see Vivian's Rembrandt locks over Collin's shoulder. Like my dispatch stuff, there'll be no pay for Vivian, only the honor of affiliating with Playboy. And on top of it, this kid is out six hundred dollars for her wardrobe.

"Come with us. We're going into the Quarter. Don't be such a pussy, Dick."

"We're here at the world-famous French Quarter Market," Vivian says, voice halting, "and . . ." She trails off, looking lost.

"Is there some local story about it?" Vince asks. "Something to add?"

"I don't know," she says. "This is my first time coming here."

Our next stop is the obligatory New Orleans tarot card reading. The guy admits to Vivian that he's just started and only charges the video guys a beginner's rate. She tells me after, as we walk on, that it was the best reading she's ever had. As the video guys walk briskly ahead looking for the next shot, I ask Vivian what he told her.

"He just talked about how I've had to be very resourceful in my life. And how I've had to depend on myself . . . and how it was the result of a early tragedy in my life . . . and I don't know. He said a lot of things that were right."

I hand Vivian napkins I pilfered from a restaurant so she can blot the sweat from her body—it's roasting out—then ask how that applies to her life.

"Oh. Well, my parents both died when I was seven. And then when I was fourteen I moved away from my grandparents' home and got my own apartment."

"Woah. Sorry, " I say. "How'd they die?"

"In a refinery fire. They worked together. Bodies never found."

I've barely said I'm sorry again, when Vince, who's standing in front of a Baskin-Robbins, calls back, "Hey, Vivian, how about an ice-cream cone?"

Vivian smiles tentatively. "I guess."

We enter the blissful freezer-enhanced air-conditioning of the ice-cream store, as dark clouds form over my psyche. I've never seen a

Playboy video, but somehow I picture ice-cream cones in each one: "Down here in New Orleans, there's nothing we girls love more than licking a nice big ice-cream cone . . . well, almost nothing!" Collin, can we get that in slow motion?

Collin and I pass the glassed-in freezer section. "Hey, Collin," I say, pointing to the merchandise, chocolate-covered bananas on a stick. "Wouldn't one of those work better?" I'm of course, kidding, however ruefully, but Collin calls Vince over for a mini-conference.

"Vivian," Vince says, "change of plan. How about ordering one of these?"

I can't tell—did Collin think I was serious, or is he just a very unhappy person inside?

A horse-drawn carriage clip-clops past. Vince, who is again walking up ahead, turns back and asks where that Mardi Gras street is where women flash for beads. That's Bourbon Street, Vivian and I tell him—it's straight ahead.

Vivian and I are talking about her being on her own at fourteen. As a product of a boy-in-the-bubble suburb in a region where Garrison Keillor famously jokes, "All the children are above average," I can't fathom being on my own at that age. I'm sure I would've quickly perished.

"Well, this is New Orleans. And you'd be surprised what people will agree to if you have cash."

So Vivian was bartending at fourteen. Nice. It turns out her grandmother owns a small strip club. According to Vivian, it's a tough place, and while she's never worked there, she's gone to Las Vegas, to a convention held for strip clubs, and taken on the role as fresh-young-thing representative of her grandma's strip place. The suburban mind reels.

Collin is up ahead, aiming his camera up at the street sign, which reads: BOURBON STREET. Vince is pulling out the beads he'd purchased earlier, trying to untangle the things. I hand Vivian a fresh batch of napkins. When Vince asks if she's okay with this, flashing for beads on camera, she says, as my stomach sinks, "Actually, I've never done it before, but, I guess."

Though the street was empty when we arrived, two couples have already stationed themselves ten feet away from us. They have giant cheese wedges on their heads, signifying their allegiance to the Green Bay Packers, and huge hurricane daiquiri glasses in their hands. They wait.

Vivian slowly unbuttons her shirt, all but one button, as we look up and down the street. It's all clear, but the sound guy isn't ready, and then a huge garbage truck rumbles by, and then a sad-looking clown on a bike, and then a police squad car.

"Vince," Collin calls out in his cranky voice, "it's not going to be any clearer."

I'm stand at a distance, on the premise that my dispatch will be about covering the making of the bus documentary, and have chosen an angle where Collin's camera will block Vivian's breasts.

"Vivian," Vince calls out, while holding out the beads, "on the count of three . . ."

Is it just me? Does this seem sad to you?

"One."

This angelic young creature, surviving extreme early adversity, for this?

"Two."

Am I too puritanical? Do I have some hang-up?

"Three."

There's a pause in which Vivian bites her lip, then she woodenly says her line, something about beads and New Orleans, and unhooks the last button and the shirt comes open. As it does, Vivian shifts position, jutting hip out to the side, instinctively accentuating curves and flexing tan washboard stomach. Light—corny as this may sound—seems to emanate from her. She radiates. Her smile gleams. The hair gives off a halo. And the breasts . . .

The breasts . . . one of the cheeseheads actually groans. I believe I would be borrowing from my colleague William Shakespeare in describing them as pear-shaped. When women express dismay over men's fascination with breasts, arguing the bit about them just being fat deposits, and men make the counterargument that they've evolved through natural selection not only for function but for desirability to the male mating mind, Vivian is Exhibit No. One for the guy side.

As Vince belatedly throws the beads into the frame—so obviously tossed from a few lame feet away, falling like a dead duck at her feet, causing everyone to laugh—it occurs to me I've forgotten something. Forgotten to take the picture.

So it's a relief when Collin calls for a second take. When Vince runs through the countdown this time, I shift forward, taking up a position that will give me an unobstructed shot. And, with the beads airborne, flying into frame, above the perfect torso, I catch the picture, reminiscent of that first volleyball breakthrough at the Mansion, and immediately prepare to argue with my boss.

We're walking back to the van. Now that the money shot is in the can, the video crew has dropped its former minimal pretense about getting shots of local color. My heart pounds in overdrive from all these forces—lust, work success, momentary belief in a supreme being—but I still manage to rally a nice-guy thought that at the very least I'll insist that Vivian join us for what will surely be an expensive dinner this evening. Then I see something.

"Can we stop for a second?" I ask.

By now it's late afternoon and as we pass between the shadows of two taller buildings, we enter golden fading light. I back Vivian up against the wall of an old home of orange bricks, unevenly stacked and shaped. She leans against the wall, hip jutting out, the warm light bathing her hair and bricks in a way that has them looking related.

"Do you mind unbuttoning your shirt?" I say, wanting the color of brown skin to balance in with henna hair and orange brick. "And just let it hang open, but not all the way."

She does what I say without question. Shirt parted to reveal the swell of breasts, she looks down at me as I go into something of a Rich crouch, shoot up, giving her that heroic stature—heroic but confident, with a nearly wanton glare. I fire off a quick couple shots—Vivian, *dios mío*—and then thank her, tell her she can button her shirt back up.

I pass the camera around, showing crew and Vivian the image on the preview screen. They all nod, say, "Wow" and "Great shot." Vivian even utters the line, "Is that me?" I'm asking myself the same question: *Is that me? Is that my work? Am I responsible for that image?* On top of all I was already feeling, I suddenly have the odd conviction I just created art.

"Fearless!"

"Herm," I say, holding the bus phone, "today's dispatch, I took a picture, there's going to be nudity, but it's related to the situation, which is me covering the video guys. And she was flashing for beads, which is obviously part of life down here, right? Because if we can't show that, well, there's a point where it's kind of ridiculous, not being able to show breasts. And it sets up a good contrast with another shot I took, without nudity, but very sexy. Come on, it's Playboy, you know? Playboy. Let's grow up a little."

"Leif," he cuts in, "relax. I'll look at the picture. If it's like you say, we'll put it up."

"We *will*?" I ask, still catching my breath. "Are you saying I could have been doing this all along, that there's a policy that if the nudity is related—"

"Leif, I didn't say it's a policy. I said I'd go to bat for this one, and let's leave it at that."

As we say good-bye, I'm relieved. No, more than that. I'm soaring on the adrenaline rush of victory, this barrier broken down. I pick up the phone again, dial, hear a sleepy Sophia answer.

"You're taking a nap. Sorry. Go back to sleep."

"It's okay. Just run-down. The stupid bus is getting to me."

Run-down? How could she feel run-down?

"Real quick. Video worked Vivian all day, can we buy her dinner?"

"Of course."

"Good. Second, the McTeeanay's bikini contest—do you know anything about that?"

"They called, but I was thinking of blowing it off."

"Can we go?"

"You want to go?" she says, sounding more awake. "McTeeanay's is worse than Hooters and you hate Hooters."

"Well, I could use the piece. Especially if I could be a judge. Can I be a judge?"

"Of course, baby. No problem. This I've got to see."

The restaurant is candlelit. The wait staff wear long white aprons. Vivian sits next to me, wearing another new purchase: a sleeveless silk dress, navy blue with small white polka dots. Taste is the great equalizer; that a girl whose parents died when she was a kid, whose grandmother runs a strip club, and who was on her own before she could drive, knows how to wear navy blue is reason for hope.

For people who work on the road, giving up their personal life, dinners like these are the great solace. My colleagues and I are an odd group, but once we start joking, sending up each other's quirks—Sophia's ass appreciation, Rich's split personality, Vegas's tingles—we become family. I am forever linked with the Kandi story, and I am embarrassed to have Vivian hear it, but with the candlelight tinting her hair with gold, I just feel proud to have brought her along.

Which reminds me. I pass the camera around so everyone can see the Vivian shots. They all make "Ooh" and "Aah" sounds, compliment the photographer and model. Vivian blushes.

"Did you get a chance to take some shots in the studio?" Rich whispers.

"Not really, just with Video out in the French Quarter."

"Boy, she worked that camera. I wasn't expecting it, with that cherub look, but then we got in the studio, and . . . *wham*."

"You think . . ." I ask, taking our hushed tones lower, "you think she's a stripper?"

Rich nods purposefully, with eyes closed, as if there can be no doubt.

"No. I don't think so," I say. She was so nervous, that look on her face when she was asked to flash. "Her grandmother has a strip club, uses Vivian as some kind of rep, but she's a bartender."

"Maybe," Rich says, not that concerned one way or the other. "But you should have been there. There's no way an eighteen-year-old girl is going to have learned that stuff."

After dinner, we all walk back to the hotel, though I sense the guys are going out to a strip club. I offer to walk Vivian to her car, but she wants to go into the hotel first and use the ATM. We find it down at the end of a dark hallway. I stand behind her and she inserts her card. Her hair smells of one of those conditioners that has managed to capture the scent of rain.

Standing in the dark . . . am I about to sweep the hair aside and kiss the back of her neck? She's taking forever to work the machine, which makes me wonder if she's having the same thought, is waiting for me to make some sort of move.

But is that where this should be headed? Taking that last photo of Vivian, and bringing her to dinner, it feels like intimacy. Then again, orphaned, emancipated minor—we're on different planets, haven't connected in a single discussion, other than my interest in her foreignness. And what of Brett? Is this me sabotaging myself, getting off track? This is one of those times where it would be nice to have Burt on walkie-talkie . . . and we're still at the ATM. . . .

"It's not working."

"Not working? You punched in your code, right?"

Vivian turns, biting her lip.

"Your code, is it the same as your account number? . . . I just got this."

"Not usually. Usually they send along a secret code in a separate envelope."

"Yeah, I don't have that," she says sheepishly.

"You didn't know . . . ? Vivian, have you used one of these before?"

She shakes her head. No.

"This is your first time?" I ask, struggling to compute, wondering how she could have survived on her own without using a cash machine. "And you have to have cash?"

"My car's in the hotel lot. I didn't know I was going to be here all day."

"Oh, right," I say, reaching for my own cash card, when the obvious hits me. "Hey, sign it to Video. Just give them Vince's room number."

"But it's going to be, like, forty dollars."

"Sign it to them. Promise me you won't pay for this?"

"If you're sure."

Somehow Butch gets lost en route to the competition. You'd have thought I would see this coming, would by now factor my cursed luck into what is potentially my last night on the road, would have mapped it out myself, perhaps taken a cab, had another cab follow, in case the first broke down.

McTeeanay's, for those who don't know, is the inevitable franchise copycat to Hooters, Burger King to McDonald's. Only, where Hooters features busty waitresses in tight orange polyester shorts serving famous chicken wings, McTeeanay's waitresses wear tight pink terry cloth shorts and serve the famous McTeeanay's biscuits and gravy.

Finally, totally lost, we stumble across McTeeanay's, but the place, crushingly, is deserted.

It's the wrong McTeeanay's. Butch is all for giving up, going back. Though his days are mostly free, he tends to begrudge this night work, especially since his girlfriend joined us on the road. Sophia, eyeing me, tells him we're not turning around. We keep driving, a circuitous tour of the small towns neighboring New Orleans, each one looking like a more ideal location for a meth lab than the one before.

And then we see it. From a distance, it looks more like a penal institution, with the inmates given some evening exercise time on the asphalt yard, which is actually the parking lot behind McTeeanay's. There's a sprawling throng of men, milling, surging, even dancing, under towering parking lot floodlamps where millions of bugs dash into the light.

As we get closer, the scene becomes clearer. There's a temporary stage, on which a woman stands with a microphone, and in front of the stage, a line of men seated in white plastic garden chairs, undoubtedly the judges. But the girls are filing onto the stage at the very moment the bus pulls to a stop: This judge is too late. F--k, f--k, f--k.

Bus stopped, I take off at a run. I immediately spot Ashley, another of our candidates—Ashley, what a body!—but Brett's nowhere to be seen. Once again, I have picked wrong. Vivian. She was the one. *Idiot!*

The MC introduces the competitors, who then strut across the stage. As they sashay, he announces a few of their favorite things: television show, *Ally McBeal*; car, everything from Mercedes to BMW; food, invariably Italian.

Flustered though I am, I'm still aware that I neglected to cover the bus today. Instead I cruised voodoo stores with Sophia, ended up buying a little red bag of love gris-gris, which I was promised would put an end to any trouble I was having in this department. Without dispatch material, I have no alternative but to work through my grief and cover the event.

Ashley takes the high road, not sneaking in any stripper moves. If anything, she looks shy. She's just another of the candidates who wears her insecurity on her sleeve, or thong. She couldn't be any more beautiful if she'd been grown in a petri dish. Still, she resorts to this jailyard extravaganza (and the audition on the bus) hoping to be reassured. *Ashley, for crying out loud . . .*

"You must really love Ashley."

Just because your job isn't at a desk, people think it's okay to talk to you as you work.

"I'm sorry?" I say, completely missing whether the current contestant is a Mercedes gal or a BMW gal. The interrupter is a woman in a taupe Armani knockoff suit.

"You're taking so many pictures, you must really be in love with Ashley."

I look down at the camera, then up at the stage. *In love with Ashley?* I process it for another second or two. "You think I'm . . . that I'm stalking her?"

"You just seem really, really interested in her."

The nerve of this woman, to mistake the focused work of a writer-photographer . . .

"Listen, I don't want to give away Ashley's personal business, but I'm covering her on behalf of a major media conglomerate. This is something she's pursuing, not the reverse, so if you'll excuse me . . ." I finish, turning back. *In love with Ashley!*

"Oh. Are you with Playboy? I'm sorry, I just, we get some *unusual* characters at these events. I like to keep an eye on things. I'm Stacy. I do PR for the five area McTeeanay's."

We shake hands.

"Weren't you supposed to be one of our judges?"

"Yes, but regrettably our bus driver messed up."

"Oh, well," she says, smiling, "you can still judge the second heat." *Second heat?*

The girls are in the kitchen between heats, knocking back wine coolers. I make my way in, staggering at a scent that would have Sinclair Lewis writing *The Jungle II,* and not wanting any part of the "famous" biscuits and gravy. I pick my way through the crowd of women in bikinis, and am surprised to be the one feeling like a piece of meat—*Am I getting really carried away with myself, or are they all looking at me with lust?*—when I see someone running at me, about to attack. I turn just in time to meet the assault, the assailant midair, aiming straight for me. . . .

Brett is in my arms, long model legs wrapped around my hips, arms clasped around my neck, lips planting a kiss on my cheek. It's without question the most exuberant greeting I've ever received. It's the way I've always wanted to be greeted. I just didn't know it.

"You made it!"

"Good evening, Brett," I say.

Picture! Moron, get a picture!

I hand off the digital to another competitor and tell Ashley to join us. Sandwiched between the two ladies, I flash a broad smile. *Click.* We check it out in the viewer and it's a keeper—the grin on my face so unrestrained, so certain to send my readership into paroxysms. We're back in the zone, on the way to a dispatch that will make them truly miserable and strangely happy.

I take back the camera, begin choreographing a mock Playboy bikini shoot. Washing skanky dishes, in bikinis. Taking out the garbage, in bikinis. Working the deep-fat fryer, in bikinis. And for each shot, they turn, bend knees, stick butts out, arch backs, smile as if these menial tasks appealed on a profoundly sexual level. We're cracking up, deeply amused by ourselves.

This is all such a relief, such a salvaging of the tragedy. But I need to collect myself, make sure I don't miss judging the second heat. I do have work to do.

It's actually easier than it looks, judging a bikini contest.

I grade on arbitrary hunches about the inner contestant, trying not to let audience hooting and hollering affect my intuition. Arguably, I should recuse myself from judging Brett, especially when she's asked about her penchant for dating older men. Instead I blush, mark her down for first place in her heat. For once, it's a pleasure to sweep aside my usual scruples.

After the heat ends, the girls are then brought out again to hear the judges' verdict, to see who goes on to the final. I've never seen the McTeeanay's business model for bikini competitions, but my suspicion is that it says something about drawing them out all night to maximize beer and biscuit sales.

I know myself better than to go back into the kitchen during the break. Brett and I've already made plans to go out later, so to go back would be to risk jinxing myself, saying something odd that would throw off the night's rhythm.

Instead, I take to the parking lot, where huge speakers are blasting out hip-hop. Some of the audience have taken to dancing, though there are no women in sight. And I'm riding such a wave that I join in, showing some of my West Coast I-know-what-you're-thinking/there-must-be-some-chocolate-in-these-skim-milk-Caucasian-genes dance moves.

I begin on the outskirts of the circle, minding my own business. But very quickly the group is pulled, as if magnetically, in my direction, and before I know it, I'm in the center, shaking it, as they say, like I just don't care. I'm not alone in the middle, though, because an enormously wide, maybe four-hundred-pound bald brother shares my space. I dance around the big man, tailoring my moves to hug the planetlike curvature of his body, working in an impossibly close orbit, in a way that must have been rehearsed and earns the applause of the nondancers.

Song over, I head into the restaurant, find my co-workers around a table of chicken bones. They look up at me, trying to smile, but either they're experiencing bikini contest ennui or that suspicious kitchen aroma is wreaking havoc. Whatever, I'm too high to be brought down. And I tell it all to Sophia. About the bikini contestants checking me out, and being jumped by Brett, literally, and not only that, but "all these guys were dancing with me, here, you've got to check out the picture. . . ."

"Fearless," Sophia says, laughing, as I take a sip of beer, "don't you see what's happening?"

"What?" I say, though I think, *I'm finally not letting anything throw me off course.*

"The gris-gris."

"What?"

"The gris-gris. The love voodoo. It's working."

We exchange looks of amazement, hers exaggerated by greasy McTeeanay's sheen.

"But I forgot to focus it."

Ashley wins. Brett finishes a respectable third. (Even I voted the other woman second—I can be only so corrupt.) And the girls are ready to go, will be driving their car, meeting us at the hotel. Hearing this, I sense trouble, potential separation.

"Hey," I say, innocent as can be, "why don't I ride with you all?"

Unfortunately, Vince from Video senses what is happening, pegs me as a man in the zone.

"Hey, can I ride with you guys, too?"

Absolutely not. Go away. I've been plotting this for days. Scat.

It's not that I don't like Vince, or that I'm particularly greedy, more that I'm wise to Vince's rap. It is too much me on a bad day, all men on a bad day, the me I'm fighting so hard to leave behind. But what can I say?

As I let him slip in the back, I mouth one simple word to Sophia: *"F--K!!!!!!!!!!!"*

We peal out of the parking lot, a friend of Ashley and Brett's behind the wheel. Brett, who sits on my lap in the passenger seat, slides a CD into the player, filling the speakers with the mellifluous wail of fellow Minnesotan, Prince Rogers Nelson. It's a song I've never heard before, about . . . "pussy control." We speed through the wasteland of outer New Orleans, heading for the Quarter.

"So," Vince shouts over the music, "this is where you girls grew up, out here?"

Vince! Here's my ATM card. Whatever I have, it's yours. Just don't make chitchat.

"What did you think of the Playboy bus?"

They're twenty-year-old bikini contestants singing about pussy control. Dude, stifle!

"Brett," I shout, needing to act fast, "I voted that other woman for second."

"You bitch!" she says, and then tries to elbow me in the stomach, which I fight off.

"Yeah, I had to be objective—in terms of 'hotness' I gave her a higher score."

"Then we're going back, you can ride home with her on your lap, you f--k."

We reach our destination, deep in the Quarter, a shack of a bar that features karaoke singing, but rather than the usual hokey songs, they're playing current pop music. On this Friday night there's a brawl outside to get in, but when the bouncer spies the girls, he smiles like a little boy and throws bodies out of the way to let them and us in.

We're dangerously low on alcohol, so I grab Vince and we head for the bar, which is dominated by a row of slushy machines dispensing fruity tropical drinks in big plastic cups. Still in the zone, I take the server up on his suggestion that we double the alcohol on all the drinks.

Finally. Drinking. In the Quarter. With the girls. Major land mines avoided.

I take several long slurps from my flammable piña colada. As my nerves settle, Ashley and I start talking about her bikini victory. She shrugs off the win, but inquires about her chances with Playboy. I explain to this doe-eyed dream woman that beauty doesn't work in tiers, that the only difference between her and women in LA is that she's intimidated, hasn't been to the big city, doesn't yet know that she is prettier without makeup in a grungy bar than most of the women she idolizes.

And then we start talking about her semi-boyfriend, who's a jerk, treats her like dirt. I suggest to her that this guy will soon recede in the rearview mirror, that she should dream a little bigger, that she can likely have anything she wants—hopefully, she'll manage not to lose the sweet side. We're getting kind of close together and . . .

Brett. Brett. Can't get sidetracked.

I tell Ashley I'm getting another round and slide through the sweating crowd. Fresh round of piña coladas in hand, I locate Brett and drag her into the crowd. We toast. Do some drinking. Sing along to the songs. Snap pictures for the dispatch. The MC knows the girls and insists they come up. Their singing is forgettable, but these three lovely young women, synchronizing their steps—no one seems to care.

Another round. My T-shirt is soaked through, my hair wet as if I'd showered, and I'm starting to get dizzy. The crowd surges. A fight breaks out. It involves a preppy-looking guy and . . . *Brett.* With barely any clothes on, she's trying to swing at him. While the crowd holds her back, the guy calls her a cunt. If this were a movie, my fist should be meeting his jaw before his tongue could hit the roof of his mouth and make the *T* sound. But . . . well, you can guess my concern. Another land mine. I defer to the bouncers, who toss the guy out.

"Brett, I had your back, there. You sensed that, didn't you?"

"Sure I did, baby," she says.

Hours have passed. Brett and I are off to the side, near a bar that is elevated, so we look out over the crowd. We're kissing. Total sweaty, hair pulling, in full view of the entire bar, public drunken macking. And it's wonderful, though not so nice that I forget my work, take the occasional picture of this all—holding camera out with one hand, self-portrait style—at one point catch Brett with my lip in her teeth. I mentally caption it, *Bikini judge enjoying the spoils.*

It's close to four. We stumble down Bourbon, everyone zombified by tropical doubles. Vince is in tow with the friend who drove us from the contest. Ashley, Ashley is . . . I don't know. Just gone. The girls want to take us into a gentlemen's club. What *is* it with women taking men to gentlemen's clubs? I feel like I'm inside some horny sixteen-year-old guy's fifth-period daydream, expect at any moment to wake up to Mrs. Crabtree quizzing me about algebra homework.

As we enter the strip club, my eyes adjust to the familiar dark writhingness that is such an establishment's interior. Soon I'm transfixed by the surreal sight of a fat, cigar-chomping customer who's looking up appreciatively at a petite young thing who's climbed up on his lap. Expertly, she moves her hips, lap dancing, and, with dress pulled off shoulders and bunched up around waist, works her breasts—*familiar-looking breasts*—with great theatricality. Her own face—an angel's face, but covered in heavy makeup, a little girl trying to look grown up—feigns ecstasy, as if to say, *Ohmygod, sitting on your fat lap, as you smoke that rank cigar and drool on me, and as I wonder if I should stop at the store so I can cook my boyfriend breakfast in the morning, the whole situation makes me want to come.*

But then the young stripper realizes what *she* is seeing—me, T-shirt so wet as to be see-through, eyes wild, with some tall thing in little black dress playing pit bull with my lip. The strippers' orgasmic frenzy momentarily vanishes as she says . . .

"Don't rat me out!"

Rat you out? Electrical impulses slowly move through the piña sludge that is my brain. *Ohmygod, it's that candidate, the young innocent, Vivian. Vivian, you're a stripper! But . . . you . . . lied!*

"Vivian, ditto."

The four of us are back in the hotel room, raiding Vince's minibar, laughing at everything. How funny it is to open expensive macadamia nuts and just throw them across the room! The continued making out is fun, too, though all of this is still fraught with peril. I see the way Brett's friend—the one who drove—looks at Vince, who's still asking questions like, "Do you enjoy bikini competitions?" Conscious of the need to come up with some pretext—and quickly—I say, "Oh, I forgot something downstairs that I told Brett I was going to show her, and . . ." blah, blah, blah. Any other time,

I'd honestly care about leaving these two in an awkward situation, but tonight I'm on a mission.

A few minutes later, I'm throwing Brett on the bed, while she's saying that her friend is going to kill her. But I stop her, drop my full weight on her, and resume our making out, when the phone rings. I answer laughing, hear the friend asking for Brett. "Ha, ha, ha. No, she's just using the rest room for a moment," I say, sounding stopped-by-a-cop sober. "Do you want to hold on? Actually, we're just coming back up." I don't rip the phone out of the wall; instead find the jack and carefully take it out. But I do throw the thing, which—in my present state of inebriation—is also funny.

Next I pull down Brett's strapless top because, strapless, that's just fun to pull down. So is the short bottom, fun to pull up, and, though the underwear—thong!—have so far to travel over such long legs, it's gone in a flash. And she's shaved!—this is turning into such a cultural graduation for me, coming from a generation of bikini-cut panties and pubic hair. In another moment, my pants are at my ankles, and I'm on Brett, our legs hanging off the side of the bed, which feels nice. I just wish I wasn't so woozy—critical synapses are refusing to fire.

As our pelvises grind together, I pause from the making out and look down at Brett. Our four eyes all make different attempts to focus, and I may be doing that thing guys do where they grab their penis and kind of present it to the vagina, just making contact, knocking at the door, as it were. But not sure myself, or itself, what our intentions are, having only been committed to at least approaching this point. It's funny that I'm thinking of my penis knocking on the door, because I actually hear the knocking in my head, my penis is really pounding on a door, adamant about getting in. It's serious wake-up-the-neighbors pounding . . . but wait, it's the friend, the friend knocking, telling Brett she wants to go.

"You're not thinking you're going to f--k me, are you?"

It's weird, because I never thought I'd know Harry Connick Jr., let alone hear him utter those words. Weird, too, because, what—do I have a digital readout on my forehead?

"Well, no, of course not."

"Because I'm not some two-dollar whore you can f--k the first night."

"I didn't think that," I assure her over the damn pounding. "But it would be fun, just, you know, for a second, just to try."

I know that sounds stupid, that it's what everyone says: *just for a second.* But given that I can't even remember what nonmasturbatory sex feels like, I'm telling myself that it's important to get the old feeling back, *just for a second,* like a slumping slugger looking to feel the ball on the bat, make contact, even if it's a foul ball. We're still sort of grinding as the pounding on the door continues. I'd consider this another example of my being cursed—the annoying friend, that is—if I didn't sense a stalemate anyway, and if, to be honest, I didn't on some level consider myself lucky to have made as much progress as I have. The New Me took an important step tonight. So I help Brett back into her clothes, give her my most gentlemanly smile. I grab panties, slide them back on, pull dress down, trying to factor in a little of my old gentlemanly ways to the New Me, just to keep her guessing.

"I had a great time," I say.

It's quarter to six. The girls have gone. The sky is lightening, with dawn on the way. I plug in the phone, call down for coffee, sit down at my desk, and, smiling, look out over rumpled bedsheets. But there's so little time, so I start uploading digital images.

Gazing at the photos—voodoo shops, being jumped by Brett, the McTeeanay's kitchen mock pictorial, judging, dancing with the big man, girls at karaoke, Brett biting my lip—I can already see the onslaught of mail. My readers will want to know how far things progressed, of course. But the beauty is, I can claim duty stood in the way: "However charged my libido, nothing trumps my obligation to my readers . . ."

Somehow that's strikes me as the perfect solution to the concerns I've been having about how far to take things. The readers will assume I shagged her silly, because at that point—the sweating, the lip-biting—who couldn't close the deal? And yet, as far as what appears on the web—and thus gets back to Playboy—I can still plead relative innocence.

I stumble to the bed, fall in exhausted, and catch sight of the clock, which reads nine forty-five. My still-drunken eyes have barely closed when the phone rings. I pick up the receiver, hear Sophia's voice: "You've got to get down here. There's a beautiful Hawaiian doll here who flew in from Florida just to meet you and teach you the hula."

Still buzzed, I slap myself in the face, reach for my camera. I want to stop myself, take a pass. But it's not happening. I'm already in the hallway, pressing the elevator button. And not only that, I can already see the dispatch in my mind, envisioned it the moment I heard *hula*. While video still isn't a reliable Internet option, my web designer has been wanting to introduce animation to our site. Fearless's hula lesson, with animated photos—are you seeing it?

Days later my hula teacher will write: *Leif, MAHALO NUI LOA!! (translation: THANK YOU VERY MUCH!!) How did you do it? The way you brought me to life in your writing was amazing! Needless to say, my husband is too pleased with himself to be sleeping with "the Playboy girl." And the hula lesson, the way you could see us moving, that was too great. We can't wait to show it to my grandmother, who will be so proud. E HUI HOU KAKOU (UNTIL WE MEET AGAIN). Aloha.*

Los Angeles, California IV

I'm back home. The bus is on a mid-Search break and I'm at the Mansion. Herm hired the Fearless Reporter to cover Hugh Hefner's Labor Day party for the website.

Bob Saget laughs when I ask if I can take his picture for Playboy.com. Does he think fans of his show—the one where people send in home videos of various caught-on-tape accidents—wouldn't be amused to know he spends his free time tomcatting around the grounds of the Playboy Mansion? But what choice do I have, other than to honor his request?

Drew Carey couldn't be more jovial, to the point that he, too, is a tough interview. I've gotten him on the subject of his good fortune—his own show, great pay. It's such a dream, especially the improv program he hosts, for which he does almost nothing. He can't help chortling. It's all so funny to him, "and centerfolds on top of it . . . with these looks." He can't stop laughing, is going to swallow his tongue, and I don't know CPR. I must get away.

I suffer a moment of brain freeze trying to decide whether Dick Van Patten or Weird Al Yankovic has more cultural relevance at the moment, when I spy someone I actually appreciate.

"Excuse me . . . David?"

David Spade looks up to me. He's sitting with a friend, under a tent, eating a Labor Day hamburger and watching through a plastic window as Playmates play a spirited game of volleyball. His eyebrow rises, arches up, just like on television.

"Um, can I talk to you for a second?" I say, holding out a microphone to him. "I'm the . . . uh . . . Internet reporter."

The words, etched with so much uncertainty, feel strange coming from my mouth, a regression to the early days on the bus. Am I really intimidated by people who've been on TV?

And then this guy, who's made a fortune off his sarcasm, says, "Internet reporter?"

Internet reporter? It suddenly has all the caché of "professional infomercial audience member." It occurs to me that, as cushy a job as this is, I really don't have any interest in collecting celebrity Labor Day anecdotes, especially when said celebrities are clearly here for other reasons. I wander off from the David Spade interview, nearly tripping over a peacock crossing my path.

The embarrassing thing is the attitude I had coming into this party. Just back from New Orleans, and Brett, and I thought I had it all figured out. I arrived at the Mansion around noon and, as I was heading over to the tent from where we'd webcast the party, peeked in at the Grotto, the legendary cave/underground pool/hot tub, with its nooks, crannies, and beanbag futons. I was feeling such new confidence that I thought it was possible that I, too, by the end of the party, would manage to get busy in the Grotto, arguably one of the planet's great vortices for celebrity sexual coupling. It would be something to tell the grandkids.

I'm in the middle of marveling at my surge of hubris when Herm approaches with great news: The triplets are here. The triplets, he explains, are the Dahm triplets, the first triplets to be named Playmates in the history of *Playboy*. Since their issue isn't out yet, getting their photo will be a coup with our readers. But the best part is that the triplets and I share the same midwestern homeland.

I practically skip up to their table, thrilled at the prospect of connecting with someone, and am about to sit down when I notice the strange expression mirrored on all three faces. I wonder for a moment if, this morning, I accidentally put on that feces-scented novelty cologne.

Clearly, the triplets are shell-shocked from the culture change and all that has happened to them. They must be thinking I'm another of the questionable types they've been hounded by. I just need to explain the situation, that I, too, am from Minnesota and am the guy who's covering the Playmate Search 2000.

But the expressions don't change. They appear to be frozen, like after a bad day of ice fishing, though it's eighty-two degrees out. Actually, one of the sisters invites me to sit down, and I resume congratulating them on landing the pictorial, remarking on how exciting it must be.

"Playboy has given us a great opportunity. We have met many famous people. Hef is so generous, so fun, and has taken us to all the hottest spots in LA."

Herm must not have said they're from "Minnesota" but rather "Android Factory-a."

"Wow, that's great. And how long have you been here?"

They look at each other, communicating by 'droid telepathy. "Forty-eight hours."

Only two days and they have this kind of attitude? These girls make David Spade seem like a veritable teddy bear. Prematurely wrapping up the interview, I ask to take their picture, encourage them to smile. . . . *No, not that, not a frightful imitation of a smile, rather a natural, happy smile. . . . No? . . . That's it? . . . Best you can do? . . . Okay, that'll have to suffice.*

Back at the tent, I switch out the chip from my camera so that the designer can start posting images on the site for the live party coverage. Meanwhile, Herm is typing at a computer, the screen scrolling up with chat-room conversation.

"Hey," Herman says, "talk to these guys while I go to the rest room. I'll sign you in."

Then he's gone. The scrolling suddenly picks up speed, the text jumping up the screen. *Hey, Fearless. . . . What's up, Fearless? . . . What's going on Fearless? . . . Remember me, Fearless, the one who offered to clean out your toilets for you? I'd still clean them. . . .*

How do they know? I don't see a camera, so I don't understand how these guys can see me. That's when I notice the words Herm has left at the top of the screen: *Fearless enters.*

These guys who are chatting with me are the diehards. The premium subscribers, about whom I was so spooked at the beginning of the trip. Though the coverage of this Labor Day party will be archived on the site indefinitely, these are the guys who actually stay home to catch it as it happens, the only advantage being that they may get to chat with some Playmates, maybe even Hef.

They keep peppering me with questions, have been rushing like a piranha to a guppie ever since Fearless entered, but I've yet to speak. Chatting. It's embarrassing, too close to memories of trying to talk on the CB radio back in the seventies.

"What's going on?" I type.

Not much is going on. They're kicking back, waiting for things to get going, one of them chilling with a six-pack of Coors Lite (Coors Lite???), and this admission leads to a discussion about what the others are drinking. Nothing against what these guys are doing, but it's so foreign to my experience, spending a beautiful holiday weekend like this. I should be typing: *Boys, save yourselves, shut down the computer, run outside, grab the first human you see, and talk.*

They're back to discussing the Search. I can't recall all the women they're asking about, particularly in the minute detail with which they write, but gradually we reach more comfortable terrain. I tell them that they don't know the half of it, the line I must walk, constantly throwing myself at all these women, stoking up these messy situations strictly for my readers' pleasure, but then excusing myself as things are heating up so I'll live—or not be fired—to bring my readers stories another day.

They respond in a frenzy. I'm a scoundrel, they write. I'm the luckiest man in the world. I make them sick. That Brett, they say, that was too much! If they were in my situation, they'd have their cake and eat it, too. If they were in my situation, they . . . they . . . they're not even sure where they'd begin, but it would be great.

And they want to know what's going on at the party now. An accurate response would be, *Not much,* and there won't be for several hours until the night portion kicks in. But I don't have the heart to say that. Instead, I look on the bright side, tell them about the pictures I recently took of Hef, dancing with eight women—images that should be coming up on the site any minute.

"Yeah," I type, "it was cool, I cut in on him, started dancing with all eight myself." *Yeah, right,* they exclaim. *You wish.* And then one asks if Karen McDougal, the Playmate of the Year, has showed up. And I write, "Not yet, but I hope she gets here soon, because the two of us have some unfinished business, if you know what I mean." *Dream on, Fearless, dream on.*

The party goes from dead to raging in an instant. One minute it's just me, the food servers, and the bartenders, and the next it's— *wahoo!*—a raging party. Apparently, it's all true—as has been reported, the Mansion is back. And considering that several of the journalists who've written about Playboy's resurgence are in atten- dance, still covering the story, this shouldn't surprise. For me, it's time to really get to work.

I worm my way in and out of the sprawling crowd, in search of the famous or the sexy, all the while trying to shake off Bob Saget's rejection and that "Internet reporter" stuff, and the sneering android triplets, and that exchange with my premium posse.

Ben Affleck—regular guy hanging with his boys, not talking to women—consents to a picture. The grown-up kid actor from *Witness* is spooked by my request, though, like he really is Amish and has never seen anything like this before.

I take pictures of Playmates. A few seem to know who I am, know about the webcast, know I'm a cog in promoting their myth, and thus pose politely for my shots. Only one snaps at me when I make the mistake of standing her in what she considers substandard light.

In addition to Playmates, there are Cameron Diaz and Alyssa Milano and celebs of that stature, and beyond them a whole other strata, similarly striking, but not yet familiar—apparently the next generation of attractive famous women.

Making another pass through the thick of the crowd, eyes constantly looking for subjects, I can't shake the feeling there's something weird about this party. And of course there *is*. It's not just that all the women are beautiful, but that the ratio is backward. Women far outnumbering men. The women aren't allowed to bring boyfriends, only other girlfriends, and the only men invited are famous or Hef's buddies. Another stroke of Hefner genius, but it gives the place a vibe like Superman's Bizarro world, a land where everything is reversed.

I join several other photographers shooting Bill Maher as he does a tequila "body shot," licking salt off the neck of a comely party attendee. But then he sees the cameras and asks if we wouldn't mind getting lost. The photographers laugh like he's being funny and keep shooting, but he says, "Seriously, please, go away." And I think, *Good for him.*

Moving along, I note something else weird about this event, though I can't quite identify what it is. Staring into all of these exquisite faces . . . it's like my zipper is down. No, on second thought, it's the opposite, like I'm conspicuously not being noticed.

"Excuse me, Leif."

"Huh?"

"You probably don't remember me."

She's changed her hair color, to a coppery red, and the name escapes me, but . . . "You were in Seattle, right? You visited the bus. Blue bathing suit, bunny logo tanned into your butt, right cheek."

"Left. No, you're right. Right. Not bad."

"Scary—you can say it."

"It's flattering."

"Did you ever see your picture on the site? You could see the bunny, and then we copied it into this circle and enlarged it. It looked good, like some textbook from the fifties."

"No, I don't have access to a computer. So are you having fun?"

"I guess. I'm working. I don't know. I feel like I should be."

She's cute, sex-kittenish, not someone I fell for, but she seemed sweet.

"It's actually strange that you saw me, because I was just experimenting with invisibility."

That's it, isn't it? In LA of all places, where everyone at least glances at everybody, at a Mansion party where the pond is stocked and the women are all gunning for the famous or wealthy, and it's so clear I'm neither, I actually achieve transubstantiation. . . .

"But I saw you."

"It's not perfected yet. I'd appreciate your silence if you see me in the ladies' room."

"Your secret's safe with me," she says, "and maybe you can teach me and later we can sneak around upstairs, see what happens after the party."

I'm feeling better, was kind of on the way to freaking myself out with that invisibility stuff.

"Hey, there you are," a familiar voice says, a voice that calls to mind some really terrible TV, but, more relevant to the situation at hand, is the most notorious of modern-day Playboy Mansion party regulars. Ladies and gentlemen, a warm round of applause for Mr. Scott Baio.

"Hey, come on over here," Mr. Baio says, grabbing my candidate friend's arm just above the elbow and beginning to lead her away. She looks back to me, trying to mouth, *'Bye* and *Talk to you later* as he continues, "I want you to meet some friends of mine."

"You're supposed to go, 'One, two, three.' Everybody knows that," Shannon Doherty says, abusing me for taking her photo without the standard countdown. Because she's kidding, as well as seductively communicating a level of restlessness with the party, the posing, and the world in general, I summon the courage to introduce myself, and am on the verge of devising a plan to make love to her . . . when my nascent Fearless intuition kicks in. I'm missing something.

Excusing myself, I find it in the Mansion entrance hall: disco dancing. Hef has emerged from his private wing upstairs for the night portion of the party and has taken to the dance floor. He's surrounded by women, including the four women widely reported to be his girlfriends. They've all changed into tight, minimalist evening wear.

Hef's personal photographer, Lynn, a woman of angelic disposition, is firing away, as is his personal videographer, so it seems safe to join them. A too-hasty move, it turns out. A security man—a purported ex-KGB agent—asks me what I think I'm doing as he takes my camera. Lynn has to intervene, explain that it's all right, I'm with the company.

The first shots are all blurs of blonde hair, with Hef's iconic mug in the center of it all. There's an interesting collage there, if everything would line up right: Hef's face surrounded by female anatomy—arms, cleavage, hair, and faces. But I can't quite get it.

Watching them all together, Hef with four girlfriends, it strikes me how accepted taboos have become, at least with regard to the face of Playboy. He's just an altar away from polygamy, and with two of them being twin sisters, well, the word *incest* comes to mind. And yet this rule-flouting is part of his charm. It also strikes me there's something familiar here, in the dancing with multiple women and flashing cameras—but I'm too in the hunt to think about it.

The twins, Sandy and Mandy, have paired off. They dance spoon fashion, dipping dangerously far back, like Siamese twin limbo dancers. They smile sensuously, Pepsodent-white teeth against impeccable tanning-parlor pallor. The sibling thing isn't on my personal turn-on menu, but something about the twins is undeniably compelling. Suspecting they could get me to do things à la

Kathleen Turner in *Body Heat,* I force myself to stop taking their picture.

I scoot back to Hef, who's now surrounded by the Dahm triplets. Though they're trying their best to affect the lurid charm of the twins, they come closer to the Osmond family trying to be sexually suggestive. I snap their pictures anyway.

I fire away, bobbing and weaving, still looking for that perfect shot. The triplets and the twins and Hef and his two other girl-friends—everyone has their fingers sticking up behind their heads and are kind of hop-dancing, little bunnies all. It's kind of cute, certainly a good photo-op, and I'm in tight on the whole thing.

Content that we have more than enough images, Herm begins packing up the gear and tells me to go have fun. I head for the back bar, detouring past the volleyball court. Cameron Diaz and two guy pals are playing volleyball with an enormous beach ball, the plastic sphere looking like the shadow of a UFO as it falls from the night sky and repeatedly knocks Ms. Diaz to the ground, much to her amusement.

At the back bar, I order a Jack and Coke, but am corrected by the bartender.

"Jack and Pepsi."

"No, Jack and Coke."

"Jack and Pepsi. Hef's drink."

Hef's drink. I've been drinking Hef's drink the whole trip, didn't even know it? And shooting the big man just now, that whole familiar scene: that was me in Austin. I was surrounding myself with all those women, dancing with them, cultivating—quite unwit-tingly—a certain image. Now I see that all I'd done was appropriate Hefner's formula. That night out in Austin, and then in New Orleans, the Fearless Reporter had become a Hef homunculus.

I suddenly want to sit down with Hugh, share stories, my little version, his big. I remember Hef talking about his midwestern back-ground, something we share, and what a repressive influence it was in his early life. I want to ask him how much his readers factored into his liberation, feeling he was a character in their imaginations. I feel like he's the only one who could understand. Hef, we should talk, bond, if you'd just stop dancing like a bunny.

But the reality is, he's busy, and I'm sipping from our drink, in the middle of a writhing party crowd. Everyone is talking with great animation, on the edge of shouting. What should I do? Find Cameron Diaz and ask to play night beach volleyball? Or Shannon Doherty? Act on my hunch that she is hungry for life, convince her I'm worthy of a starlet's attention?

For a moment, I imagine myself like George Bailey from *It's a Wonderful Life*. I call up that part of the movie where he's out walking, full of frustrated dreams, and runs into Violet, the good-time girl who had a crush on him as a kid. They talk about making a night of it, but she's thinking dancing and dinner while he's proposing driving up to the lake, walking barefoot, feeling the dew. Soon a crowd has gathered, all laughing as Violet lays into him for such a suggestion.

I really am invisible, standing in the middle of a crowd. I watch mutely as everyone pairs off and hungrily converses, then notice the dark cave that is the entrance to the Grotto looming black and mysterious off to my right. Clearly the guy who's standing solo amid this seething party isn't Grotto-bound. And yet I can't make myself leave. Imagining myself months from now, back in my isolated writer's life and wistfully recalling this opportunity, the sheer ratio, I know I'd be consumed with a particularly acute attack of self-loathing if I departed now.

Talk to someone, Leif.

"Fearless?"

It's Herm, lugging a box of computer cables, catching me just as I'm edging away from the mass, having admitted the obvious: Nothing's happening without that bus.

"Hey, how come you haven't signed and returned the new contracts?"

"Contracts?"

"For the second half of the trip. Son of a bitch, this thing is heavy."

"I haven't received any new contracts."

"Really? I bet I forgot to send them. Well, send 'em back as soon as you receive them."

I was starting to think . . . There'd been no word. I assumed I was done.

"Okay."

"Great. I got you a nice raise. Keep up the good work, you freak."

I nod, slink out of the party unnoticed.

"The first time I had sex, my girlfriend started crying."

I let the line hang out there. Burt is stone-faced.

"I guess some things are so disappointing . . . one is left with no other option but tears."

Odd, that I'm only getting to this now, talking about sex in therapy. After four years of off-and-on counseling? Isn't exploring one's feelings about sex one of the fundamental reasons people *do* therapy? Shouldn't I have brought up the subject before—you know, so it wouldn't be so obvious I've been avoiding it?

In general, I look upon that first experience with extreme gratitude. Experiencing romantic love for the very first time with someone who's also experiencing it for the first time, as I did, I could understand what all the fuss was about: the poems, the songs, *Romeo and Juliet*. I guess I'd mentioned her in the past, but never this part.

The tears weren't a shock. They jibed with the "discomfort" they tell you about in sex-ed. Still, the silvery beads trailing down that frightened, so-loved, so beautiful face . . . I whispered, "Should we stop?" and she shook her head resolutely, wrapped her arms tighter around my back.

My emotions were a complete jumble. On one hand, there was the physical ecstasy and emotional peaking—on the other, guilt over causing this person I would have taken a bullet for repeated pain. My mind called out, *Stop, go back to making out.*

We tried to talk about it, but, both of us being shy and new to the experience, we were at a loss. We'd been primed, as we all tend to be, to expect something that would be nothing other than simple bliss. She spoke of her love for me, of enjoying the closeness and wanting me to feel good. It was a touching attempt to see the glass as half full, but there was no mention of her deriving any sort of sexual pleasure from the experience. Tears with orgasm would be one thing, but tears and a pleasure that was at best vicarious struck me as unacceptable.

Ignorant as could be, I shifted my sixteen-year-old noggin into overdrive, determined to make sex pleasurable for this love of mine. I was convinced there must be a mechanical solution, and yet worried that the real problem had something to do with—you guessed it—the inadequacy of my penis. I spent the next several years failing to solve the riddle.

"Was there ever a moment," Burt wants to know, "when it occurred to you that her lack of orgasm from intercourse is really the norm for women when they're young teenagers, that her tears had to do with her own issues, that this wasn't just about you and your perceived shortcomings?"

It should have been blindingly obvious, but this is the therapeutic moment:

"No, that never occurred to me."

And come to think of it, now that we're on the subject, now that we're rolling a bit, my next serious relationship was off on its own less-than-sexually-savory path as well.

She was a lovely brainy blonde, a young urban planner just out of college. When we first got together, she rather tensely explained to me that she could only come via the missionary position. Eager to expand her horizons, I patiently eased her into as many permutations and combinations of male-female coupling that I could think of.

And, miracle of miracles, she achieved ecstasy in each and every one. Often multiple ecstasy. Good news, one would think.

"Okay, we proved we can get off together, but . . ." she said after one robust session.

But *what*? I wanted to respond.

Instead, I listened as she roundabout explained what was on her mind. There must be something more. Something deeper, that was it. She decided that what we needed to do was to . . . to reinvent sex.

Come again? I'd just assumed sex was one of those things that the supreme being upstairs had gotten right the first time. Like, if only on top of all the sensory delight cappuccinos would stream out of our genitals at the big moment?

She wasn't joking, though. And I was willing to bow to her authority. So the search for a new, undefined sex ensued. There was lots of not-touching touching, attempts, I guess, to stimulate each other's auras. It was a bit like the sex scene in *Cocoon* between Steve Guttenberg and Tahnee Welch, except that neither one of us was a space alien. All in all, some of the most frustrating, humiliating moments of my entire life.

Tragically, all our efforts to reinvent sex proved unsuccessful. The cappuccinos did not flow. And instead of going back to that ridiculously dated, albeit readily orgasmic version of sex, my partner suggested that perhaps the problem had to do with the balance of power.

The problem was that I was always initiating. What she thought might work best was if *she* took over initiating for a while, see how that worked. Fair enough, I thought. I'd just lie there in bed at night, hands neatly folded on the covers, looking as desirable as possible, and wait to have my brains initiated out.

Night followed night with no sign of initiation. No matter how cute I looked, what sort of lingerie I wore—nothing. And to add insult to injury, she was having wet dreams. She'd wake up glowing, eager to pass on tales of crazed sexual encounters she'd had in her dream world. I was reduced, on nights sleep wouldn't come, to quiet self-initiating.

"I know, I know," I say to Burt. "What the f--k was I thinking?" Taking his benevolent smile for encouragement, I continue: "Reinvent sex? What kind of idiot would put up with someone making that demand? Answer: me. But this is an issue beyond the realm of therapeutic intervention, isn't it? We're talking about gross stupidity, aren't we?"

He's still smiling, because the thing is, overwrought as I am, it's working, the therapy. This is me getting better, outraged at what I used to consider normal, unconscious behavior rising to the level of conscious and the conscious not being impressed, at which point there's actually a chance of *changing* behavior.

"I was just wondering," Burt offers, "if you're able to enjoy oral sex."

I'm about to enthusiastically answer in the affirmative, when Burt catches me. . . .

"*Receiving* oral sex."

"Oh, that."

Voodoo! It's voodoo. How does this man see into my head? The fact is, I don't enjoy it. My reaction is always the same: *Really, thanks, that feels nice, you must be cramping your neck, I don't want to be a pain, why don't you just scoot back up, it sure could be bigger, couldn't it?* I've *never* enjoyed it.

"So," Burt continues, "when you *should* be thinking, *This feels incredible, I can barely hold on, this is going to be the explosion of all times,* you're really thinking, *I'm such a bother, she really doesn't have to do this for me?*"

"Well, yeah, kind of . . . uh . . . exactly."

He smiles, like I should get it.

"How do you think you're ever going to feel anything if you're preoccupied by all of these other things? You're lucky to get an erection in the midst of all that, much less climax."

Erection . . . how did you know? Thinking back, that's absolutely what I'm doing, particularly during oral sex, but with everything else as well. My situational impotency, all these bizarre distractions running through my head—enough to fill a book.

There are times I wonder: Is it poor taste to tip a therapist? Slip a twenty in his Sansabelt?

My euphoria is short-lived, because a related thought hits me: Why must my arousal be tied to my head when no other man's is? Correct me if I'm wrong, but isn't this emphasis on what's happening above the neck a chick thing?

"You know," Burt says, "looking at all of these feelings, you realize that in terms of casual sex, you're kind of screwed."

He smiles. He can't resist puns.

But I'm *not* smiling. Instead, I'm screaming inside, *Are you kidding? I'm on the goddamn Playboy bus. I have to have casual sex or I'm going to explode!*

But I manage to croak, "Seriously?"

"Well, it's just my opinion."

The Ohios

I just want to say right now that these are real and I think they're in proportion and I've been told they're beautiful and I just think real is better than fake."

She's only just stepped on the bus, is dressed in a red plaid skirt, sheer white blouse, and white knee-highs. And she speaks the above the way others might say hello.

Of course, no one had suggested they *weren't* beautiful.

The bus is parked in Covington, Kentucky, across the Ohio River from Cincinnati. In an unprecedented bid for the hearts and minds of the native populations, Playboy has chosen to honor Ohio with three bus-casting stops—Cincinnati, Columbus, and Cleveland. It's drizzling out. And chilly. Fall is here. I'm writing an e-mail to Daisy, who has become a steady pen pal:

Hey, I'm back on the job, so can write to you from work. And my first message is, HELP!!!!!!!!!! It's funny that it starts to get to you, this spending excessive hours with people you barely know in a cramped space, but it does. People are getting weird, there's no getting away from it. Daisy, what should I do?

June, who's here in place of Rich, is a naturally beautiful albeit tightly wound woman whose looks make the candidates uneasy, inspiring them to ask, "Why haven't *you* been in *Playboy*?" She has a funny way of interrupting my interviews by asking, "Are you through chatting?"

Sophia has stopped calling me cheesy, and when I stop by the bus on my way for a run, she says nothing about my shorts. When a candidate with an amazing butt visits the bus, Sophia won't play along and worship the butt. During the day her smile looks forced, and at night she goes off with June to a health club to "work out," something she would have derided earlier.

At one point Vegas asks if anyone on the bus needs anything, and both June and Sophia jokingly snarl, "Tampons." I make a reference in the dispatch to our transformed tough guy returning with matching tampon boxes, and my female editor cuts the joke. Her e-mail to me reads: *That tampon joke???? You guys are losing it.*

Vegas, Seamus, and Butch, incidentally, all seem on the verge of killing each other. Their anger with each other has been simmering for much of the trip, but by now, under gray skies, with none of them having much of a break, it's getting ugly. I have to call Rich in Chicago, telling his voice mail he'd better do something.

And me, well, I'm doing a story on this stout old bruiser of a senior citizen who brings her two barely-legal-looking granddaughters to the bus. She's pretty much pulled them by the ears, ranting on about how they might as well appreciate what they have while they got it. I'm writing it down—"Look at me, all wrinkles, which, before you know it, will be you"—when I suddenly realize what I'm doing, manage to glimpse my own slippage: I'm writing a cute, or sort of cute, grandmother story.

None of which is to suggest, though, that when a Catholic-school-girl-themed candidate boards the bus defiantly proclaiming the beauty of her breasts I'm not going to rally.

We're ensconced in the changing area, with electronic doors on both sides tightly closed, protecting us from the bad bus vibe. Melissa, she of the plaid skirt, is up on the makeup vanity, having crawled up there and assumed a feline, on-all-fours pose before I've even turned on my camera. She's also slipped out of her blouse, unprompted, revealing a pretty, sheer-white bra.

There's something familiar about her, something other than the Catholic schoolgirl thing, which I'll admit has a place in my personal erotic fantasia. She reminds me of a young woman I knew in Minneapolis. Same sallow skin, sunken eyes, and general sense of a fragile constitution. In vibrant contrast to the aura of illness, though, both women project extreme sexuality.

"Should I take my bra off?" she asks.

Sequestered as we are in the tiny changing area, with Melissa sitting on her haunches, plaid skirt spread out, hands poised to remove her bra, I suddenly have a fever. Nudity in these circumstances exceeds Fearless's mandate. So the answer, sadly is no.

She's still waiting. Melissa, she and the woman in Minneapolis, here's what they're like, some short-lived flower that must smell all the sweeter to pollinate in its brief existence.

"Um, the thing is . . ." I say, feeling a sheen of perspiration trying to cool my face. "Why don't, um yes, why don't you take your bra off?"

The photos are searing: reflections in mirrors, plaid skirts, white underwear, carnal gaze of ailing health. And let's call a spade a spade: genius breasts. I almost think I should say something like, *You weren't kidding, they're exceptional, and I feel really glad to be alive right now.*

There's a sense that we're both only warming up. But I'm worried that the door is about to open, revealing me and topless Melissa . . . and I'm worried that it *won't* open, leaving me trapped in here with this ailing hothouse flower. A tingle? Yes, Vegas, that's what I'm feeling, which could easily escalate into something that is distinctly improper in a work situation. . . .

"I think we got it that's great why don't you put your top on very nice to meet you."

I feel ridiculous, retreating across the parking lot, heading for my hotel room to be alone. Alone to have my way with these Melissa images, but at the same time I'm glad I got out of there when I did—

before tingle segued to visibly inappropriate. *Please* tell me this was an aberration.

"Leith, vat do you sink you're doing?"

Her name is Greta, another new member of the crew, my current technical assistant. She's a lanky woman with spiky short blonde hair and a thick silver stud through her tongue that renders her nearly unintelligible Polish accent impenetrable. The way she takes in the bus, spies her surroundings, I have the impression she's not a fan of the group dysfunction. Or is it simply all too much to take, going from formerly Communist Poland to the Playboy Playmate 2000 Search bus?

"Vat? No, no, gib me dis, please," Greta says, taking the digital camera from my hands. She holds the camera up, considers it admiringly. "Whose is dis?"

"Um . . . Playboy's," I say, feeling mellow, back from my little time-out in the hotel.

"Bullsheet no. Whose is dis?"

"Mine?"

"Okay, yes, ahsome," she says, and I translate: *awesome?*

"So dat makes you . . ."

"A guy with a camera."

"F--k, no." Greta pauses to look out the window, momentarily distracted. "Dis Ohio, it reminds me of home, you know? F-----g depressing. Okay, camera, what is guy with camera?"

"Guy with camera is photographer?"

"Ahsome. Photographer. So why don't you start being photographer, okay?"

"I'm actually more of a writer . . . well, even that is open to debate . . . anyway, forget that, but I'm not exactly, you know, trained . . ."

"Trained? I've got photography master's degree, but I working as graphic designer. So?"

"Yeah, *so?*"

"You have job with camera, you photographer. They pay you. I see these pictures, in Chicago, I see. Der good, okay? But you too much afraid. Voyeur, is okay for sometimes. But, Leith, not all voyeur. And I watch, this morning? Here I see you apologize, with the girls, 'Is okay I take your picture, I'm sorry, is okay?' Leith, come on, no f-----g way, man. You're photographer. You're good. Enough. You take picture, for them that should be privilege. Okay? Take pictures, man. If this is okay for them, ahsome, if not, f--k them. Okay?"

Greta, who sent you? And who else is studying me? But I just respond, "Okay."

"Ahsome. Now, let's take some pictures. Let's make dis something really cool."

She wants to know what I want to do, what I might have been avoiding, and no sooner have I mentioned that "maybe, it probably sounds dumb, but at least by the end of the trip it just seemed like, well, it would be a shame not to use the bus shower," then Greta has the shower stall open, is tossing aside all the photography equipment cases and casting paraphernalia that had been banished there. And she has me crossing the street to the Kwik E Mart for dishwashing liquid. And by the time I return, there's a candidate under the water, wearing only her thong, waiting for the soap.

"Ahsome. Now we make bubbles, take some pictures."

Ohio passes by. In a dispatch, after a dismal jog on a cold gray afternoon—past check-cashing places and pawnshops and the dinner theater where Toni Tennille is appearing in *Victor/Victoria*—all the while narrowly avoiding stepping on one pancaked cat after another, I christen our location on the periphery of Columbus the "run-over-cat capital of the world."

Sophia and I have our first fight. It goes down in front of a busful of candidates, when I learn that the bus won't be departing on the usual Sunday, but instead on Saturday night, my only approximation of a night off. I can't stand the thought of spending it on a bus driving and resent not being consulted, to the point that I stay behind and catch up with a rental car.

My Greta apprenticeship is the only thing that keeps me inspired. For one of our escapades I suggest a down-and-out swimsuit edition, set around our hotel's dismal seventies-era indoor pool. As usual, the words are barely out of my mouth than Greta has a handful of candidates scattered around the pool.

We haven't asked permission to shoot here. In the windows that surround this indoor courtyard, an increasing number of faces appear in parted curtains. Greta tells a candidate who stands in the pool's shallow end that she must lose the top because "this will be ahsome shot" with her blue eyes against the pool water. Directly above, a family of five, including three young kids, stare down motionless. Twenty-five years from now, the youngest of the kids will be in a therapist's office, calling up this memory.

I begin shooting more on my own now, in the back studio when things are slow, just me and a model. I'm back there with a young woman who resembles supermodel Naomi Campbell. When I utter the standard photographer exclamations—*beautiful, awesome, mommy!*—she seems genuinely touched. So caught up is she that, though I managed to request she keep her top on, she pulls it aside, to reveal small, firm, divine breasts, which she—*I'm not making this up—insists* on grabbing. . . .

Damn it . . . and again I make hurried excuses, exit the bus.

This is getting ridiculous. I'm becoming positively feverish. What happened to my decorum? My situational impotence? Somehow the Hef-cribbed Fearless persona, combined with the ongoing Burt work, has me less and less preoccupied with candidates' issues, and more and more . . . intoxicated. Increasingly, I doubt my ability to pass a sexual sobriety test.

And the whole time, Greta keeps pushing for more.

That afternoon I get a call on the bus from Herm. He mentions the recent photographs, the nudity. We've been through this before: "You should avoid stepping on the magazine's toes," etc. But since crossing that line with Vivian and finally getting nudity on the site, I'm no longer listening.

As for love, I've finally got it all figured out. Looking back—Eve in Portland, Daisy in Albuquerque, Brett in New Orleans—I see the common denominator: a candidate I have a connection with, who also expresses less than full enthusiasm for the magazine, *and* who makes some overture. The more aware of this formula I become, the more I see how reliably these situations arise. If only the gods weren't so amused by my failings, insisting on manipulating fate to keep my plans from reaching fruition.

Take, for example Alex, a psychiatric nurse and part-time model. We meet late in the Cincinnati stay, but she suggests she take some time off from work and drive up to Cleveland to stay with me a few days. An hour before we leave Cincinnati, I get a call from her.

"Are you guys okay over there?"

"Hey, we're great. I can't wait for Cleveland—"

"Haven't you heard the sirens?"

"Sirens? Actually, maybe . . ."

Turns out there's a manhunt going on. One of her patients fatally stabbed a guard. She mentions grief counselors, a possible funeral, a memorial service for her co-worker.

"That's terrible. Awful. I guess, um . . . are we still on for Cleveland?"

In Cleveland, so desperate do I become, that I decide to call a cute candidate at home, though I'm uncertain whether she meets all my ask-out criteria. She definitely made the overture, repeatedly suggested I call, and we hit it off. I just don't know her feelings about *Playboy*. But it's our last night in Cleveland, and my plight is becoming ridiculous. . . .

She's thrilled that I called and the burgeoning journalist in me is soon getting her story. At eighteen Katie was supposed to move to LA—had already been out there and met with an agent who represented several *Baywatch* stars and wanted to sign her. Then she learned she was pregnant. She decided to keep the baby—*babies* actually, twin two-year-old boys who're the little voices I can hear in the background as we talk on the phone. She can't even put into words what they've meant to her. But she also wonders what might have happened had things been different.

She's already suggested hiring a baby-sitter and meeting me out somewhere, but I'm suddenly seized by a notion: What if I came over to *her* place, hung out, maybe rented a movie and made dinner, took care of the kids? I've even convinced myself that it's what the readership would want—photos and an essay of Fearless enjoying the pleasure of a nice wholesome evening at home.

I mention that being on the bus isn't all fun and glamour, that one can actually "grow a little tired of the whole thing, if you know what I mean."

She doesn't. It seems so exciting to her, traveling the country, meeting people, doing what you want to be doing. . . . She can't imagine a bad moment.

I talk about burning the candle at both ends, about how the constant relocation can be tiring. *Say it, just ask. . . .*

"Actually, Katie—"

"For me, to have you pick me out of all those girls . . . it really was such an honor . . ."

She's still talking, I hear words, but . . . the movie, cooking, the kids . . . it's fading.

"I know there are thousands of beautiful girls competing for this—baby, Mommy'll be just a second—sorry, Leif. But if something were to come of this, it might—"

"Ba-bo, ba-bo," a little voice interrupts.

"Just a second, boys. Well, everything happens for a reason, I guess, and if something happened, maybe that would be a way—I'd still have my sons, and could have my dream, too."

It's gone. The snuggling on the couch, the wine buzz, the food coma, the kissing. . . .

"Ba-bo, ba-bo."

"No—no, not now," she says, sounding a little embarrassed. "Still want to go out?"

Yes, as soon as I'm able to rid my mind of "honor to work with you" with a blunt object.

"It's getting late, and unfortunately I've still got to write my column."

"Oh, I understand."

Hollow silence, which I fill with, "But I hope we can . . . keep in touch."

"Ba-bo."

"No, not now. They're going through a phase. Not happy they're no longer breast-feeding," she says, laughing. "A little obsessed . . . with Mommy's breasts."

Oh, Katie, you said a mouthful.

Instead of Katie, I head out with Greta. We find a surprisingly raucous scene in a warehouse on the outskirts of town. Greta, drinking vodka, praises my Jack and Coke order, glad to see I drink the hard stuff. This praise, and more drinks, leads to my praising her, confessing to her my jealousy and admiration for her work, her self-assuredness, her visual sense.

But she's jealous, too, wants me to know that this job I have, the freedom of it, is unbelievable: "Take it from someone who's known what no freedom is."

The drinks keep coming and soon we're posing what-ifs about *Playboy*. What if this legendary magazine were to recruit some young blood, let its time-capsule aesthetics be shaken up? Might it once again be able to shock, return to the forefront of public consciousness? And Greta admits she's considering angling for a job as photographer at the magazine: "How cool would this be, female photographer for *Playboy*?"

A couple of drinks later, a pretty young woman stands before us, says hello. It takes a second, but yes, we recognize her as one of the candidates from the swimming pool. She thanks Greta for taking such great pictures of her. I can't hear what they're saying, but it's funny, the look of gratitude and flirty respect this candidate is giving Greta. It's the look that James and Raj get, but different.

It's an innate trust issue. Like with a female gynecologist. And working these last couple stops with Greta, it's taken the unease out of my shots, or at least started the process. Watching her work, it's not only relaxed me, but highlighted what should be my strength. After all, didn't I tell Brett in New Orleans that I've been told I'm a woman trapped in a man's body?

"Greta, what if we *both* start shooting for *Playboy*?"

"Dis would be so ahsome."

Detroit, Michigan

◆

How long can you go before running out of material?

That line is one of the most repeated in the mail I get—from friends, strangers, co-workers. How long, they want to know, can I keep it up? Evidently, the answer is: *Until* Detroit.

Aldonza and I walk through a nearly abandoned swath of downtown. My original idea was to check out the State Theater, see if we could shoot in there. But somehow I've gotten us lost, the awareness of which has my shoulder muscles tightening.

What will I tell Herm? Will this be the day the dispatch went blank? And what about this candidate, Aldonza—what is *she* thinking of this aimless walking? Where does she suppose I'm taking her?

We walk in silence. Were Greta still on the road with us now, she'd just barge into one of the dive bars we pass and throw Aldonza on the pool table. But I need something more. I probably should have put a little more thought into this, considering I had the entire day to myself.

Aldonza caught my eye this morning. She was holding a folder on her lap. It was green, with a big cartoon picture of Garfield the cat saying, "Well, duh!" I made some joke about helping her with her homework. "Back in my day I was a pretty mediocre student. . . ."

She continued looking at me blankly, so I said, "The folder. You brought homework?"

"Oh, no," she said, with a faint accent, which she explained was Puerto Rican.

I flipped Garfield open. There were some unsettling snapshots— of Aldonza naked in a hotel room, taken by a boyfriend, perhaps. But behind those were professional shots of her in a bombed-out- looking warehouse, her body aglow in afternoon light. Her figure was so vibrant, lush, not at all what one would imagine, seeing her dressed in secondhand slacker clothes on the bus. Her posterior was particularly noteworthy.

"The men must worship you down in Puerto Rico."

She showed the hint of a smile. "I do get attention on the beach."

"Is that true, that the men down there have a thing for butts the way men here have a thing for breasts?" I ask. I'd heard that the Puerto Rican version of *Playboy* is all booty.

"My sister, she has a big chest, and yes, in Puerto Rico, they barely notice. But up here, she always has dates. We're opposites."

I managed not to make a joke about there possibly being a land where women, too, have drastically different preferences—some Shangri-la where neurotic, sexually stymied, questionably potent males are the hottest things around. Sometimes you just have to let 'em pass.

Aldonza had something else to show me, an issue of one of *Playboy*'s Newsstand Specials. Her picture was in it. She handwrote a letter, and a couple weeks later they called to arrange for her to fly to New York. Given the hundreds of stories I've heard of women sending their pictures in to *Playboy*, only to not even recieve a rejec- tion, it's surprising to hear of the ploy working.

We flipped through the issue, "Bad-Girls Next Door." The photos didn't do her justice. And, judging by the way she was clasping the issue, she didn't want to show the last page. I asked if there were any photos I hadn't seen. She blushed, said she didn't like the last one, looked away as I turned the page.

There she was, bent over a couch, shot from behind, looking back.

She was wearing lingerie, but it was completely sheer, creating a nearly gynecological image, racy even by Newsstand Specials' more permissive standards. *Well*, I thought, after getting over the shock of seeing her so exposed, *I can do better than that*.

There's a brilliant red door on a little row house down a side street, and I suggest that Aldonza sit in front of it so we can just get *something*. But as she sits down, wraps her arms around her knees, and smiles prettily, a shrill yapping erupts on the other side of the door, causing both of us to yell out and run away from the little guard dog.

"Does it bother you," I ask, "that I have no idea what I'm looking for?"

"No," Aldonza says, and proceeds to tell me a story about the Newsstand Special shoot. "We drove out from New York City into the country, but the guy didn't know where he was going. We were in the car for hours. And I started to think about the situation, that I had just written a letter, and now I'm in the car with all of these people I don't know. I'm thinking maybe they're going to turn me into a sex slave, you know?"

By the time they arrived at the location, she needed a drink, so they found some champagne. But imbibing on an empty, nervous stomach only made her instantly drunk and sick. She spent the shoot trying not to throw up.

I feel better. Not because of her story, but from speaking up, admitting to being clueless about this shoot. Burt will be pleased. It's one of his deceptively simple lessons for combating anxiety—actually saying what's on my mind.

"So," I ask Aldonza, "I seem normal in comparison?"

"I wouldn't go that far," she says, laughing.

"How about here?" Aldonza asks, pointing to a little shop that sells vintage clothing. There's an ancient woman behind the counter, her white hair pinned up with a little hat and wearing a long dress. The place is filled with clothes from all different eras—flapper,

Marilyn Monroe, sixties—and we're the only customers. It feels right.

The changing area is just a couple kitschy old Chinese screens brought together. Aldonza goes behind and I hand her this pink psychedelic sixties wife pantsuit. When she's ready, I slip in with her, try and get far enough back so she's in the frame. Then—gritting my teeth because the shop is going to fill with flash—I take the picture.

We hold our breath, waiting to hear some complaint, but the little old lady says nothing.

We put Aldonza in a fifties black lace cocktail dress, then a red silk kimono, then a seventies wraparound thing. Each time she changes, I step back out into the store and allow her some privacy. But when I hand Aldonza a men's vest, ask her to put it on with nothing underneath—wanting the sides of her breasts visible—she starts changing before I'm out, so instead of leaving, I just tilt my head down. There's still the proximity to a woman changing. As I open my eyes and see the vest and that full curve beneath it—just what I was hoping for—it's all starting to feel nice, intimate. . . .

"Excuse me," says a craggy old voice. Aldonza bites her lip. I push open the screen.

"We're taking pictures for . . . her boyfriend . . . of her in cute clothes. He's on an aircraft carrier. For six months."

"For his birthday," Aldonza adds, stepping behind me.

"I close up in fifteen minutes, just so you know."

We step back in, pulling the screen behind us, trying not to laugh. I want to buy Aldonza something, want Playboy to buy her something. She deserves some payment for doing this, giving up her afternoon. When I suggest the black dress, which fits her like it was made for her, her cheeks flush, and my only sadness, as I ask for a receipt, is that I won't be taking her out in it.

Back out in the cool gray day, I look at my watch. Things should be winding up on the bus. As I take note of Aldonza's bag and the sexy outfits she'd brought from home at my request, the obvious hits me: "How about going back and shooting at the bus?"

*   *   *

It's a little tricky getting rid of everyone, or at least the men. Sophia and June barely pause to smirk at me and Aldonza, but the guys linger. Vegas and the current photographer—they're very interested in my work all of a sudden, as well as the nice young candidate. "What was your name again? We didn't catch it."

I have to repeatedly reassure Vegas that I know how to lock up the bus. He *knows* I know this, but he still must be escorted to the door. Our current photographer, too, who in his daily life is more of an assistant, is very interested in our work

"You're very fortunate. I yearn for the opportunity to do something more creative."

He begins waxing on about the constraints of taking Search Polaroid shots, how he feels his gifts are wasted, and that he'd love to work with a talent like Aldonza, free from restrictions of his daily work.

Yeah, whatever, buddy, explore those yearnings with your own candidate, I think, as I show him to the door. A part of me, though, is distantly aware of how different I'm acting, never before using the bus after hours, let alone kicking co-workers out.

Aldonza upends her bag and a delightful tangle of tiny colorful outfits spill out. Selecting a pair of little blue shorts and a white mesh top, I send her to the dressing room. Once back in the studio, we get down to work, to the faint sound of the digital camera and our breathing, which rises and falls together.

"You're good at posing me," she says.

I've chucked my shoes, work from my knees for many of the shots, catching the heroic angle.

"Honestly. You're not like other photographers. It's very comfortable."

I know what she means. The Greta conversation—I'm not lurking on the periphery, but am front-and-center, being my sensitive self. There's a moment, though, when my mind would like to take these thoughts in a neurotic nosedive: *But is that being manipulative, using this nice-guy b.s. to lure a woman into taking off her clothes in the back of a bus . . . ?* But I remain calm. I keep shooting, her back to me, legs crossed and up on her toes, the combination accentuating the amazingly full, amazingly perfect Aldonza butt.

She steps in the changing room to change, during which time I hear something, some noise outside. I turn to see that a gang of preadolescents has climbed up on their bikes to scope out the bus's interior. They are flashing crazed smiles. They nod frantically to me, giving the thumbs-up approval of little dudes. Back in the studio, I close the door.

We shoot her in a little two-piece black lingerie outfit. Then in a white French bathing suit I can't really explain. It's technically a one-piece, but barely there, comprised of a white strip that wraps around the neck before coming down and covering, barely, both breasts, then joining at the bottom. Aldonza's lying on her back. I stand over her, straddling, looking down.

"Can you pull the strips off to the side, like that? . . . Right. Now hands over breasts, but don't actually cover, and then, not like ecstasy, but close your eyes, okay, and turn your head to the side."

I love this shot, think, with her nipples poking through, that it puts a twist on every recent magazine cover that features an actress or singer on the cover topless, save for her or someone else's hands. It's also not a *Playboy*-type shot. She's neither feigning pleasure nor pretending to be alone, is instead aware she's setting a scene.

But as I'm about to take the photo, I realize the thrill is escalating—surging, if you will—and I can either step off her, excuse myself for a moment, think of something safe—impending tax code changes, the debate over school vouchers, Señor Wences—or get this picture.

I take the shot, repeatedly.

Aldonza's bag is empty. We're out of outfits, which causes momentary panic, but then I think of the obvious—Aldonza naked. Actually, I decide to use a robe—the famous Search robe—as a cover, but imply nudity. My voice croaks as I ask if she'd mind taking the last shots with only her thong. The shaky voice isn't about nerves, as in the beginning of the trip. Now it's the by-product of lust.

I arrange Aldonza in the corner, pull back the robe, and pose her in that shot where the model's knees come up to shield her breasts, and feet are close together so you can't see if she's wearing underwear. I tell her how beautiful she looks, how great these pictures are turning out, and as I'm taking them I stand up to adjust her hair, realizing too late that . . .

Well, there's no polite way to say it. The fact is, I'm *beyond* tingle.

It gets worse. As I bend over to make the adjustments in her hair, I catch sight not only of the ludicrous tent in my khakis but—it's almost *too* humiliating to reveal—a spot on the fabric. It's not *that*, not ejaculate. Rather that stuff they tell you about in sex-ed, the male body's contribution to lubrication. That spot is right at Aldonza's eye level. Precome. Classy.

Run. Run away. Tell her you're ill, you freak.

It's ridiculous, insulting, embarrassing, possibly illegal. I know all that, and am leaning toward the door, when, *f--k it.* You know what I'm saying? For crying out loud, what the hell? This is absolutely one of the most erotic experiences I've ever had, and am I not supposed to, you know . . . react? It's just, as absurd as my situation is, calling a halt to it—yelling, *Cut!*—seems more absurd.

I pick a new pose: Aldonza lying on the Playboy robe, the robe standing in for a bearskin rug. I keep firing away, encouraging her all the while. And that feeling I've had in my loins now spreads. Every nerve ending becomes an erogenous zone—fingernails, hair follicles, everything.

But what about Aldonza? *What is she thinking? Is she aware of what is going on, that we have been breathing in sync?* I position Aldonza so she's leaning against the base of the studio couch, robe between her legs. At this point it seems that the only really strange thing would be for us not to be together.

Reach down, slip off the thong, slide inside her—that's what an atavistic voice calls out from deep inside my cortex. I take a photo. Take another. Stalling.

Though I can already vividly sense how good this is going to feel, there's still the small chance that I'm wrong, will wind up on the cover of *USA Today*, the headline reading, "Desperately Horny Internet Reporter Attacks Innocent Would-Be Playmate."

But is that what's holding me back? There's something else, something that calls to mind some of the other young women from the road, like Vivian in New Orleans. Certain of these candidates, there's a fuzzy vagueness about their personalities, like countries without clearly defined borders. Too yielding. And for me, even like this, furnace about to blow, I'm too aware of it, that not saying no—particularly in my role as apparent Playboy designate—is not the same as saying yes.

And then it's gone, the moment of temptation. Once again, I've given matters too much thought. Already I feel my systems powering down. I already hate myself for this, but . . .

"I guess we're finished. You can put the robe back on."

Having said good-bye to her with a hug, I return to lock up. My breathing is slowly approaching normal and I remain thrilled about the photos, but still, I want to know whether that was good judgment or fear. Stepping back in to lock up, I notice something lying on the couch. It looks like a notebook. She's left it behind, the cartoon cat.

"Well, duh!"

With a coffee in my hand and a computer bag over my shoulder, I weave my way through people speed-walking to work, and I take in the old-time buildings of Detroit's business district. Emerging from the city core, stepping out of building shadows and into the morning sunlight, with the river and bus now in sight, I start chuckling, though I'm not sure why. Soon my socially acceptable slight giggle escalates to full-out laughter. It reaches a point that I have to stop walking. I double over, amid the pedestrian flow, wiping away tears that are streaming down my cheeks.

It's everything. Going to work so matter-of-factly, after yesterday . . . being alone with a candidate in the back of the bus, becoming beyond aroused, out of body, and taking it all so seriously. So ludicrous, and no friend to share it with, the experience of the proverbial tree falling in the woods. And now here, laughing hysterically, the decent citizens around me living their normal lives, not knowing who I am, nor bothering to ask if I need help.

I continue laughing, catch my breath, then break into peals of laughter again, acutely aware of how close I am to losing control.

"Call Herman," Sophia says as I step into the bus. "He sounds pissed."

It's not what you're thinking. No call from Aldonza's lawyer. Rather, Herm wants me to know that the production team back at the home office is screaming at him. Am I crazy sending *all* those images? And requesting they animate the images, so they'll appear on the site like a live photo shoot? And with *all* that text? Don't I realize the time constraints they're under?

I shift to grovel mode, pointing out that I'd left everyone apologetic voice mails last night, warning them, explaining it was a one-time thing. It's also why I mentioned that if it was too much, Greta had offered to do some of the tech work, that if it *still* was a problem, they should call me and I'd tell them what to lose.

Unfortunately, adopting the angry logic of the put-upon worker, the team's reaction to my wish list was to do nothing. There is no dispatch up.

Nothing?

Since I came back for the Search's second half, people have been dragging their feet over the amount of work that goes into the daily dispatches. Having heard the praise, no one remembers how we got to this point.

"And another thing, Leif, about some of those images . . ."

"What?"

"We just can't . . ."

"Can't what?"

"She's feeling her breasts with her eyes closed."

"So what?"

"It's a little too . . . too sexy."

"Herm!"

"Leif, this isn't the magazine. Actually, they wouldn't allow that in the magazine."

"They're great pictures."

"That's not the point."

"They're sexy because they're a little different. That should be good. I busted my ass."

"Listen, I'm going to see what I can do, but please, go easy out there."

"Herman, did you see her?"

"Yes."

"Come on!"

"I'll do my best."

Too sexy?

I spend the next two days in the stairwell. There's a fold-out jumpseat for riding shotgun, and it occurs to me that if a candidate sits in the jumpseat, the surrounding white surfaces bathe her in perfect light. And if I wedge myself up on the dashboard, back smashed to the windshield, I can just get the shot. So that's what I do for two days, photograph faces.

The women are all so different, but in the flattering light, and without the complications of their being nervous overexposing body parts—not to mention my own nerves—I can get them to smile so naturally, the sort of unguarded smile that occurs between friends. They keep letting me "in." And when I show them the images, one woman after another gives me the is-that-me? response. My editor in Chicago writes: *Love these images!*

Taking everyone's picture—the stunning, the plain, and everyone in between—the experience reinforces another recent epiphany from the road. Having studied hundreds of women day after day, appraised all with a critical eye, eventually it comes to this: Either everyone is flawed, or everyone is beautiful. The idea calls to mind the claim James made about his ability to find the beauty in any candidate. Working with candidates in the stairwell, it's clear how much more attractive the latter attitude is.

It's not until late in the first day of head shots that it occurs to me what I'm doing. Not to undermine the preceding sensitive observations, but come on, cutting off the bodies after what I went through with Aldonza? Take that, folks in the home office! Just a bunch of heads. Not even a *hint* of cleavage. Fully cognizant now of the passive-aggressive game I'm playing, I keep shooting heads.

It's late in the afternoon, Day Three. Our last day of casting. I should have made arrangements for a date by now. It's a Saturday night. There've been one or two possibilities over the past couple days, candidates slipping me their cards, but nothing I've been excited about.

There's a candidate who's willing to rescue me from my predicament. Part-time bartender at a club owned by her brother, she also runs an escort service, presumably recruiting talent from the club. She sweetly suggests that she can hook me up, should I be in the "unlikely" position of needing company.

As I continue shooting portraits, I find myself wondering, with horror, if I'm seriously considering the offer. That thought sends me out to the parking lot for air. Amid the usual last-day rush of candidates frantically filling out applications, a new arrival catches my eye. But since I don't want to offend the other women, I persuade Seamus to bring the others in first, leaving her to me.

Her name is Dolores. I ask if I can take a picture of her face. She shrugs. She's wearing a long black skirt and heavy sweater, not revealing an inch of skin. Her blonde hair is pulled back and haphazardly twisted up. She has a graceful mouth, but slight bags under her eyes, and her nose is the tiniest bit bulbous, like her great-great-grandfather might have been W. C. Fields. When I raise the camera, she makes no effort to smile.

I make some comment about the scowl, to which she replies that I don't look so cheery myself. And just like that, we're staring each other down. Naked staring. I don't know what passes between us, how this chemistry thing works, but something's going on. And I must say, after Aldonza, and all the others, it's comforting that she isn't abnormally pretty, that deeper feelings are finally happening, and that they aren't directed at a freakishly sexy woman.

I get the door for her. She hitches her long skirt to take the big first step, then gets stuck for a second on the stair, so that I almost bump into her, face into butt, which is when I get the bad news. It happens in a flash, a mere glimpse of skirt pulled tight around rear, but with my now-seasoned eye, I'm afraid I may have praised her for exclusively possessing inner beauty too soon. Dolores, I suspect, is at the very least covering up a phenomenal ass. *Damn.*

She's supposed to be filling out her forms, but instead our faces are inches apart and we're arguing about who is more lonely. It turns out that we've both been planning to adopt goldfish in an attempt to solve the problem. I tell her about the little lake in Echo Park, where I live, with the huge koi swimming among the lotus blossoms. My plan is to release my fish anytime I go out of town, so they can grow up to be big.

"Or eaten," Dolores suggests.

She also explains her extra clothes and semi-surly attitude—a friend wouldn't take no for an answer, insisted she come down to the bus. But Dolores professes zero interest in Playboy, and wanted to look as undesirable as possible for the occasion.

As we continue talking, I can feel people staring, including Sophia, whose jaw is open. I send her a glance, telepathically assuring her this is out of my control. When Dolores laughs, which she does with abandon, she rests her head on my shoulder. It's all I can do not to kiss her.

"So what are we going to do about this?" I whisper, so all the eavesdroppers don't ear.

"I don't know," she whispers back.

"Are we going to get together tonight?"

"I'm going out of town for the weekend. My family rented a cabin in the woods."

She lowers her head to my shoulder again. A wave of warmth surges up my spine. Who spiked my cornflakes with Ecstasy?

"New York," I say, not giving a damn about jeopardizing my job. "We'll be there for Halloween. You're coming to New York."

Just then, a candidate who's finished her casting walks by, exiting the bus. "It was nice to talk to you," she says as she passes. But I don't remember talking to her. A moment later it hits me . . . *Oh, sarcasm.* Sarcasm sounds so brittle when you're in love.

Buffalo, New York

The new crew members, Tashi and Elaine, are telling stories about their work as a photographer-producer team in New York. They like to work covertly, often using hand signals to communicate, as they conduct their shoots on the busy city streets or down in the subways.

Elaine, the producing half, speaks in a Broadway-dame, baby-doll voice. She was a Wall Street computer analyst before overlapping stints as a professional singer-dancer, a "Women of Broadway" *Playboy* model, nude body double in movies, and Playboy producer.

Tashi, her cohort, is a hairstylist turned fashion-world hairstylist turned fashion photographer turned erotic photographer. He races around the bus like a little kid laughing, styling candidates' hair, and suggesting I take pictures of him diving in the air to catch a bikini top as a candidate tosses it off.

There are tales of Elaine's donning a sexy outfit to charm Navy brass into letting Tashi shoot on their ship, and of models they've dressed in short skirts, without underwear, striding past construction crews on lunch breaks, with Tashi following along, crouched down, shooting up, catching long legs, skirts, dazed workers. It all sounds familiar, similar to where Greta and I were headed.

The rest of the crew are getting frayed around the edges: The police arrive to interview Vegas about some complaint they've received, which evidently proves groundless. We all fail to notice when a candidate brings her baby onboard the bus at the same time a reporter is taking a tour. At one point I'm sitting outside with Seamus, autumnal winds whipping away at the tent flaps, and when I try to lighten the mood, joke about what a sexual free-for-all our Playboy life is, he scowls. "Don't piss on my neck and tell me it's raining."

Given the mood and the cast of characters, I've set modest goals for this stop. A simple image I've had in mind since we pulled into town: photographs of a couple candidates flashing in front of Niagara Falls. Kind of "Ansel Adams, the Naughty Years." Unfortunately, I'm having a hard time even managing that, finding two lovelies with the right Playboy zest for a trip to the local natural wonder.

In the meantime, candidate after candidate laments how "dead" their city is. Ranking with Albuquerque's hopefuls in their desire to flee their hometown, they spin fantasies of escape—essentially beg us to take them away, preferably to Florida. Enmired in the melancholy, we find ourselves clinging to Tashi and Elaine's joie de vivre, with me picking them as my subject for the day's dispatch.

"So, much of what I do," Tashi says into my tape recorder, "is acting out the fantasies I had when I was in my teens. I'm bringing them to life, with Elaine's help."

I nod vigorously, remembering my own explosive sexual awakening, and realizing that much of what drives my picture-taking interests is tied to that time. Even the shots with Aldonza behind the changing screen had precedents—memories of sneaking into changing rooms with my first girlfriend.

Something still gnaws at me, though. It takes a second to figure out how to put it into words: "Tashi, given that you *are* making those adolescent fantasies partly real—I know everyone asks this, but does the situation ever escalate?"

"Keep in mind, what we do is very expensive—there's the model's time, the crew, the equipment, the location. So there's pressure. And with all those people . . . the more people involved, the less likely you are to achieve the chemistry I think you're talking about."

I imagine Aldonza and me in the midst of a five-person crew and having to be conscious of the ticking of some time-is-money clock. But still . . .

"Some of the situations I've been in," I say, "well, they're all one-on-one, and I haven't known . . . I mean, it's been much more *heated* than I anticipated. It's a strange situation where it's almost my job to lust after the model, be the eyes of all the other men who will see her image."

In the way Tashi stares out into space I see I've triggered some intimate memory. But then he makes a funny face, a conspiratorial face, a face that says, *We photographers have secrets.* Which gets us both to laughing, in the midst of which I realize Aldonza's shots must still be on my laptop. I decide to share my work.

"Ooh," he says. "These are sexy. With that little camera? You're good." He keeps flipping through images, then looks up. "And just the two of you? Lucky man . . . wait a minute. She's—I know her—that's . . ."

"Aldonza."

"Right, Aldonza. Elaine, come here, you've got to check this out, remember Aldonza? What a nightmare. Is that really her? You got better shots of her than we did."

Better shots than the photographer? The compliment reminds me of an e-mail I received from Rich this morning. *Hey, buddy—about the Puerto Rican. She looks beautiful. Someone we should be keeping an eye on, or was that just great photography?* And I remember Greta's and my alcohol-fueled scheme to become Playboy photographers, which is the moment I wonder, should this be—could this be—a *sober* ambition?

Tashi and Elaine take turns telling their side of what happened when they shot Aldonza, and amazingly it's the Rashomon version of the story I've already heard. They comment on how oddly jittery she was and I give Aldonza's side, explain that the length of the drive made the girl somewhat paranoid that they might not even really be from Playboy. Tashi laughs. "That's right, the driver did get completely lost."

They then mention that she was so on edge they gave her a drink, but that only seemed to make her worse. I describe how she hadn't eaten, and the alcohol didn't agree with her, so that she was worried about vomiting in the midst of the shoot. Elaine and Tashi laugh sympathetically, concluding that the way she looks in my photos, like a different person, says a lot about how significant is the model's state of mind.

As I step outside the bus, Vegas follows me. He has a last detail about the Aldonza shoot, a detail Tashi and Elaine left out, which, he suggests, really explains her nerves. For Vegas, attempting to be diplomatic is a confusing experience, but he mentions that all of the lingerie that day had to be thrown out, that the model really should have canceled the shoot, that she suffered from a medical issue—"a sexually transmitted outbreak of a recurring nature." And that's all, he suggests, he should say on the subject.

VD? That's apparently the suggestion, and I remember Aldonza showing me the pictures in the magazine, not wanting me to see that one shot of her bending over the couch. My heart goes out to her. It says a lot about what she was willing to endure in order not to avoid missing her big chance.

But wait. Didn't we almost have sex?

I recall my perception of her, of a young woman who was not saying no, and I'm intensely relieved—relieved in a way that has me breaking out in a cold sweat—that things with Aldonza ended like they did.

I don't land my waterfall shot until our last day, which is not to say Day Two passes without material. A candidate visits the bus who lists her job as "magician's assistant" and I end up convincing her to persuade her boss to come down to the bus and make some magic. To the bewilderment of my co-workers, I photograph the two of them—he turns out to look like a long-haired Gothic version of David Copperfield—back in the studio, he levitating her, she wearing a see-through blouse.

Elaine, perhaps sensing she should help me with my Niagara tribute before the bus antics get even more bizarre, calls me in my hotel room the morning of Day Three, tells me she has two candidates who match the description I gave her. So my assistant, the two friends, and Seamus squeeze into the rental and head off.

Seamus is actually not on the clock, has opted to take the day off, and is technically along as a tourist. Studying his lined face in the rearview mirror, I can guess why he's taking the personal day. He looks terrible. He wears an expression one would see and say, *Good lord, what happened to you?*, never expecting the answer to be, *The Playboy bus.*

Once at the Falls, it becomes obvious I haven't fully thought this out. There are people everywhere, thousands of people. And it's freezing out. But there's no going back. By taking this road trip, I've blown off all other story possibilities for the day. I've also rented a car without asking Herm, raising the stakes further.

So I ask the girls to go in the rest room and, if they wouldn't mind, lose their bras and shirts, come out with just their jackets. When they return, I position my assistant and Seamus to the sides, a vain effort to conceal our activities. Seamus, Mr. *NYPD Blue,* is trying to talk me out of it, whispering something about getting hauled off to jail.

People are too uptight, you know? If two women can't expose themselves in front of one of the world's natural wonders, regardless of the throngs of families around, then can somebody tell me what the point of it all is? Seriously, the more I do this, the more I see the looks we get in public, the more convinced I am that we're right and everyone else is wrong. I know the line "It's just the human body" is a cliché, but really, isn't it true?

The girls do it once, blink-of-an-eye fast, but before everyone can run off, I tell them to hold on. We need to do it again. They think they opened all the way, but the picture reveals they didn't. And once again, we're going to animate this, like the hula lesson in New Orleans, so I need multiple pictures, including one or two where they're fully exposed.

The girls do it again, opening their jackets all the way, in the freezing air, with a thousand or so eyes on them, and an awesome mass of water plummeting off the cliff behind. Their expressions are wildly wide-eyed, as if they were in fact going over the falls in a barrel. As for the breasts, all four are revealed to be extremely . . . well, Elaine knows her business.

"*Now* we can go," I say, meaning now we can go stop by the Harley dealership where they work and take pictures of them in their bikinis straddling hogs, and then we'll go have an expensive lunch on Playboy, because I can't do this without a trade-off.

Seamus, though, lingers.

"You're a twisted f--k. You know that, don't you? Huh? You know you're losing it?"

It's Dolores, on the bus phone. We're about to pull out for NYC. She sounds well. She's sorry for not getting back to me sooner, has been distracted with midterms, but has been thinking about me. It's nice, this expression of interest without mention of a boyfriend, or ongoing manhunt, or wanting a possible threesome.

Turns out, though, it's more than me that has her feeling good. I'd known she was in college, studying business, but hadn't realized she had a job on the side. Stripping. The place is only topless, and her mom, she tells me, sat in the audience the whole first night she worked, making sure nothing happened. Dolores, a lifelong dancer, enjoyed the movement aspect, and the money is ridiculous. But she recently decided it isn't worth it. She quit this morning and is feeling buoyant.

"It's time to get out when you suspect you're starting to hate men."

Though I'm a little taken aback by the news of stripping, had no inkling of the sideline from my brief time with her, I'm happy to hear about the choice she's made.

"So Dolores," I say, thinking it's a long shot, extremely last-minute, and will cost me big in airfare, "are you going to let me fly you to New York?"

Were Burt or certain concerned friends here, there'd likely be a cheer at this tentatively bold gesture, and I'm pleased to have asked. Yet I can't shake the reality I'm inviting, i.e., hiding, a woman from my co-workers for an entire weekend.

"Definitely," she says, "as long as my mom says it's okay."

New York, New York

It all begins with The Donald—Donald Trump, that is—surrounded by cleavagely gifted candidates in front of the Playboy bus. Skyscrapers reflect in the bus's towering windshield as he shoots a jet of white liquid—champagne, technically—all over the bunny logo. I capture the image and a Playboy publicist tells me she wants to distribute it to the wire services.

Later, I'm with Greta, who's back on the road, the two of us eluding security guards in Rockefeller Center in an effort to make it up to the studios of *Late Night with Conan O'Brien*. There, one of our candidates, an actress, is taping a Conan skit, playing the buxom blonde. We take pictures of Conan and Andy Richter for the site. Conan signs our photo release, saying, "Something tells me this is the sort of thing I pay a lawyer to advise me not to do."

The real excitement for me, though, is that New York is the first stop where a friend will be able to see in person what I've been doing. Thus far, people have tended to listen to my bus stories with mock belief, like my friend Estella back in LA, who's convinced I've been working at Jack in the Box this whole time. They act like they're humoring me. And a part of me shares their disbelief.

So it's a great relief when my longtime pal Wayne arrives from LA and I'm able to bring him back in the photo studio and persuade a representative segment of New York womanhood—a commodities trader, a lawyer, a designer's fitting model, and a hip-hop DJ—to surround him, lay hands on him, kiss and fondle him, as I capture the moment for my dispatch.

Wayne is tall and smartly dressed, with an infectious smile and deep brown skin. If you saw him, you might think you'd met him before, or maybe that you'd even gone to school together. He's a member of that unsung Hollywood caste who make a living acting in secondary roles on TV shows and in films. Most recently he's appeared on *The Steve Harvey Show*. Apparently, it's a must-see program in the African-American community, because Wayne is hailed by every black man and woman we pass during his visit.

This is all to say that Wayne is no stranger to odd perspectives. Still, as the girls help him up from the studio couch and escort him through the *Star Trek* doors, back up front to the bus's lounge, where I introduce him to more women and show him some of my high-tech gadgetry, he's no longer looking at me with that sure-you're-working-on-the-Playboy-bus way.

"See?" I whisper to him, "It's real, isn't it?"

"Sure it is. And even if it's not, who cares?"

The plan was that Wayne would take Dolores around during the day, freeing me up to work. But on Day Two Wayne and I swing by the hotel lobby to collect her, fresh from the airport, and I first see that cheery beaming face, see Dolores step out into the street, look up at all the tall buildings with the thrill of a first-time visitor, repeatedly exclaim, "Ohmygod," I realize I've been kidding myself. I will be doing very little work over the next two days.

The afternoon passes in a blur of New York tourist must-sees. Pretzels, the Empire State Building, and, to Dolores's great joy, shoe shopping. She and I hold hands every minute. At intersections, when we're fortunate enough to get a DON'T WALK, there's kissing, the two of us a living, breathing Robert Doisneau image.

A funny thing about taking to the streets with Dolores: While I'm the Playboy guy, and Wayne is the Steve Harvey guy, next to her we're the nonexistent guys. Everyone—men and women—fixes their eyes on this luminescent force we're strolling with. They see her and smile. She has that kind of spark. Which is fine by us, because as her companions we reap benefits, foremost among them that we rarely pay for things. The pretzels are free, the virtual-reality ride atop the Empire State Building is comped. Such is Dolores's world.

Wayne and I are kidding her about the phenomenon, and at first she just says, "What do you mean?" and acts as if it were normal. But when pressed, she tells of a French guy, an alleged count, who was recently at her strip club. He'd been tipping her in hundreds, telling her in broken English that he was in town on business. The guy claimed to be a great cultivator of roses in his spare time, and if she told him her real name, he would create a rose in her honor.

She assumed it was a line, but told him anyway, and just recently they'd called her from the club. There were roses waiting for her—not cut roses but an actual plant. The label identified the breed as The Dolores. Accompanying the plant was a letter from the count inviting her to the château whenever she wanted.

Toward the end of the day, we locate a costume shop. It's Halloween eve and the place is under siege, a mob of panicking shoppers. A lisping goth salesman/boy assists us, fetching costumes for Dolores to try on that are all variations on the same dress. Nurse, witch, French maid—all feature an extremely short, extremely tight latex dress. Each time Dolores pulls back the dressing room curtain, activity in the frantic store momentarily ceases. She has enough vah-vah-voom in her life, though, so she opts for pinstripe shorts and double-breasted blazer.

"I'll be a gangster," she says, satisfied. A moment later, she pulls an electric blue flapper dress off the rack and announces, "And Leif, you can be my flapper bitch."

There's a great rollicking outing that night on the bus. I hadn't been sure we should go, nervous as I am about the crew catching on to where I know Dolores from. But the bus is heading out to an old hangout of Seamus's—an infamous Italian restaurant in Queens frequented by cops, ballplayers, and the occasional gangster—and my bus confidante Sophia settles the matter by insisting she'll squeal on me if we don't come along.

It takes what seems like hours to get there. On the bus, the music never stops. Crew members are dancing. Everyone takes Polaroids. Playmate Rachel Martinez is supposedly along, but I never see her. I've been introducing Dolores as someone I met while we were in Detroit, saying that mutual friends put us in touch. Realizing no one's in a mood to be skeptical, I grow quickly comfortable, pull Dolores into my lap, where we practice our kissing. Wayne keeps saying that he doesn't care if we ever get where we're going. "I'm all about the ride."

Back in our hotel room, Wayne snores in his bed while Dolores and I kiss and wrestle in ours. She wears men's-style pajamas, smells somehow of vanilla, and continues exhibiting such adorableness, good humor, and lust-worthiness that I'm concerned I'll botch this somehow with a patented example of Leif self-sabotage—perhaps some sexy hives.

Since we're both about to pass out, and have known each other for less than a day, and *do* have one more night together before she must get back on the plane, I decide the best course of action is to let things taper off at this point and we're soon both fast asleep.

At five A.M. I wake up to the alarm and shut the thing off before either of my roommates stir. With my head feeling as though it might crumble, I ease myself into the bathroom, shut the door so as not to wake the others, and set up my laptop on the cold tile floor. I can't procrastinate any longer. I must write and file a dispatch. I can't forget, after all, I have a job.

Eyes blurredly fixed on the keyboard, it's a strain just to remember the way words go together, let alone be funny. But I must cough something up and send it to Chicago, so I plod on, only occasionally coming to a complete halt—each time the hideous realization sneaks back into my head that I'm on the bathroom floor, working at five-thirty in the morning, while my bed is being kept warm by the most desirable pajama-clad body.

Two hours later, with a terrible dispatch uploading over the phone line to Chicago, I slip back into bed, pull Dolores in, and re–pass out. Around eleven, all three of us wake up, Dolores leading the charge and telling us we have to get out and see the city. Wayne and I ask her to kindly shut up.

"Hey," Dolores says, "were you working on the bathroom in the middle of the night?"

"Yes."

Wayne bursts into a phlegm-filled schadenfreude laughing fit at this news.

"I think that got into my dream," Dolores says. "We were down in the Bahamas, hanging out in some little bar on the beach. It was this cute shack that was also an oyster bar. But the whole time we were there, Leif, you were freaking out that you couldn't find an outlet for your computer. The walls were all made of thatch, and you kept looking, insisting there had to be an outlet somewhere, because you had to plug it in."

I scan Dolores's face for signs of recognition, any indication that she knows what she's saying. The overt sexual metaphors are almost too obvious. But all I see is a happy-girl smile. Leaning over, she gives me a quick kiss on my lips and announces, "I'm going to take a shower."

Stepping out into the night in midtown Manhattan, I feel like I'm having one of those dreams of being out in public without any pants on. The first moment is horrifying free fall. I am, in fact, *not* wearing pants, have on only fishnet stockings, a black garter, polka-dot boxer shorts, and a very short dress. What really makes me feel naked, though, is the shoes. Tottering down Madison Avenue in search of a subway, feet torqued up in marabou-trimmed mules, I feel like a bunny tied to a rope that a hunter has staked to the ground in the hope of luring bigger prey.

Once on the train, I notice Dolores and I are the only ones in costume, and I'm wondering why we didn't take a cab. I want to crawl under the seats, or make out with Dolores, but instead hear myself talking.

"I see you. Yes, I see you staring. Looking at me like I'm the weird one. Fellow subway riders, don't you know what day it is? Hello? Rhymes with spleen? Halloween? Does that ring a bell?"

I'm getting blank looks. New Yorkers stare at the guy in the blue flapper dress, look on with no change in expression. Nonetheless, I continue.

"Friends, they give us one day when they say, okay, we recognize the pressure of conformity, so here's your one sanctioned day to let off some pagan steam, and we won't ostracize you, and look how you respond. New York—the cage door is open and you're sitting on your perch."

Still, nothing beyond seen-it-all indifference. That is, aside from the old guy in the buttoned-up shirt fixating on my garter. I demurely pull down my dress, feeling exhilarated. In my mind, I'm already composing the dispatch to my readers about the need to rediscover the true spirit of Halloween. There must be a liberating side to being crazy.

Several minutes later we arrive in front of a bar called Cortez, where we're to meet friends. Unfortunately, the aspiring professional wrestler guarding the door won't let Dolores in without an ID. The monolith won't even take a twenty-dollar gift, money that he could surely put toward a flashy cape or new wrestling tights. I'm tucking the twenty back in my fishnets when he comes up with a counter-offer. We're all welcome in, he says, "If I can get a look at her tits."

Dolores steps in front of him—he outweighs her by two hundred pounds and is a foot taller—and with undaunted gaze opens the gangster blazer, pushes back her bra, lifts her palm-size breasts, lightly squeezes one, tugging at her nipple. The mountain man is frozen, as is Wayne, whose mouth is agog. Dolores and I could go on a crime spree, she freezing men, me taking their valuables.

That is, if I weren't a little frozen, too.

Cortez is an overcrowded freight elevator taking the express route to the earth's center. People are shoulder to shoulder, shouting out conversations, laughing in shrieks and roars. Several women are up on the bar dancing, and over their shoulders are the bras, hanging in clumps on a series of hooks, like a long coatrack.

We find our friends deep in the crowd. I've been having that feeling you get when you're about to introduce your nineteen-year-old potential Playmate to your brainiest friends, they of the Ph.D.s and perfect SATs. But Dolores is quickly surrounded by said pals. I can't hear what she's saying, but they're throwing back their heads in laughter, whatever it is.

Did I mention the mushrooms? I may have ingested psilicybin mushrooms, something I was offered the moment we located the gang. I rarely use drugs—my freewheeling mind not needing any encouragement—but, well, I once lived in Colorado as a ski bum, a lifestyle for which recreational drug use is mandatory. And I took only a minuscule amount, just the crumbs in the bottom of the bag. Enough to provide an energy boost. But considering I've already been ranting on a subway tonight and am in a flapper dress, the drugs may be just enough to send me over the edge.

Wayne and I are near the bar when one of the guys pushes past en route to the rest room.

"Thanks for bringing the little Pam Anderson doll. She's great."

Pam Anderson? As in Pamela Lee? As in former *Baywatch* babe? I don't know what he's talking about. And then I do. Take away Anderson's breast augmentations, the cartoon makeup, the psychological mayhem wrought by her career, and you'd probably have something similar to Dolores. Both women display a certain infectious innocence combined with unbridled sexuality.

"She's a doll," Wayne says.

"I'm just glad I'm old. Imagine the younger me: I'd be making such an idiot of myself."

I gag, horrified to find a foreign object in my mouth, relieved that it is only a pale blue feather from my boa.

"But do we ever *really* get past making an idiot of ourselves?" Wayne asks.

There's no light in the bar, giving the party the frenzied look and feel of an impromptu celebration during a blackout.

"I don't know," I say. Already I can feel the damn drug making it hard to conceal emotions. "I just . . . she's never been to New York before and I'm this guy working for Playboy, inviting her to visit. You know? Is this obligation?"

For a moment, we see Dolores dancing with a friend of mine, her fedora moving to the beat. She flashes a big smile and waves, then gets swallowed up again.

"I don't know, buddy, but it seems to me she likes you. She came to visit. She's staying with you. Sleeping in the same bed. Kissing you. Seems to be having fun in your presence. These are some classic signs of 'like.' "

I'm unconvinced, take a strong swig of Jack and Coke, gag when I realize there's something in my mouth. The boa again. Then, speak of the devil, Dolores pinches both of us on the ass. She grabs my head, plants a big smooch on my lips, and says, "I told you I didn't want you talking to other men, you sexy bitch."

She pulls me to her, moves my hips in an effort to get me to dance. Being pulled in by Dolores, it feels good, in my toes and in my earlobes, but the heels . . . Dancing might mean a broken ankle. She's looking up beaming, yells over the crowd, "I'm having so much fun."

Over her shoulder, the girls are still on the bar—thick-waisted, drunkenly beaming from nondescript faces, dancing to a rhythm only marginally related to the music. Dolores can barely move in the crowd, but the little movement she is managing is graceful, sinuous, and I'm instantly fighting my new, improved circulatory system.

I take Dolores's drink, hand it to Wayne, and lift her up to the bar's top, just as a new song begins. The other girls scoot back, making room, and at first they keep dancing. But then Dolores takes off her fedora, tosses it down to me, permitting waves of soft blonde hair to cascade down. The crowd falls nearly silent. The other bar-top dancers go still.

"Oh, man!" Wayne yells. "Oh, man! Go, Dolores, go!"

Dolores moves up and down, swaying and swinging, losing herself up there to the music. She smiles serenely and this whole crazed, dangerously-beyond-capacity bar looks on. There's applause as the song ends, and as guys nearby exchange high fives, the crowd starts chanting, "One more song, one more song."

"That's a story we'll never know," I shout into Wayne's ear.

Wayne looks to me from Dolores.

"That aura she has. We're obsessed with it. The world is obsessed with it. She's a catalyst. People name roses after her. That's something you or I will never experience."

"Not in that dress, you won't."

My own effort on top of the bar does not go so well. Even when I go for the cheap appeal, grabbing my breasts, looking heavenward in the ecstasy of it all. Even when I wrap my boa around the woman in front of me, pull her in for some girl-on-girl grinding. Even though, as Sophia might point out, from my hemline down, clad in the fishnets, I could pass for a woman.

What I was saying to Wayne before, about being jealous of Dolores as ingenue—it's true. A part of me has always envied women in general, for so many reasons: emotional integrity, maternal instincts, multiple orgasms, to name a few. Is there such a thing as vagina envy? And yet, dancing on the bar in heels? This isn't what I want.

As the song ends, a female bartender yells, "Don't ever do that again—girls only." And so I take to the air, leaping out over a barstool and descending into the mass. Wayne's shoulders somewhat slow my fall, though not enough to save one of my heels, which is badly bent under. I'm thinking, *She's right. I'm not a girl, even with these legs.*

"Leif, we're going to split," a passing friend says, motioning toward his waiting girlfriend. "Best to have sex before the drugs wear off."

A couple hours later we're standing at the door to the Vault, the S/M club. I read about this place in a magazine and am surprised I remembered the location. The doorman, with shaved head and bulging eyes, wants forty dollars from each of us, even though it's already four forty-five and the club will be open only for another hour. Single men, heads down, push past us, handing over the money and disappearing through the door as I ask the doorman to be reasonable.

I plead for a volume discount but am met with the blankest of gazes. Desperate, I pull out the big gun I've so far left in its imposing holster: I mention the name Playboy. "See, the thing is," I say, confidential-like, "I'm with Playboy. There's a trip across the country and everything I do is fodder for my column. With this being an obvious contender and there being the possibility of favorable press, well . . ."

He almost laughs. He doesn't actually do it, but almost. Of course, I'm not seeing what he's seeing: an apparent drag queen with a broken heel, gangster girlfriend, and square-looking buddy who looks strangely familar in new Banana Republic–wear, trying to use the world's most famous hetero men's magazine to swing a late-night discount at a primarily gay bondage club.

"Are you tripping?" he asks.

"A little bit, but at this point, it's more the alcohol."

"Well, I don't think this place is your answer, whatever you're looking for."

Thirty minutes later we belly up to a diner counter in the meat-packing district. The place is crawling with attractive, drunken people. Wayne is deep into an obscenely large hamburger. And I'm talking to Dolores.

I'm trying to set things straight. I tell her I don't want any confusion or games, because I think so highly of her. If she wants to be romantically involved, that's great, but if not, that's great, too, because I'm different from other guys.

She looks at me a little wounded.

This damn outfit—the fishnets are constricting, the air circulating up my dress sucks, and my lone bare shoulder is distracting. And these shoes.

"I thought . . ." Dolores says. "Aren't we having fun together?"

"Yes," I say. *Honestly, I hate these clothes.*

"I thought we were having such a great time."

"Yes." *Force Wayne to trade outfits. You need firm ground.* "Dolores, what I think I'm trying to say is . . ."

And then a voice in my head suggests I stop. Just shut up. So I kiss her on the cheek and suggest I may have had the tiniest amount too much to drink. I then excuse myself to go to the bathroom. As I wait outside, a tall transvestite or transgender woman says, "Come here, sweetheart," and with a tissue, holding me by the back of the head, dabs under my eyes.

"Your mascara's running, darling."

I've been asleep for hours when my slumber is interrupted by a low moan. Through the fog of waking I feel pressure against my pelvis. Dolores has spooned back up against me and is grinding, moaning. Is she awake and trying to start something? Or dreaming again?

My genitals, disappointingly, seem not to have noticed. After all my changing, after creating the New Me, I can't believe it. I can't fathom how I can be in this situation and not feel a thing. Amid my self-chastising, an old memory surfaces.

I was at the age where I was still playing kid's games, but almost too old, nine or ten. A game of hide-and-go-seek. I wound up hiding in a closet with another kid. She was younger, probably five. Blonde, perfectly featured, the neighborhood princess.

It was a small closet. And pitch-black. I remember hearing some kid calling for everyone to come out. And as the girl started to stir, I remember telling myself, though I knew otherwise, that we needed to keep hiding, so when she tried to get up, started to pull away from our spooned hiding place, I held her, hands on wrists. Her struggle escalated . . . until she let out a quick piercing yelp. I let go and opened the door. Rejoining the others for the next round, I felt rattled.

That's it. That's the only time in my life I've ever, even for a moment . . . It wasn't even a thought—I was devoid of sexual desires. But there *was* a wanting something and an understanding of the potential to want someone who doesn't want to be wanted. Back in the eighties—during my coming of age—there were those who argued that all sex is violence against women. Have I always feared that it might be true?

I am, oddly enough, alive.

In fact, I'm safely in bed. Well, my three middle toes are numb, appear to have suffered mild nerve damage—and will feel this way for the next five months—but I'm otherwise in one piece. Actually, there's also that matter of what I said in last night's dispatch. All I had were pictures from a brief visit I paid to the bus yesterday, a test run of the outfit, Fearless in drag taking pictures with candidates. Strangely, I'll have to go online to find out what I wrote to go along with it.

Wayne coughs in a way that says he should have stopped at one pack of cigarettes.

"Angel, why don't you get Uncle Wayne the ice bucket so he can spit up a lung? Then find something heavy to bash in Uncle Leif's skull."

"What about me?" Dolores says. Her hair is tangled and her face is pillow-creased, but she still manages a cherubic grin.

I push the face away, asking, "Any good dreams?"

She yawns, looking up toward the ceiling. "I had a horrible dream," she says, with Wayne moaning in the background. "I'd gone back to stripping and was dancing for this man, and as long as I did everything he said, everything was okay. But the minute I stopped, he got really mad and started yelling in this horrible way. . . . It was terrible."

She's off again to shower, leaving me to notice that our window does in fact open.

"Wayne, I don't want you to get all weird about this and ask me not to, but as soon as they bring up the coffee and I have the energy to get out of bed, I'm hurling myself out that window."

"Can I have your digital camera?"

"Ten thousand women have been on the bus and I insist on picking the girl who has nightmares about men controlling her every action? No doubt the dream was inspired by my drunken effort to define what is going on between us. And why do I pick the girl skittish about men? Because I *identify* with the sentiment. So that's it, I'm going to put an end to this."

Wayne answers with a cough.

"I realize it's selfish, that you and everyone else who loves me will be inconsolable."

"We'll manage."

"Just know that my limit has been reached and I truly have no other option."

"No problem."

I've got to go, join the bus, continue on. But before I leave—I dread doing it, but I decide to log on, check my e-mails. As expected, there are plenty—expressing displeasure, no doubt.

Dear Fearless, as a devoted fan of your dispatches, I look forward to logging on every day to see which girl-next-door will be in the bus in search of her break. This recent stop, though, has been a waste of my time. That goof Donald Trump? Day Three was the worst, with that gnarly chick in the blue dress. I could see one picture but not an entire dispatch. New York must have much better stuff. I hope you get back on track!

Washington, D.C.

◈

There's a naked candidate on my lap, holding my hands to her breasts. I actually try to pull away, saying, "People might get the wrong idea," while making a concerted effort not to feel the breasts. Obviously, it's impossible not to feel, but I try to feel in a more objective way, like a doctor.

"Oh, come on, lighten up," she says, tightening her grip and telling our photographer to take the picture. Then telling him to take another to be sure we have it.

There're four of us back in the studio: Leslie, the naked woman; the photographer, Dan; Leslie's friend, still in bra and underwear; and yours truly, the objective one. It's our first day in town. I just woke up.

"You've got soft hands," she says, finally letting them go. "I love that. I love men with soft hands touching me. Most of my clients are lawyers—well, who *isn't* a lawyer in DC?—some of them get manicures. Isn't that hot? A man's hands with a manicure. That rocks."

Dan and I shake our heads, conceding that it *is* sexy. But I can't help but mention, "Don't most strippers hate that, if they're actually touched?"

"Seriously? Not me. That's the good part."

Leslie had piqued my interest by listing stripping in both the job and hobby blanks of her envelope. I'd merely asked to take a picture of her, of her big move, whatever she did that really brought out the tips, and suddenly I was pinned.

She isn't a pretty woman, but the body, while probably ten pounds over the weight currently considered fashionable, has a curvy softness that feels nice. I don't doubt she does very well at drawing out tips.

"Aren't you going to have April take her clothes off? What are you waiting for?"

April, who is nearly six feet tall and has a pixie face, blushes. Dan, the photographer, obliges Leslie, asks April to strip. I must admit to my own Leslie-like enthusiasm, but as April slips out of her bra, I wince. The boob job is one of the more botched I've seen. Which is saying something, after what I've witnessed on the road.

It's worth noting that this is the ugly secret of breast augmentation. Those new and improved mammaries all tend to look impressive in clothes, but so do rolled-up sweat socks. Get those clothes off and it's a different story. Anyone looking to discourage the procedure based on side effects could make a more visceral argument on cosmetic grounds. One look at this candidate would do it.

"Isn't she hot? April's a bank teller, but sometimes, when I get asked for girl-on-girl, I bring her along. How sexy is that? Yum. Don't you want to just molest her?"

Again, Dan and I are caught politely nodding: Sure, we would like to molest her.

"Here's some stripping trivia for your article. You know that Clinton thing, with the cigar? He didn't invent that. Believe me. That's been big here for years. I bet this is the most kinky city you guys visit."

What does one do with candidates like this? I can't help but appreciate her energy, but she's so out of my moral sphere. I feel paralyzed.

"I can't wait until we're done here. April's playing hooky. I'm going to be all over her."

All I can think to do is stand the friends in the changing room together and have them snuggle up for one little kiss, which I plan on telling the folks at the home office is just the candidates demonstrating a scene from their act. That's different from actually having a girl-on-girl scene on the site, right? They're merely pretending for illustrative purposes. Of course, though I ask for a peck, what they give me is the last days of the Roman Empire.

Given the full nudity, the line-crossing photos of me with my hands on a candidate's breasts, and the girl-on-girl action, I'm feeling ahead of the game. My thoughts turn to the following day, for which I already have a plan—something along the lines of the trip to Niagara Falls, substituting national monuments for water. I only need to find the right candidate.

I'm hanging out, meeting women, going over a strong contender's portfolio. There's a shot of her in a sort of farmer's daughter outfit stretched out in a real live haystack. Other shots show her in a swing, by a stream, and in a wheelbarrow. All feature sexy clothes and cheesy poses, and it takes several patient explanations for me to understand where she got the shots.

"So a company arranges these photo weekends, they find a location, charge photographers for setting and willing models, and your only payment is photos for your portfolio?"

"That's it. They match up dirty old men with young girls and get paid for it."

She has her hair pulled back in a ponytail, revealing a broad, beautiful face, sans even a touch of makeup. It's a face that reminds me of those composites *Time* or *Newsweek* occasionally run, along with the heading, "Is This the Face of the Future?" I think I can see Mediterranean, African, Egyptian, and Indian in her lovely face.

"Cynthia, what are you doing tomorrow morning?"

A man in black fatigues and a black cap patrols the perimeter of the White House. He has an M-16 slung over his shoulder and held in ready position, though a black canvas cover has been thrown over the weapon, giving it the look of a gun-shaped purse. The guy walks past us, just beyond the fence, face devoid of acknowledgment, as if he thinks we can't see him.

I take a first picture of Cynthia against the famous background. Even though she's dressed, even wears an overcoat over her dress, the two of us keep looking around.

"Okay, Cynthia, that's good. Now smile for Aunt Edna."

Are there microphones around? Why wouldn't there be?

"Why don't you start opening your coat, slowly, show your aunt that pretty dress?"

Truth be told, I'm not in love with the dress. It's wool, coarsely woven, with a square neckline and bland oatmeal coloring. She's wearing a teddy underneath, which is more interesting, but how to access it? I want to have pictures for yet another animation—Cynthia flashing in front of the White House—but I already feel conspicuous, am sure a security team has cameras trained on us.

As I continue taking forgettable shots, I say, "I guess, um, I guess that's as much . . . um." I pause, not yet totally without scruples when it comes to asking a woman to expose herself at eight A.M. on a cold day. Before I continue, Mr. Invisible with the M-16 makes another pass.

Then she says, "Should we find a bathroom so I can take off the dress, then come back?"

"Yeah," I say to the young mind reader, "I think Edna would like that."

People are on their way to work on this gray morning. Business-people, in business clothes. Cynthia and I walk among them, arm in arm. The neighboring structures are office buildings, with stark marble lobbies, populated by security men massively filling out their blue blazers. They politely shake their heads when we ask for the bathroom. We stroll on, the bureaucrats and lobbyists and business types all clipping along at a much quicker pace.

We find a deli in one of the buildings, and when they, too, deny us rest room access, Cynthia tells me to distract them, which I do with a probing question about the process by which water bagels are made. She then slips past a THIS SECTION CLOSED sign and tiptoes up the stairs to perform her quick change.

Back on the street, we return to the rapid current of grave-faced worker people, until we're again in front of the White House. We need to do it quickly, we agree, wondering aloud as we say this if we're doing something illegal. A large family is looking to get the same shot, so Cynthia and I stand close together for warmth, smiling for whatever cameras are watching us.

"I'm having fun," Cynthia whispers to me. "My best friend and I wanted to do this. We wanted to go all over DC, take pictures of each other naked in front of all these buildings. She's going to be jealous."

I don't have time to ruminate on her comment or to wonder if there should be some secret society for people who find this a pleasant way to spend time. The family is finally walking away. The security guy is nowhere to be seen.

"Let's go, Cynthia."

I step back into a crouch as Cynthia opens the black coat, stretching her arms wide so that the garment takes on the look of huge wings, body in white teddy popping out against the background, figure held gracefully in a sweeping curve. I get the shot, then snap off a second before she closes her coat. Looking around, I see at least half a dozen law enforcement types standing within sight range, as if they'd just stepped out from behind the trees.

"That Edna is one warped aunt."

An old-fashioned cab takes us to the Washington Monument, the overly heated air producing a cozy, sleepy feeling. The old cabdriver, his dashboard covered with photos of grandchildren, whistles softly, tonelessly as he drives. Cynthia drops her head to my shoulder. I turn to her, bringing my mouth and nose to her hair. I kiss the top of her head. She snuggles in closer, so I kiss again.

We do the Washington Monument, and then the Lincoln. With that awesome stately figure behind her, I'd like to get more than the lingerie. Again Cynthia reads my mind. She slides her index fingers over her teddy's lace cups, slips the material under, and unleashes her breasts.

We hop a cab and ask for the Watergate. We're thawing out; Cynthia leans against me. We laugh about the close calls with The Man and about how Cynthia loves to do this. She wonders why everyone doesn't indulge in such exhibitionism. Smiling, she looks up at me and says, "You're going to end up a fat dirty old man taking pictures of little girls."

I freeze up for a moment, feeling unpleasantly exposed.

"And . . . what about you?"

"Probably the same—a fat dirty old woman taking pictures of little boys."

There doesn't seem much chance we'll get past security at the Watergate. Nonetheless, we walk arm in arm into the groovy, well-appointed lobby. And when no one stops us, we take a seat, slumping down into a white leather love seat, cuddling together. Again, people are streaming by, presumably powerful people, moving in and out of the doors.

Massaging Cynthia's palm, I think about Monica Lewinsky. She's supposedly holed up here, has yet to be seen in public. If I could just get my butt out of this love seat, leave Cynthia behind, I almost believe I could track the ensconced intern down, wrangle her onto the website, scooping Diane Sawyer and the conventional competition in the process. Delusional, yes, but such is the nature of my increasingly detached thinking.

But on the couch, it's just so nice, sitting with my model. I don't get up.

"Cynthia, I can't thank you enough," I say, back in the Mayflower lobby, staring down at her excellent bangs, which hang over sleek eyes. "You made my day."

"I had fun."

"Make sure to give my room number when you leave the garage, okay?"

"I will."

"Actually," I say—this is a perfectly sensible suggestion, much as it feels otherwise—"do you want to come up?" I look around. "Put your dress back on? We can get you some breakfast. Playboy owes you that much. I've got work, but you can hang out."

Up in the suite, Cynthia comes out of the bedroom, into the salon, wearing the Mayflower bathrobe. My idea, but she was immediately game. I hand her a menu, then log on to my computer.

Fearless, reads a note from Herman, *you must have been kidding with those photos, right? The hands on the breasts? Those two chicks making out? That was a joke, yes? You can't think we can run that? I'm faxing you guidelines from Standards and Practices. Give me a call ASAP.*

There are other e-mails, from past assistants, telling me how the picture of Fearless the Breast Fondler has been printed out and stuck on everyone's cubicle. What, they want to know, will I do next? But I'm not in a mood for fun, instead bang out a response to Herm— some indignant rant about how as long as people read the text, see the context, they'll understand. And what do I have to do anyway, go work for *Hustler* to get creative freedom?

Screw work. Cynthia and I sit on the floor—I can't tell you how handsome the room is, but Mayflower, please consider this advertising. I'm on the phone for some time placing our comprehensive order. We're going to pig out; we've earned it. Still sitting on the floor, waiting for food, Cynthia tells me about her art school, where she studies sculpture.

"It's so great, sculpting a head, the way it comes into being," she says, speaking in hushed tones. "From a lump of clay or some big stone, how you just make it appear, bit by bit, uncovering that person in this inanimate object. It's so cool, who wouldn't want to do that?"

For some reason, we hadn't ever talked about this—what Cynthia does—until this moment, but it turns out she's an artist, has been a professional since she was sixteen, specializing in sculpture. She's had several shows, is represented by a gallery. In the past, I would have seized on this, wanted to know more, incorporated it into the dispatch. But I barely hear her. Instead, I take her in my arms, slowly lower her down to my lap, gently cradle her head.

"There's so much to heads, so many of the senses, so much of a person's experience can be captured in their head. Don't you think heads are amazing?"

She has perfect skin. Not a blemish. Her eyes are gray. There's a moment of thinking of Dolores, whom I feel myself missing, but this reclaimed virginity business is becoming ridiculous and the moment is so perfect. I lower my head, softly kiss her perfect cheeks, her straight nose, the beautiful eyes. It's slow kissing, keeping with the morning's dreamy rhythm.

"You're kissing me."

I softly kiss outskirts of lips that have just spoken.

"I know," I whisper, kissing along her forehead and then asking, "Is it okay?"

"I don't mind," she says, looking off as I bite gently along her ear. "It feels nice."

I brush my lips against hers, not stopping to kiss. The bed is just through the door, around the corner. Maybe twenty feet away. A superb mattress. Cynthia has closed her eyes. It's amazing how long it's taken for everything to line up. I just need to lift her up, carry her into the room. I'm feeling a rush of knee-weakening elation. If she'd only *do* something, if she'd seek me out, pull me in. Without that, I'm not totally sure.

I keep kissing. There's plenty of time, I think. I'm here all weekend, and surely this is a done deal, one even I couldn't botch. So I cradle and kiss, while stroking her fine hair. Several minutes later there's a knock on the door and a cart is pushed in bearing our break- fast of eggs and bacon and pancakes. We devour it.

*   *   *

A woman in a blue blazer and floppy women's tie hands me the Standards and Practices fax as Cynthia and I pass through the lobby. Violence, rape, incest, bondage, bestiality, etc.—nothing about two female friends simulating a kiss, or even a reporter placing his hands on a candidate's breasts. It just seems so arbitrary, what gets them going. What about some of the really tacky photos we run? Shouldn't there be a clause prohibiting bad taste?

"What's that?" Cynthia asks.

"Just a note from my boss telling me to keep up the good work."

Seamus shoots me a leer as Cynthia and I board the bus. We plop down next to a candidate named Sybil who's in the middle of telling a story. While I'm still stewing about the fax, at least I've retained the warm and tingling sensation, the residue of my morning with Cynthia.

". . . so, first question I miss, off goes the skirt," Sybil is saying. "Second question, I lose the underwear."

She's talking, it turns out, about going on a local radio show— whatever the DC Howard Stern ripoff is—and playing strip current events. I take the bait, asking, "You weren't interested in the more traditional wristwatch, one sock, two sock progression?"

"No."

"Why not?"

"Well, because I'm not like other people, and because I wasn't intimidated, and because to be a tease in a situation like that would be ludicrous. And because I'm a little strange."

"Well, why didn't you just miss all of the questions?"

"Because I'm not stupid."

Sybil's another former emancipated minor, now putting herself through grad school. There's something familiar about her. The independence. The mild craziness. The appearance: polyethnic, face-of-the-future look, buxom figure. There's even something familiar about her address, a Maryland suburb. I show the address to Cynthia, who's sitting on the other side of me.

"Hey, that's my street."

"Cynthia," I say, "meet Sybil. Sybil, meet Cynthia. You two should be best friends."

Though part of me senses trouble, I show Sybil some of the morning's shots.

"She's totally hot," Sybil says matter-of-factly, looking from my camera to Cynthia.

The tone is that of a connoisseur. I can't help asking, "You're interested in women?"

"Most definitely. I just broke up with my girlfriend."

Leif, don't do it. Change the subject.

"Do you think *she's* cute?" I mouth to Cynthia. She nods her head. I can't seem to stop it, whispering to her, "Have you ever . . . ?"

She shakes her head no. The doors to the studio open up and Collin, cameraman from Playboy Video, appears.

"What's up, Dick?" he says.

"I didn't know you guys were on for DC."

"Just a quick one. Who're your friends?"

It must look a little funny, the bus is effectively empty, but I'm tightly sandwiched between these two. He knows something is up, must have developed his own instincts for this kind of thing. If I were to lie, to say there's nothing here for him, he'd laugh in my face.

"Actually, it's kind of a coincidence," I say, my stomach churning as the memory of Cynthia in the hotel robe grows more indistinct. "They live on the same street. . . ."

We're back in the studio. The four of us. The girls are naked. Collin is on a knee, in tight, taping. He runs through the usual lame questions and is quickly rewarded with Sybil's candid stories of threesomes, intimidated boyfriends, and her attraction to Cynthia.

The girls are turned on a forty-five-degree angle toward each other and it's like a mirror. Both have voluptuous figures and the type of breasts you won't see in the magazine. They're not once-small breasts enhanced, but naturally large, with a slightly distorted shape, like vegetables that have been left on the vine beyond the usual growing time.

I take pictures. They really are beautiful young women, and with the mirroring and the attraction . . . But there's Collin in close with his camera, and I've got the Standards and Practices fax, and my sweet, quirky Cynthia suddenly feels far away.

I know what Collin is going to ask before he says it, seem to hear his request for a kiss a second time, so strongly does it echo my own thought. But because I apparently can't use women kissing in photos, I'm stuck looking on, a voyeur peering over the video camera as the Botticelli mirror closes in on itself. With enthusiasm, Sybil takes hold of Cynthia's head, brings Cynthia's mouth to her own. The two kiss, tentatively but seriously.

Cynthia has once again taken a seat on the couch with me, while Sybil remains back in the studio, having her actual photos taken. "So would you want to . . . to be with her?" I ask.

Cynthia brushes her bangs aside before nodding yes.

"Fearless, come talk to me for a second," Collin says as he steps out the bus door.

I meet him on the sidewalk, across the street from an ABC News studio.

"What's the deal? They seem wild. Will they get together for us?"

I don't know what to say. I strongly desire to be far away, and yet I have relevant information. I know that both women are planning to join us on the bus's excursion tonight. I know that Sybil is bi, thinks that Cynthia is hot, that Cynthia is bi-curious. And it could be argued that this is part of my job, helping Collin get footage of the two of them together. Also, there may just be a part of me that wants to be there. . . . But my Cynthia, the great hotel room, our dreamy morning together, ordering room service—standing there, filling in Collin, it's like watching the petals of a flower wilt.

It's not until I've completely finished bringing Collin up to speed and forecasted the likelihood of his obtaining the sort of shots he's looking for that I notice Cynthia. She's been listening to every word. She must have slid open the window and has been leaning out, eavesdropping on this professional consult. It's so sad, looking at her face. The goofy smile is long gone, along with the morning's sweet feeling.

I've turned into the guy in *Star 80*—the PG version, but still, it's just degrees of sleaze.

Herman won't budge on the photos. They go too far and he won't put them up. He won't even put up a version where the image is mostly dissolved, barely visible, and further obscured by the word CENSORED emblazoned across. It's infuriating.

So I call it a day. I slip on running shoes, and head out for a long one. I'm back in the civilian world, though this time moving faster than everyone else. With music from a mixed tape blasting in my ears, I weave my way through pedestrians like a runaway ski racer, striding until I'm totally lost and not finding my way back until almost six. Just as I'm in sight of the Mayflower, my pager goes off. It reads: 911.

I call the bus from a pay phone. It's Sophia. There are two women at the bus she thinks I should interview. When I tell her I have plenty for the day, she suggests I think again.

Tess apologizes for the way she's talking, lips immobilized, but she's just had her lips and chin done. It's embarrassing, she says, speaking like a master ventriloquist, but what are you going to do?

With her friend Isabel nodding on, Tess explains that they host a show. They review porn, or maybe it's the inside story on porn—I'm not sure what they're talking about. I don't follow where the show airs, or if it's actually a reality, and I'm still in running clothes, smell like a locker room, and don't feel like dealing with whatever the ventriloquist is trying to tell me.

What to say, how to get out of the bus without being insulting? Is *Don't call us, we'll call you* too harsh? I'm about to speak up when I hear the bit about the live sex show.

"Live sex show?"

"That's what we do," Tess murmurs. "It's how we're financing our video show."

"By *sex show,* you mean, like the two of you get together and strip?"

Tess shakes her head as though I've just accused her of using the wrong salad fork.

"It's not what you're thinking. It's not two strippers getting together, bringing a vibrator to a gig. Not at all. That's just a cheap attempt to capitalize on the girl-on-girl craze."

"It's much more," Isabel agrees.

"It's more like a well-choreographed orgy. With anywhere from two to six girls—"

"Or seven—"

"Well, yeah, or eight, whatever they can afford, but there are props and sex toys. . . . It's hard to describe, if you haven't seen it. It ends with all of these women going at it, and the men watching us going crazy."

"Tess's amazing with the strap-on. She can out f--k any guy I've ever been with."

Tess doesn't even blush.

"Wow," I manage to say, a really naughty image in my mind. "And you do this often?"

"All the time. On weekends we're booked from early evening until morning. And we make at least five hundred dollars an hour."

"You do? And do you . . . is it acting, or are you all into this . . . ?"

"Ohmygod, I always come," Isabel says. "I've never not."

"It depends on the crowd. Sometimes they get a little obnoxious, the guys. We don't like to be touched, or really even a lot of screaming. As long as they're behaved, yeah, we get off."

"Here's something you should print," Isabel says. She proceeds to mention a revered professional sports team. "They were the worst. Of all the professional sports teams we've had, they sucked the most.

F-----g professional athletes are used to getting this stuff for free, so they act all entitled."

"How about . . . I mean, maybe this is a dumb question, but what about your boyfriends?"

"Tess and I live together," Isabel says. "You should see her house. Tess's got the most beautiful house near American University. Those people don't have a clue what we do."

"Well, they know we're not a sorority."

Isabel's zeal, Tess's cool plastic face, the two women expounding on a lifestyle about as removed from my sexual existence as the earth is from the Andromeda Galaxy—it's enough to make me dizzy. They go on to explain their video show, which in detail makes sense. I'm startled to hear that they've already invested fifty thousand dollars in cameras and editing equipment.

Knowing she has a rapt listener, Isabel talks about her first time. About how she began by answering phones for the sex show company, then came along to a show, just to give lap dances on the side. But one of the girls didn't make it to the gig, so Isabel went out there, wild with fright. The next thing she knew, a girl was going down on her, another was nibbling her breasts, and she was coming and then she was reciprocating.

"So the first time I went down on a woman in my entire life, it was in front of fifty people. It was all so insane, and then there was all the money. I thought, *There are worse ways to make a living*."

When I suggest that this all plays into deep-seated male fantasies and fears, that women secretly want each other and that we're superfluous, they only shrug.

It's half past six and everyone else has called it a night, so we're the only ones on the bus.

"Shall we head into the studio and get a few images to go with your story?"

The girls stand before me, waiting to go, in surgically exaggerated glory. In my mind, I see a writhing Dante-esque vision of their sex shows.

"I have to clear out some images from the camera, and we're ready to go."

It's a refreshing change, shooting these women who're used to doing things I've never imagined. I certainly don't feel that I'm luring them into something they'll regret.

I take a first picture, just to get the two of them together, clothed. I wish I weren't in these running clothes, wish I were feeling more professional, but there's no point in changing.

"Okay," I say, "I guess we'll just . . ."

It's a little tricky, though. What to do? Infinite possibility. They stand before me so seriously. Just provide some guidance. But why isn't something coming to me? Especially after a run, my mind is usually reliable. Nothing. They're waiting. . . .

"It'll just be a second. I've got to think of how best to do this. . . ."

Standards and Practices. That fax. All of this opportunity standing in front of me, but each time I think of something, Herm and the fax come to mind, and I'm back to nothing.

"Sorry about this. I just need . . ."

There's nothing I can do. They apparently do the greatest sex show on earth, and none of it can be shown on Playboy's website. Even if it's real, even if this is what they do, both personally and professionally. There's that lingering line: *She can out-f--k any guy I've ever been with.* It's hard not to be curious. But lawyers and faxes add up to full-on creative block.

"This is really . . . it's hard to explain, but I got this fax, kind of got in trouble. It's really a shame, but I . . . don't think there's anything I can do with you two."

Back up in the suite, the first thing I notice is the Mayflower robe, and think of the morning. Screw Collin. Salvage the weekend. It's possible she didn't hear me after all. . . .

"Cynthia?"

"Yes?"

"It's Leif."

Silence

"How are you?" I ask.

"Fine."

"Well, the bus is definitely going out tonight. I was just checking to see if you're still coming."

"I don't think so."

"You're busy?"

"No."

"All right. Well, I guess I was actually thinking we could . . . well, have a good night."

"Good night."

Ugh.

The phone rings fifteen minutes later

"Hey, sweetie," says a woman's voice. "There was something else we wanted to tell you. You know when you asked if we ever missed having sex with men? Well the truth is, there *is* a guy. He's our business partner and he lives with us. We didn't want to say anything without asking if he minded, but he said he thinks maybe it makes the story a little more interesting, that the three of us are a couple."

Tess. It's funny that she called, because I was just imagining her and Isabel having at each other on the Oriental rug right in the center of my expensive suite.

"Well," I say, "that does make it more interesting."

The idea of the girl-on-girl exhibition in my room had occurred to me moments after Cynthia and I had said good-bye. I was imagining a column: Fearless paying for his own sex show.

"Wow. I'd wish I'd known. It would be good to talk about it some more."

"Sure, call us anytime, honey."

"Yeah, I've got your number."

My only qualm in having Tess and Isabel go "Live from the Mayflower" would be the stuff they said about not liking their customers to get physically involved, because I also want sex. And the idea of paying for sex, after all I've been through, now seems like the only sensible remaining option.

"Are you all busy this weekend?" I ask.

"Seriously busy. We've got a packed weekend. You should come along, check it out."

Really! "Really? Would that be okay?"

"Of course. Come along with us in the limo. It'll be fun. You'll get a kick out of it."

"Yeah, that would give me a great story."

"Okay, sugar. I've got a run, but plan on about eleven tonight."

I don't even know what to say about The Judge's house.

"William, this is amazing."

It's a spectacular four-story Georgetown townhouse, the castle of a man for whom making two hundred and fifty dollars in a twelve-month period would be unfathomable. William isn't a judge, is actually a DC lawyer. "The Judge" was a name he picked up back in college. When the rest of us preoccupied ourselves with deconstructing the mechanics of beer bongs, he'd already moved on to matters less philosophic, such as organizing panels of the Washington elite to come to our campus and discuss weapons procurement.

With William out back flipping the steaks on the grill and striking wife Marcy upstairs looking for a photograph, I'm left in the kitchen to keep an eye on the kid, Chris. Chris has huge brown eyes, sandy blonde hair, pink cheeks, and a Band-Aid on his forehead.

"You and my dad were friends in school," the four-year-old says, not looking up, face trained down on a little plastic horse in his lap. He's combing the mane.

"That's right," I say, the ice in my Jack and Coke jangling every time he shifts his weight, and I lunge, thinking he's about to fall.

"But you and my dad haven't talked for a long time."

"Yes, that's true, too," I say, amazed at what a conversant little kid he is. Furtively, I check my pager to make sure the batteries are working, that I haven't missed a page from Tess and Isabel, who've promised to pick me up in the limo after I'm through here.

"My, my," Marcy says, laughing, "how boring our lives must seem to you."

Chris is softly patting my shoulder, having adopted me as his new buddy. Dinner—complete with a PG-rated summary of my exploits—is all but finished, the food tasting wonderful, but having a strangeness that I can't put my finger on until I remember . . . *home-cooked*. Marcy, whom I'd never met before, is enviable—funny, intelligent, pretty, and a photographer.

"Boring can seem really attractive," I respond, feeling the little hand on my shoulder.

Maybe I could blow off the sex show? Just say, *Thanks, but no thanks*. We could tuck Chris into bed, read him a story, then come back downstairs, have after-dinner drinks, light a fire . . .

My butt is vibrating. The pager.

"Would you like coffee with your dessert, Leif?"

Visions of tangled flesh.

"Thanks, Marcy, coffee would be great."

Once again, I feel the vibration, and instinctively imagine the girls and I twisted pretzel-like on the Oriental rug. I wish it were different, but . . .

"William, can I use your phone?"

I've come too far not to make this call.

"Hey, darlin'."

Tess, you term-of-endearment-spouting sex worker, you came through.

"I've got some bad news."

"Tess . . ."

"I'm sorry."

"Tess, say it ain't so."

"We talked to the clients, explained that we'd be bringing a journalist along, but there're going to be too many people there who wouldn't be comfortable, a couple of serious VIPs. It just won't work. But if you could stay longer? Or maybe you could come back?

Anything, really, we'd love for you to see the show. It just can't be tonight."

Sunday. We're leaving for North Carolina, but on the way out of town I'm supposed to take a picture of the bus passing in front of the White House. A comic adventure ensues, with me on Seamus's shoulders and Butch having to repeatedly drive past, backing up traffic in the process. Cops chase us away. We're laughing about our antics while stopped for hotdogs and sodas at a roadside cart when some men in uniform approach the bus. Their patches read, SECRET SERVICE.

For a cop, Seamus cracks surprisingly quickly, is a model of contrition as he apologizes for the suspicious behavior and the photos. Butch isn't much better. Nor, in fact, are Vegas and I. We're all outapologizing each other. Playboy headquarters wanted the picture, that's why we had to keep driving past the White House.

"So," one of the guys says, interrupting our babble, "you got any Playmates in there?"

Which is how we end up in the White House. We show them ours, they want to show us theirs, including areas regular tours can't go. We're even treated to an off-color story.

According to one of our guides, early in the Clinton years Bill and Hill hadn't yet learned the full extent of panic buttons in the White House, specifically the ones in the third-floor quarters, next to the bed. One day they accidentally kicked one, causing a squad of agents to blaze into the bedroom, only to interrupt the President and First Lady, who were tangled up in the sheets.

"Boy, was he mad," says the Secret Service guy. "It's true about the temper. He read everyone the riot act, then had the bedroom buttons shut off. Apparently she's not a lesbian."

Later in our impromptu tour I end up in the pressroom, in front of that blue curtain and behind the lectern—the one with the presidential seal. In lieu of a candidate's flashing I unbutton my own shirt

and ask Seamus to snap a picture. Observing my efforts, Vegas
motions to the daughter of a WASPy-looking family that is also on
a private tour.

"We're from Playboy," he says, wearing his staple leer. "Would you
do that?"

Her face floods with a look of such disgust, such raw offense.
Damn Vegas. Damn me.

Charlotte, North Carolina

"They still haven't tested Eve."

"You're kidding!" I say. Eve was the godess I'd met in Portland, the one I went on a date with, along with her boyfriend.

"No, I've asked," Raj replies. "Repeatedly. They say they don't see it."

"That's crazy." Insane crazy. What do they want if they don't want Eve?

We're eating dinner—Raj, Vegas, Seamus, Butch, Sophia, and I—at the hotel's restaurant, which smells as though there's been an environmental accident involving the kitchen's fryer.

"How about that funeral plot broker, Emma. She's going to at least land Playmate, isn't she?"

"Not even tested."

!!!!

"I know. I know. Don't look at me."

I mean, what the hell? Is this just someone's idea of an expensive joke, sending us around the country? We continue grousing, hashing through a long list of our favorites, none of whom are being tapped by Chicago for follow-up. Innuendo, the sort that flourishes at any corporation, cresting tsunami-like as the tour nears its end.

I'd be in better shape to contribute my own gales of outrage if my mind would quit replaying the DC experience, which has me wanting to vomit. Or is that just the fryer smell?

"They tested Daisy," Raj says. "I didn't shoot her. Was she good?"

"Ask Fearless," Sophia suggests.

"How would I know?" I respond. Daisy, the Wal-Mart-employed future doctor. And my e-mail pen pal. She's written of breaking up with her boyfriend, joked about falling in love with me and encouraged me to masturbate, but no Playmate test.

As I walk away, I hear poor devoted Raj lamenting, "At a certain point, it's almost like you're not supposed to care, you know?"

I'm sitting down to check my e-mail when there's a knock at the door. I open it and am met by the lone eye of a video camera. "Please, Fearless, tell me what I've missed. You were so good in Austin, about the threesome. Give me one more video confession. No one's going to see it."

Sophia takes a seat on the bed. I fall back into my desk chair. I still don't think this is wise, committing things to tape, but screw it, maybe this is the way to process the whole thing.

I begin back at the point where we last did this. I give her New Orleans, going out with Brett but running into Vivian, my increasing arousal in Ohio, capped off with Aldonza, Tashi's Aldonza news, Dolores and her dreams. I wind up with a description of DC—my kissing Cynthia, Cynthia's leaning out the bus window, the sex show gals, little Chris patting my shoulder, Vegas's crack in the pressroom, the WASP daughter's scowl.

"So what do you think? Because after DC . . ." I say, searching for a point. "It's the first time I've seriously considered that I could be permanently damaged. I'm at the point where I can see how . . . Much more of this, and it would be hard to follow the bread crumbs back to myself."

"Fearless, I think it's mostly in your mind, you know? I'm guessing you could take this all a lot further before getting into trouble."

"Nice of you to say, but you're not sure, are you? You don't *say* it like you're sure."

Sophia laughs. "No, I'm not. Maybe you are f----d."

Must all of my friends be aspiring comediennes?

This all reminds me of one of my favorite Burt-isms; sometimes its hard to tell if it's light at the end of the tunnel or just an oncoming train. Sitting here across from Sophia, feeling sick to death of the bus and myself, I'm flashing back to that moment outside the bus when Cynthia leans out the window and hears me setting things up with Vince. Rich's line returns to me yet again: *It's a slippery slope.*

"Keep in mind," says Sophia, "it might be you've been on this bus a little too long. It's not human. I couldn't do what you do for two days, much less—how many *has* it been?"

At first I shrug off her comment. It hasn't been *that* long. But then I start counting up the recent stretch—realize to my near-horror that it's been more than forty days—and nights—since I've had a break. Maybe she's right. I'm just tired. If I can just make it through the next two cities, I'll go home, get a well-deserved rest, and finish off the trip with a clear mind.

With Sophia gone, I return to my e-mail. A letter from Daisy awaits: *Leif the Lucky, long time no talk. But great news: my aunt agreed to pay for my ticket so I can come out and visit you during your break. Are you masturbating?*

Athens, Georgia

"Did we do your butt yet?"

Just three days to go. Finish up, go home, sleep, go to therapy, don't think about aspiring Playmates, except the twenty-year-old who's apparently visiting.

"Why don't we stretch you out on the floor, get one that shows off those long legs."

I'm shooting a candidate named Becky—pretty smile, complementary stylish short blonde hair, and inconceivably long legs (thirty-six-inch inseam, but only average height)—and I'm just going through the motions. I could be shooting a bowl of potato salad.

"Okay, Becky, hip out to the side . . . yes, like that, now mess up your hair."

The only reason I mustered the energy to shoot her was that she mentioned working for FedEx—not in the front office, but in a distribution center, handling the heavy packages—and I guess I still have a thing for that: outrageous beauties innocently working away in dead-end jobs.

"Should I take my top off?"

"Um . . . did Raj already get some with your top off?"

"Yes."

"Well, I guess we've probably . . ."—*snap out of it, man!*—"already got it." *Idiot!* "Not to say they aren't worthy of more photos. I'm guessing they are." *Stupid, stupid man!*

"That's too bad," Becky says, pulling on her jeans, replacing her bikini top with a T-shirt.

The implication of her last statement totally eludes me. I'm too busy trying to rally the will to invite her to the Fearless Reporter Chat.

Herm called to remind me about it this morning. It was planned weeks ago, a live chat with all of my fans. He wanted some ideas regarding how he should be promoting it on the site. Exhausted, just wanting to get him off the phone, I said, "Well, make it a pajama party. And, actually, it was my birthday yesterday, I guess, so make it the Fearless Reporter Live Chat Slumber Party Birthday Extravaganza," or something.

"I'd love to come to your party," Becky says, once I finally ask the question. "But I'm leaving right now to go visit my parents for the weekend."

Her hometown is in Alabama. A burg of less than two thousand people. I picture Granny on the porch with a plug of chewing tobacco in her mouth. The return of this beauty is probably headline news for the town paper.

"Are you going to be able to check out my photos of you?" I ask.

"What do you mean?"

"Do they have computers there?"

"Are you kidding?" she asks. "Leif, they have computers everywhere."

As I come out of the studio into the packed lounge, I spot a woman I'm instantly drawn to. She's by the entrance, talking to Seamus, and I guess it's her clothes that get my attention. She has taste. Tailored pants, stylish white blouse, good shoes. She's pretty, too, and her bobbed hair is well cut, flattering. Above her mouth and off to the side, a beauty mark, à la Marilyn. But she's turning back, leaving before I can meet her and ask her to the party.

"Seamus," I ask, "what was that? Where'd she go?"

"ID. It was expired. Had to send her home."

"I don't get that. Expired ID. It was good, it expired, so does that mean she suddenly turned seventeen?"

"What crawled up your ass and died?"

"Nothing. Nothing crawled up my—"

"So what're you all freakin' upset about? We've been doing it this way for months."

"Did you *see* her?"

"Dude, she was all right."

"No, she was better than that."

"Well, friggin' say something. Want me to get her?"

I peer out the window to the lifeless parking lot.

"No, thanks. It's too late."

There's a chance I might need to go to the hospital. You know, like when celebrities or rock stars are brought in for exhaustion? I think that's what I have.

But I can't even get up off the couch. It's Day Two in Athens, the day of the Fearless Reporter Live Chat Slumber Party Birthday Extravaganza, and I don't have the strength to call out for help, let alone invite a single candidate or make an effort to gather material for my dispatch.

A candidate sits down in the small space between me and the corner. She has red hair, green eyes, and a not-small nose. It's an intriguing face. If I could just . . . I'm still slumped down, head barely up, but I manage to work my digital out of its case. *Must take photo.*

"Turn this way," I mutter.

"What's wrong with you?"

Snap. I take the first shot. Then a second.

"Why are you taking my picture?"

"Please, *shhhh,* just be."

The sage eyes squint for a second, look over at the pile that is me, then seem to make a decision. They flash open, surge with life, and she, Elizabeth, brings her lips together in a full pout, *snap,* then broad smile, *snap,* then sneer, *snap.* With each shot, I find a little more strength, sit up another half inch, until finally I'm nearly upright and am closing in, isolating features—nose, eye, cheekbone is my favorite combination. *Snap, snap, snap.* Seventy-three images.

This momentary revival is interrupted by raised voices. Two candidates, one by the changing area and another by the door, are yelling across the crowded lounge. Strange that it's taken so long for this to happen. There was a time when it would have been a story, our first catfight.

"Ladies, ladies, please," Sophia calls out, laughing. "We're all sisters here."

The shouting doesn't stop. They don't care that others are around or that someone from Playboy is asking them to stop, which strikes me as unusual enough that I turn toward the front.

It's her. From yesterday.

"Boy," I say to Elizabeth. "My kind of women."

"Those two? Julie and Laura?" she asks.

"You know them?"

"Of course. They're my best friends."

Elizabeth is working tonight, can't come to the chat party, but she tells Julie and Laura to come over, introduces them to me, and tells them about the big event.

"That sounds fun," Laura says, perky, showing no emotional residue from the argument. Julie, less in the mood to smile, only reminds Laura that they already have plans.

Julie's the one, though. The adrenaline floodgates open. My heart hits that rhythm that I fear is audible. *Make a pitch, but be subtle. Get them to come, but don't be weird.*

"You've got to come! Well, you don't have to, of course, but it's going to be fun, maybe, and seriously, I'm kind of screwed if you all don't, just for a little while. *Please.*"

Sexy, very sexy.

Julie continues scrutinizing me, while Laura smiles. I write down the hotel address and, hey, look at that, my hand is shaking.

As they get ready to go, with Laura and Elizabeth grabbing their stuff, there's an awkward moment when Julie and I are standing together. *I love you.*

"By the way, I have to say, impressive fighting."

"I'm sorry?"

"The fight. I come from a tradition of repressed emotions. That's kind of a goal of mine, being able to just do that. Especially in front of strangers. Nice."

"You think that was a fight?"

"Um . . ."

"That was just a disagreement. You haven't seen a fight."

Fearless enters, the screen reads. I'm in my pajamas, at my laptop, sitting in the middle of my flying carpet, the queen-size beds pushed together and wrapped in Christmas lights. My current assistant isn't feeling well, but luckily one of the candidates, Tricia, has a computer background and, clad only in a hot pink baby-doll nightie, is trying to get the chat software running. Sophia looks over our shoulders, her face covered in a pale blue mud mask. Vegas is at the ironing board, blending up piña coladas. And Raj is breaking out his camera.

For the most part, my audience consists of the usual premium subscriber suspects, the crowd that was there for the Mansion Labor Day party. As before, it takes little more to amuse them than some good taunting. I describe the scene in my hotel room, make jokes about my using them as an excuse to lead this decadent life, and exhort them to "please, whatever you do, don't try this at home. . . . I'm a trained professional." That really gets them.

I'm making up the scene they're missing. Besides Tricia, only one other candidate has shown up so far. She's married and comes across as more like someone who should be at a demonstration against cruelty in veal farming rather than at a Playboy party. Otherwise it's just the bus crew, all in our jammies, whooping it up. But the audience doesn't need to know that.

Of course, there are additional digital attendees, including some favorites out there from the road. A Bible-thumping nudist from Austin. And a candidate in New Orleans, who refers to herself as the runaway I convinced to return home, though I can't recall her or the exchange. Also out there is an X-ray tech from Ohio who likes to send me e-mails detailing the objects her male and female X-rayees have managed to lodge in their nether orifices.

Maintaining the digital connection proves a challenge, though. During one lapse, while Tricia tries to reestablish our link, I look up to see who turned up the music so loud and spy Laura, from the bus, in baby-blue flannel pajamas. She's holding her top open like a flasher as Raj, kicked back in a chair, takes her picture. And if Laura is here . . .

I scan the room—Julie, wearing short men's boxers and a gray Nike half-shirt, is sitting on the floor with a room service tray between her legs. The lone item on her plate is a steak, which she is rapidly consuming.

I slip off the bed, leaving Tricia to work on the line.

"Hey," I say, crouching down to Julie. "Thanks for coming."

"You're welcome, and happy birthday," she says, brushing bangs out of her eyes with the back of her knife-wielding hand, then turning back to the meat, hacking off another chunk with a flair that would impress Benihana himself.

"Good appetite," I say, for lack of anything else.

"I'm training."

"For . . . ?"

She looks at me, perplexed.

"You said you're training. What are you in training for?"

"I'm not 'in training,' I'm training."

I still don't understand, but Tricia has the connection up, so I climb back on the bed and return to my public. With a start I realize my parents are online, as well as friends from LA, and Daisy. It's starting to feel a little like *The Wizard of Oz.* "And you were there, and so were you . . ."

The link goes down again. And Tricia struggles to remedy the problem. Julie has finished eating, is talking to Sophia. Then suddenly Julie is lifting the half-shirt and the pizza delivery girl is feeling her breasts. The pizza girl shakes her head in disbelief as Julie nods her head insistently, yes, they are implants. Laura has turned around, dropped her pajama bottoms, so Raj can get a shot of her butt, which, to judge by his expression, must be something else. The door swings open and the room service guy brings in a huge block of a birthday cake. After giving the guy a dollar, Sophia actually has to physically turn the guy around and lead him out the door. I'm standing by the window, fresh piña colada in hand, when the veal protester approaches and tosses off the line: "So, do you do this in every city?"

Several brief chats later, we finally lose the connection for good, neither Tricia nor I bothering to check the phone cord, which someone has kicked free from the jack. So, the ostensible excuse for the evening over, all we can do is take photos to post with tomorrow's postmortem party dispatch, create the scene the readers will imagine resulted in losing the connection. Contemplating said scene, I suddenly have another mini-vision.

Running into the bathroom, I hack out a wedge of birthday cake, stick a candle in it, while unbuttoning my shirt. Then, laying myself on the bed, I set the cake on my bare chest, light the candle, and direct all the women to grab their forks, lean in as close as possible, "and, by all means, look hungry." Okay, so it's a bit obvious. Still, as a photographic capstone to the evening, it works.

After the cake shot, I steel my ever-questionable courage to ask Julie if I can take her picture. As I bring my eye to the viewfinder and she affects the look of a searing vamp, there's not the usual mild stirring of interest that slowly builds. I just see her, and *wham,* craven lust. This is going to be a problem. I can't even risk speaking, so I motion for her to raise her shirt, slowly. The stomach is a wonder. Whatever this training is, it's working . . . but someone hands me the phone.

"Great job, Fearless."

"Herm?"

"I can barely hear you. What are you having a party there?"

He sounds pissed. "Yeah, a little one," I say.

"Leif, I'm *kidding*, you goof. Just wanted to say the chat was great. Good job. They were eating it up. Have fun."

I'm about to apologize for losing the connection, but he's already hung up.

"Is it really your birthday?" Laura, drink in hand, looks up at me with the smile of the pleasantly buzzed.

"No, it *was*, though, two days ago," I say, seeing, as I do, that Raj, still planted Jabba-like in the chair, is now working with Julie.

"What does that make you?"

"The big four-six," I say, kidding, still feeling high from Julie. "I know, I don't look it."

I'm thinking, thinking, thinking. Like the birthday cake picture, like the party, like the whole trip, waiting for an idea.

Laura is telling me about stripping, which is how she makes her living. It's funny, she tells me, that she'd end up stripping, because, well, if you knew her family, it's absolutely the last thing in the world someone from her family would end up doing.

I'm nodding, smiling, wondering if I came off as having strong feelings about how people pay their bills or if she is constantly giving this speech.

She continues talking, about the place *they* work—the implication being that Julie is not just an office manager, like her envelope said, but also strips. The money, Laura says, is *amazing*, the kind of money her family would expect her to make. Ironic, isn't it?

I've got an idea for the closing shot. I pull Laura by the wrist, hand my camera to Sophia, and ask Julie to join us on the bed. I mess the sheets up, then lay the laptop between two pillows. I place Laura down on one side, Julie on the other, plant myself between them.

"We should be tangled up," I say, as Sophia climbs on the bed and stands over us, shooting down. "And look like you've had the sexual session to end all—"

"Should I unbutton my top?" Laura asks.

We're all lying together, with the computer in the shot. Julie's head touches mine. She's breathing in my ear, feigning sleep. I tell them both to not hold back, and faux-sleeping Julie raises her shirt just so, so that the bottom half of the not-to-be-believed breasts peek out.

As my breath falls in with Julie's and music thunders in the background, Sophie stands over us, taking the photos, giving directions between blasts of the flash. I pull the Christmas lights across us, just so there's a reason to keep shooting, then maneuver the girls' legs so we're even more enmeshed. My hand, when it comes back down to rest, happens to land just below Julie's breast. Her skin is blissfully soft. . . .

My mind strains to keep this in perspective. Because I'm in bed with two women, wrapped up with them, we're portraying erotic exhaustion, my hand is in the vicinity of a bare breast, and there's a chemistry between me and this woman that sends the hairs on the back of my neck dancing, a certain primal instinct suggests, *Reach out, kiss, touch, stroke, love. Do it.*

And then the flash goes off, blinding me, revealing the false tableau.

Julie's changing. We're standing in the sink/mirror alcove outside the toilet/shower area of the bathroom, the door to which is closed, with Laura on the other side. The Nike half-T comes off. The boxers drop to the floor. There's a moment of eye contact in the mirror, me looking up from her body's reflection, catching her eyes.

Laura will emerge at any second. Laura, who wants to take me out to a bar, though Julie is going home. But it's Julie I want, and there's the rub. She's stepping into overalls, pulling them up to her waist, searching for her T-shirt, still half naked, with me inches away.

Do something! Is Laura going to interrupt? Will Julie scream? Will someone get sued? Why have I had so much to drink?

She's found her T-shirt, is looking for the tag. Is this such a good idea, having this backstage pass to the women's locker room? Because it feels like things are breaking inside, short-circuiting. I don't even want to catch my reflection in the mirror, some terrible naked look of lust.

"You're going and . . ." I say, hazily aware of something a little dangerous in this ongoing confluence of flesh, impotence, and alcohol, "and . . . we're not even going to kiss?"

She stops in the middle of putting on her bra and shoots me a look. It's not the expression of someone about to kiss; rather, it's the face that was shouting at Laura on the bus. She fastens the bra, pulls on her T-shirt, and hitches up her overalls—all quickly.

"Why would you say that?"

"I just . . . I . . ."

"That's very personal to me. I don't just kiss like that."

"I'm sorry, but . . ."

She's looking to the door of the bathroom, which is still shut.

"I thought you liked Laura," she says, her expression still one of near outrage.

Laura? I grimace, think of a lifetime of confused flirting, of sending the wrong signals.

"No!" I whisper-yell, then drop back to pure whisper. "No, I don't. I like *you*, from the moment I saw you getting kicked off the bus. I was thrilled when I heard fighting and realized you'd returned—"

"That wasn't fighting."

"Right. Listen, I've been doing this for five months and believe me, I know what I like, and I would just like to spend some time with you, get to know you."

Whew. That was like one big breath, took all my last sober energy.

So that in its wake, I feel a bit smashed, must sit against the sink. But at least that pissed-off look has eased up.

"That's nice of you to say," she says. "But it's a bad time, I got really hurt in my last relationship, and I'm still not near ready to get involved. I can't."

"That's okay," I say, dazed by the seeming statistical impossibility of ever meeting anyone when the time is right. "I understand."

"Honestly, for me, kissing is a really big deal, it's extremely personal. I'd almost sleep with someone before I'd kiss them."

Well, we can just f--k! the mind jokes.

The door is unlocking, and before we can say anything else, Laura appears, smiley as ever, somehow having managed not to hear the discussion.

"Ready to see some of Athens, Leif?"

I could absolutely scream out. This trip is all but over—only one last short leg left—and I've established myself as the country's most beyond-help male. I just can't take it any longer.

As we head for the door, Laura asks if Julie wants us to drop her home.

"Actually, I'll come out for a drink. Just one."

We're in this hipster little drum and bass club in downtown Athens. Laura is on her cell phone, trying to call a guy she's been seeing, and is expressing great frustration at not being able to reach him, which I read as good news. Not for her, but for Julie and me. Information must have been exchanged, womanly information, territorial understandings.

Sitting in a fan-backed chair, I pull Julie down to my lap, wrap my arms around her, and squeeze her narrow, muscular waist.

"Hey," she says, turning back, catching my eye, bringing her cheek much too close, given the dark bar, the tribal drum and bass music, and the smoothness of her skin. I'm forced to kiss her cheek.

"Leif . . ."

I'm about to yield to the impulse a second time, but pain shoots through my ear, into my skull, bouncing around inside. Uncomfortable, but also lively, almost pleasant, enough that I forget where I am for a second, give myself over to it.

I hear my name again. Julie is twisting my ear.

"Take it easy. This has to go very, very slowly, okay?"

I nod my head, the movement making stars drift before my eyes.

"You promise?"

"I do. I promise."

"And no more drinks. You're drunk."

"I'm wasted."

Laura's guy finally shows just in time for last call and soon we're back in Laura's SUV. The whole time Julie and I have been holding hands. We're whispering to each other, not so much to communicate, but for the sheer pleasure of whispering. So immersed am I in this interaction that I'm slow to register the car's coming to a halt and the hotel bellboy's pulling open the door. As I stumble out, it occurs to me that I haven't asked Julie about *her* intentions. I look down, see that I'm still in pajamas. Were I not so lit and unable to construct an argument for Julie's accompanying me, I'd undoubtedly be feeling great frustration right now.

But she follows me out.

"I'm going to stay the night, make sure he's all right," I hear her say.

The room is all shadows, softly backlit by city lights. Scattered everywhere are little surreal blobs, the melted remains of the candles. The smell of pineapple juice hangs in the air. As my eyes adjust, I see the birthday cake on the bedside table, only one slice taken, the piece I took for the photo. We forgot to eat the rest.

Julie's overalls slip to the ground. A woman's pelvis, that hip structure, that's the best, isn't it?

"Remember your promise."

Promise?

"We're just sleeping."

She takes off one shirt, replaces it with a half T-shirt. I lunge forward, literally sweep her off her feet, and we fall onto the sprawling bed/magic carpet with her pinned underneath. Before she can protest, I laugh.

"I'm sorry," I say, tears coming out of my eyes as I roll off, "I'm kidding."

"So, you're really not gay?"

There's something about a soft southern accent on a woman. It's almost like that hip area.

"Not that I'm aware of."

"You're sure?"

"The future's uncertain," I offer, pulling Julie into spoon formation. "Why?"

"Because," she says with zeal, as if I'd asked something too obvious to explain, "the way you dress, and you're very polite."

"So was Liberace and no one ever suggested he was gay."

"And you notice things."

When did qualities like manners and attentiveness become a form of self-outing?

"Honestly, if you're asking about sexual impulses, they've just always been about women. But if you're asking about approach to life, I'm a bit gay-leaning."

Julie takes my hand, slides it between her breasts up near her neck, so that I'm encircling her with my arms, my forearm basking in radiant warmth.

"So you really haven't slept with anyone on this *entire* trip?"

"Do you have to say *entire* with such emphasis?"

"Haven't you met lots and lots of girls?"

"It's not just the trip, it's my life of late. Sex is not a part of it."

She has the softest hair. It's as fine as an adult's hair could be and, like most people, she likes having her head stroked. As I do, she asks about my life and, there in the dark, the discussion veers toward my sexual history, so that I'm telling her the things I've been sharing with Burt lately. It's only when she asks how long it's been that I can't be totally forthcoming. I simply say, "Awhile," allude to drunken moments and half-failed encounters. The truth is, I don't know myself.

"And I have serious misgivings about my penis."

There's a thud at the door as I say this, a funny auditory emphasis, which I realize is the morning paper being delivered.

"What do you mean, misgivings?"

Julie and I haven't moved in what must have been hours. We're clinging to each other.

"I think I'm a well-endowed man trapped in the body of a guy less well off."

I'm biting her ear as I say this.

"It's tragic, really. It's both undersized and functionally erratic, which is hard to take. If there were any justice, it would be an either/or situation, you know? If you're going to have a problem penis, it should be either above average in size with some perform- ance problems, or lacking in dimension but as reliable as a Swiss watch."

Out the window, the sky is blushing, showing the first signs of pink, and it strikes me only now that this is the worst seduction ever: tales of a bad sex life followed by ridiculing my manhood. Take that, Barry White.

"I think we better get some sleep," Julie says, momentarily confirming my low self-appraisal. But then she adds, "But first I think we should kiss."

She rolls over, staying within the confines of my arms, and our lips meet. They press together. It's personal.

Pulling back, Julie says, "Thanks for keeping your promise."

Promise?

Sophia strokes my head. I lean on her shoulder, wiped out from my trip up the bus stairs.

"There, there, Fearless. Everything's going to be all right. Just tell your mama Sophia what sort of sick things you've been up to."

Judging by the way the candidate across the aisle is staring at me, I really don't look well. And considering I'm still in my pajamas, there's probably some question as to whether I smell well.

"It was great, so great, we had so much fun."

"And you shagged her rotten, you bad boy?"

"Nothing happened. She wouldn't even kiss me. It was awesome."

Remembering my professional responsibilities, I call out to the candidate across from me, "Sweetheart, will you do me a favor? Will you sit next to me for a second?"

It's funny, how I'm feeling. Raj is in the back, going to town with some candidate; Vegas is outside chatting up a hefty female city bus driver; Seamus is giving the spiel to a fresh batch of candidates—and it's all home, feels like where I belong. But the thought of doing one more dispatch, writing a story about how some girl . . . ugh.

"Sophia, will you take our picture?"

"Sure, baby."

The candidate has excellent posture and I do my best to right myself next to her, just in time for the flash.

"Okay, now, Sophia, let's have a hug."

"That's it? You're leaving? One picture?"

"See you in Florida or LA?"

"LA for sure, Florida, possibly. You're really going?"

"Sorry," I say, already turning to go. "I've had it." Bleary-eyed, I hobble down the stairs and into the rain, shuffling along in my pajamas, hand held out to signal an oncoming cab.

I'm sitting on a stool at the bar/restaurant where one of her friends works. Julie's jacket is draped over my damp shoulders. She and Laura are at the bar, eating lunch and talking about everything under the sun. With my hangover, I can only marvel at their animation. Somehow the afternoon passes, me on her shoulder, savoring the two women in conversation, warmed by a borrowed jacket, and timidly sipping a Bloody Mary in a vain effort to hold the pain at bay.

Another cab. Raj and I are headed for Antoine's, the gentlemen's club where Laura works, and Julie *used* to work, though this evening she's back on the job. Apparently she had to quit her office manager position and is doing some impromptu stripping to cover her rent. The plan was to meet Laura and Elizabeth and, between sets, hang out with Julie.

At the door we happen to mention our employer and are immediately lead to a VIP booth. I have to admit, the scale of the club takes me back. With long catwalk stage, vaulted ceiling, and theatrical lights, it looks like the set for a Hollywood movie about the ultimate strip club.

Laura and Elizabeth join us and minutes later we're drinking shots and are on our feet, dancing to the music and raucously cheering on the dancers as they make their way onto the stage. It's a localized dance party amid a sea of tall wing-back chairs, and if, as it seems, the other customers are playing some secret game—slump down in your chair and try to look sexually maladjusted—our revelry makes them play even harder.

A dancer named Kennedy appears from behind the curtain, takes her place where the silvery spotlights merge. Judging from the hollering Laura and Elizabeth are doing and the handfuls of dollars they toss to the stage, she must be a friend. Kennedy resolutely strides along the catwalk, her gaze fixed on a point beyond the blinding light. She pauses long enough to step out of her short beaded dress, then continues on, her pace unaffected by the thundering bass-heavy music.

Shooting the crowd one last look, she arches into a deep backbend, drops all the way until her hands reach the ground. From there she kicks up into a handstand, which she holds, motionless, before walking around on her hands a hundred and eighty degrees. Laura and Elizabeth continue hollering their approval as the guys in the vicinity direct their glazed-over expressions to the stage. Kennedy returns to a backbend and then manages—most impressively—to rise back to standing on her towering heels.

She turns toward our side of the stage and I get my first clear look at her face. *Julie.* Kennedy is Julie. Her hair is slicked back, so it looks dark, and under heavy stage makeup and blinding lights, she looks like a different person. It's her, though. And I think, *Wow.*

"You were awesome," I say. "We loved it."

"Thanks," she says, catching her breath. "And thanks, you all, for the tips."

I sit down into one of the chairs, and Julie follows, landing on my lap. She finds my mouth with hers, kisses me, forcing my head back against the chair, her tongue tasting of red wine.

"Maybe I'll come back with you and live with you in LA," she says.

Live with me? In LA? *But, but, but . . .*

"Well, you're welcome to come out anytime."

"Really? Because I barely have any stuff. Nothing is holding me here."

"Yeah, it's just me in my place," I say, still scrambling to understand. "You'd like it."

"You've gotten to me," she says, not smiling, studying my eyes.

"It's been great," I say, backpedaling, trying to figure out if she is actually suggesting moving in with me.

"I want to get out of here. I don't want to be working," she says, but stands up, spotting a manager closing in on us. She walks off to circulate. Laura and Elizabeth continue dancing, hooting and hollering, tipping friends. Women steadily pay visits to Raj, bestowing on him a level of attention more appropriate to your average Ottoman sultan.

I track Julie, watch as she drifts among the men. She ignores most, just wanders on, apparently listening to the music, sipping from a wine glass. Intermittently, though, she stops, slips her dress off for a table dance. I see her looking off into middle distance as the patron focuses, fighting a less-than-photographic memory, trying to stuff what he can into his brain. Watching on, I'm not feeling jealousy so much as how foreign the experience is, as in, *This is a new one.*

Twenty minutes later she's back on my lap and whispering into my ear. "This guy, before you got here—he kissed my ass."

"Literally? You're kidding."

"No. No, I'm not."

Kissed your ass?

"And they kicked him out?"

"No. He's a big customer, spends thousands of dollars here. They just talked to him. That's why I'm a little buzzed. I normally hate to drink when I dance, but . . ." She pauses, fixing her expression. "Don't tell the others, I don't want to ruin their night."

"Which one was he?"

She looks down at me over her wine glass.

"Julie," Elizabeth calls over. "You're on, honey."

"I'm not going up."

"Julie, just point him out," I repeat.

"Sweetie," says Elizabeth, "you're going to get fired."

"Good, fire me." Julie drains the wine, wraps her arms around my neck, bringing her mouth to my ear. "Leif, you're going to have to take care of me tonight, okay?"

"I grew up in foster homes, seventy of them," Julie tells me, an hour later. As she shares this confidence she pulls my arm around her waist.

We're back in bed in the hotel room, which hasn't been touched. I'd left word with housecleaning not to enter until I'd done some damage control. Unfortunately, that means the beer-and-champagne-spattered room is now filled with the sour scent of aging alcohol. As far as the cake, it has shrunken slightly, its frosting turning glazy.

I must have heard her wrong. No one has been in *seventy* foster homes, but the other options, seventeen or seven, still sound pretty bad, especially difficult to fathom for this son of loving, still-married parents.

"At sixteen, my foster family adopted me."

"That was good of them," I say, thinking how difficult it is for a teenager to get adopted.

"They did their best. It's hard to convince a sixteen-year-old she suddenly has parents. My real mother, she's dead now, but for years I knew she was alive and only that. I never knew anything about her or why I was taken away, but it must have been something."

I express my sympathies for her struggles. Trying to pick up her spirits, I suggest she must have been a cute kid back then. "It's hard to believe," I say, "that anyone would not want to adopt you." At this she bursts out laughing. She describes herself in adolescence: acne on top of acne, extremely thick glasses in ugly one-hour frames, and crooked, broken teeth.

"You're exaggerating."

"Yeah, right. Leif, I didn't have *any* friends in high school."

"You hung out with the unpopular kids?"

"No, I didn't have any friends. Not one."

No friends? That's not possible, is it?

"I took dance and competed in gymnastics. Even with moving from one home to the next, I managed to keep at it. That's what kept me sane, or as sane as possible."

At eighteen, she graduated from high school and moved out. She was looking for a waitressing job, saw an ad looking for a dancer, and was naive enough not to know what it really meant. It was just a little bar on a dead-end street, the building made from two old boxcars, close enough to the tracks that it would shake when trains roared past.

"The first day, I wore a leotard, tights, and leg warmers."

"Tights?"

"Isn't that pathetic?"

"Leg warmers?"

"Yes," she says, giggling.

"That's pathetic."

The image is too heartbreaking—this little dancer, in dance clothes, with thick glasses, in a railroad car bar that lacked even a stage. She was supposed to drift among the tables, do a little stripping, serve drinks. Maybe you had to be there, but laughing-fit tears are streaming down our eyes.

Around the time she started stripping, a woman she'd known through her dance studio took her out one night for a drink and seduced her. It was her first adult sexual experience. They were together four years.

She kept stripping at the dive, saving up enough money to fix her teeth. Eventually she was able to afford clothes she liked, as well as get a decent haircut and switch to contacts. Her skin, though scarred, had also cleared up. These gradual changes, combined with her dancer-gymnast figure, brought her increasing attention from men, which she eventually parlayed into a job at Antoine's, where she began making serious money.

The story is interrupted by kissing. Not kissing as a pit stop on the way to sex, but kissing for kissing's sake. Neither of us register the decaying room, which is bathed in the moon's pale light.

"A year ago I quit the club. I got a job managing the office of a trucking firm. It was such a change, not stripping after seven years."

"Did you like it better?" I ask tentatively, not wanting to insult the stripping option.

"This past year, working, it was the first time I've been happy—really happy—in my whole life. It was strange. And the thing is, I liked it."

Gradually, though, she started handling calls meant for the account managers. Not surprisingly, she demonstrated a knack for dealing with the male customers, selling them on ever bigger percentages of their shipping dollar. Ultimately, she brought in tens of thousands in new revenue. The only problem was that the owner wouldn't compensate her beyond her office manager's salary. She was barred from earning the commission the accountant managers pulled in. So she quit.

"Now I'm scared," she says. "This last year, having a job I was good at, I felt so good. After I left, I thought it would be okay to just strip one night now and then, make my rent. But my very first table dance, that guy kisses my ass and it all came back to me. I'm worried I'm going to slip back to where I was."

"It'll work out," I say, brushing her hair back from her face. "You've felt the difference, now. You can try to go back, but it's not going to work—not after that part of you that wants happiness knows the difference." I'm plagiarizing here, but I don't think Burt would object.

Julie and I wrap our arms around each other. We just squeeze, cinching our bodies together, her hug every bit as strong as mine.

In regards to her sexual inclinations, she doesn't think she is gay, thinks it was just being wanted by someone. She gets a faraway look as she speaks about it.

"It's funny. So many of the girls at the club sleep with each other because of the way men treat them or because they're around beautiful women all the time, or because they think it's some cool thing. My perspective on it's a little different."

It's almost impossible for her to come during intercourse. She has a little easier time if her partner stimulates her orally—and she has to admit that the first woman she dated was extremely proficient. There *is* a way, she admits, that it works every time, *snap,* just like that. But she can't do it at her home, has to go over to Elizabeth's.

"Handheld shower massager?"

"You've been hanging out with women for too long."

"You should get one for your own place. I don't think they're that hard to install."

Again, we hear the paper land outside the door, this one the Sunday edition. In bed with Julie, listening to her story, it's hard not to compare it with my more familiar nocturnal state: isolation and insomnia, neurotic pacing.

"I'm sorry we can't have sex," Julie apologizes. "I think you'd feel great inside of me."

"Well, thank you."

"Can we at least sleep naked?"

I think about it, biting my lip in thought, because, you know, I'm not as easy as I look.

"Yes, we can."

Time to shift into overdrive. My well-honed internal slacker alarm is blaring, telling me that if I start racing now—throw the mounds of papers and clothes into my bag, give the room a whirling-dervish straightening, and sprint to catch a cab—I'll just make the final boarding call.

"Hey, sexy, make me get out of bed."

Julie's eyes don't open. She wraps her arms around my waist, pulls me in.

"That's helpful."

We've already woken once and had breakfast—Julie decided to violate her carbo ban and eat pancakes, the dishes from which are on the side of the bed. Now she's using her considerable wiles to keep me in her clutches. But I can't. I can't miss my plane, can't risk not getting back to LA today, as I have a therapy appointment tomorrow.

"Julie," I plead, experiencing the discomfort of withdrawing from a dream I'd rather stay with, "I have to get going."

She still won't open her eyes, her face exhibiting that fierce implacability that is not in my repertoire. I start pushing myself up, doing a pushup, when I'm stopped—Julie's powerful arms grab hold and pull me back to her.

"I want to try," she says.

"What?"

"I want to trying coming with you."

Heart instantly pounding, erection—wonder of wonders—at full sail, I lead my penis to Julie's vagina, and slowly, slowly push myself in, sensing every new fraction of space, rapidly increasing in heat and wetness. Fully in, I stop, our two pelvises snug up against each other. We just stare into each other's eyes, don't move a muscle.

"Wow," I say.

"Yeah," Julie says. "Wow."

Sex is one of those things that words inevitably fail to capture. But remember when it was new? That's how it is with Julie, only I'm no longer seventeen. It's the kind of intimacy that has you wondering how you can ever go back to do anything *other* than having sex.

At a certain point, moving back and forth, ever so slowly, it becomes too much. When the neurological Big Bang occurs, we look deeply into each other's eyes, a look I don't imagine ever forgetting.

When we're lying still, luxuriously postcoital, Julie says, "I really didn't want us to have sex, you know, but I'm so glad we did."

"Me, too."

"I don't know why you haven't done that for so long. It was so passionate, felt so good. That's the difference between having sex with a man and having sex with a boy. A man makes you feel like a woman, a boy makes you feel like a toy."

"Well," I say, at a loss, "that's an extremely nice thing to say."

Then, bowing to the inevitable, we throw off the bedcovers and head for the shower. Julie shampoos our hair, alternating back and forth, working up a strong lather. It's hot, steamy, and nice, but I can feel sadness welling up, the thought of saying good-bye. An old-fashioned lump is forming in my throat.

The sadness escalates, metastasizes into something a little different. It's an emotion that comes on like a head rush, to the point that I worry I'll lose my balance and fall against hard tiling. It's just . . .

Five years, half a decade.

. . . There were some drunken half efforts, failed moments, but really nothing that could be called sexual union. Five years—abstinent, alone, without that form of human interaction. There's something about spending half a decade of one's fleeting sexual prime totally isolated . . . I feel grief for all that lost living. I'm embarrassed by the thought, knowing my problems pale next to what others endure. But still, it's pain.

Then again, I have to laugh. I just appreciate it so much, my mind for keeping it from me, not letting me do the math, put two and three together and getting five until this moment, when it was easier to take.

Los Angeles, California V

"And were you able to receive oral sex?"

You've got to love a therapist who not only takes notes, but reviews them before a session.

"Why, yes," I respond, "now that you mention it, I was able to enjoy oral sex."

It's Monday, the morning after my return to sexuality, and I'm back in the chair, trying to describe to Burt in fifty minutes my forty days on the road. Somehow, though, I'm focusing on Julie.

"And why do you think that was, that you were able to enjoy it?"

"No teeth?"

I feel like goofing around, but Burt is intent on salvaging something productive out of our time together. So I stare off at his neutral-toned walls, absently running my fingers through my hair, trying to summon some useful thoughts.

"I guess I just felt like myself with her," I say.

"And why do you think that was?" Burt counters, ever Socratic.

"Because she had a great body?"

He doesn't even bite on that one.

"I don't know," I say, sighing. "There was something about her. That she's seen it all, has seen some of the worst the world has to give, I felt she would take me for what I am, whatever that is, but yeah . . . I guess . . ."

More looking off into space.

"She was, I think . . . nonjudgmental, you know? We talked so much before having any contact, just spewed it all out. For hours. I told her my every insecurity, my every shortcoming. And she did the same, told me everything. I guess that was it."

"So you told her all about your insecurities, admitted what a loser you are?" He smiles at his bit of tongue in cheek.

"Yes, big loser."

"Isn't that what you're supposed to feel, as a guy, admitting all of these things?"

"Pretty much," I reply

"Men talking like that, honestly expressing their feelings, do you know what that is for many women?"

"Ammo for future fights?" *Burt, quit pitching these straight lines.*

"It's foreplay. You engaged in thirty-six hours of foreplay. It's what many women crave."

"She did keep remarking on how sensitive I am. She asked if I was sure I wasn't gay."

"Because she's never been with someone like that, she doesn't know what else to think."

"That, and I kept going on about how hot Tom Cruise was in *Mission Impossible*."

Seriously, I kill in therapy.

"I do have to give you credit," I say. "After it was over, I was aware that much of what had happened could be credited to your coaching. There was an I-told-you-so feeling in the air. The things she was saying—I jokingly imagined she was looking over my shoulder and reading off Burt cue cards."

"This is my fantasy," he says. "All that we've discussed today is very important. This is a big session. This is for me what it's all about, why I'd never want any other kind of job. I get to live out my fantasies."

With our time now up, and all this good feeling in the room becoming a little thick even for a sap like me, I mention that I still have to deal with Daisy coming into town. I hadn't taken very seriously her e-mails informing me she was planning to visit, but the trip is for real. A twenty-year-old I met for a half hour will be paying me a visit, exposing me, from a mental wellness perspective, to a veritable field of land mines

But Burt isn't having any of this quibbling. Instead, he gives me my postsession hug, then pushes me toward the door and says, "Go, get out of here, live. Live."

Later that afternoon, I sit on my rickety balcony, looking out over the valley, notebook computer in my lap. As I grapple with post-therapy thoughts, I find myself inexplicably thinking about a motorcycle. In high school, I bought a small motorcycle for transportation, but I have no idea why I'm recalling it now. Actually, it's not the bike, I realize, but the bike's manual that has started me thinking.

Like most parents, mine were adamantly against their kid riding a motorcycle. The one concession I made was to assure my pop that I would read the instructions before riding it. The manual was, as I had always feared of such documents, extremely boring, enlivened only by the occasional rocky translation of Japanese to English. I slogged on, though, head bobbing, hoping to glean something of value. It wasn't until I arrived at the section about riding basics—amid lots of advice about braking distances, defensive driving, things like that—that I sensed something beyond the predictable.

In awkward English, the manual explained that at a certain point, once the engine has been fully broken in, the time comes to test the bike's unique qualities. Wearing plenty of safety clothes, and in a clean open space, ideally in an empty parking lot, the owner was advised to take the bike and ride it hard, at uncomfortable speeds, in and out of turns where it's easy to lose control. Intermittently the owner should slam on the brakes and go into skids that might end with the bike on the ground.

The objective, the manual said, is to find your particular motorcycle's edge. Do it in the safest setting possible, but go ahead and push it, ride it beyond what you think is right, and so learn intuitively where you will have control and where you won't. That is the only sure way to become a truly safe rider of your unique machine.

I remember being shocked by the advice. I assumed it was a mistake—the work of a new employee who, once the faux pas was discovered, was promptly sacked. Taking a product to this dangerous gray area of performance and finding the edge of sustainable control—these were radical urgings for a major corporation. They were particularly radical to the mind of a sixteen-year-old.

Here on my balcony, a decade and a half later, the manual's advice strikes me as a fitting metaphor for the Playmate Search experience. What has my experience with this whole bus-borne bacchanal been about if not for exploring gray areas and losing control?

It's strange, where a little free association can lead. I'd completely forgotten that motorcycle passage until just now, and here it seemed to appear out of the blue. Once again, *Thanks, mind.*

She's among the last to deplane and looks younger than I remember—*too* young for my thirty-something tastes. Really, what was I thinking? My thing is with Julie, anyway. Well, at least I'll have a fun weekend hanging out with Daisy. Platonically.

Back at my place, I give her the quick tour, showing her the view from my precarious balcony, the creepy black room that is my office, and the kitchen, where I point out the provisions I've stocked at her request: Twinkies (they still make them) and Orange Crush. And—*ahem*—the bedroom. That's it, all four hundred square feet.

We sit on the couch talking briefly about her flight, but since it's already twelve-thirty in LA and the two of us are both still on East Coast time, I suggest that it's time for bed, feeling a bit weird as I do so. I even give the futon couch a look, briefly mentioning that it turns into a bed, "in case this seems too awkward." I've at least made up my mind that there'll be no sex. It would be like going home with someone after a shared elevator ride.

Like Dolores in New York, Daisy comes out of the bathroom in pajamas, looking quite cute. But I'm determined, and without even so much as a kiss good night, we go to sleep. Or that's what we *start* to do, until one or both of us roll over and we somehow bump into each other, bringing us face-to-face. What follows, against my better judgment, is making out, the yanking off of such clothing that covers our lower halves, and robust sex, which we engage in, off and on, into the following evening.

At some point during it all we're both on our backs catching our breath, enjoying the all-over buzz, and Daisy is suddenly curious. She wants to know if I've been sleeping with women at every stop, if she's one of many. I tell her she isn't, laughing as I do, not because I'm lying but because, if she were, this would be a funny time to ask. She smiles, too, appreciating the irony, but follows up with, "Am I? One of many?"

It's so unfair. If this visit had only been a week ago, I could even say she was the only one. Then again, she can't *really* think that I've been a monk, no matter what I say. So, chuckling all the while, I assure her, "No, Daisy, you're not," to which she responds, "You lying sack of shit." We resume our tangle, but I'm feeling the sting of conscience. Beneath the irony and sarcasm, what does she think I've been doing?

When it's all over and the bed is on the other side of the room, Daisy phones her twin sister. I try to give her some privacy, but can't help overhearing the snippet, "Oh, yeah, only about eighty times."

As she hangs up the phone and stands naked at the foot of my bed, I point out that, while I've never really considered myself a breast guy, I have to admit that her "rack," as she puts it, must rank among the planet's best, a judgment I believe I can make with some accuracy. Daisy, for her part, describes how the seasoned crew in Chicago where she had her Playmate test shoot refused to believe they were real and stood around marveling. I'm glad to hear I'm not the only one to confront this physical feature of hers and be deeply hypnotized.

She then returns the compliment, telling me I'm the biggest guy she's ever been with, blaming the "donkey dick" for her not feeling so hot.

Yeah, right. "How many are you comparing against?" I ask, laughing.

"Two."

"That's what I was afraid of."

Not a representative sample, though following certain flattering remarks Julie made on the subject I'm on the verge of thinking that perhaps I've been wrong. Maybe I am, after all, at the least average. . . .

"Trust me," I insist. "Whatever pleasure you think you felt can't be credited to the real me. I'm a small man of wavering potency, sexually paralyzed by self-consciousness, momentarily transformed by a thirty-ton bus."

"You're talking like a pussy."

"It's true. This sex—it's Playboy's doing. Working for Hef, being linked to the Playboy ethos on a daily basis, it's like kissing a sexual Blarney Stone. You, my dear, have witnessed nothing short of a miracle."

"Really . . . that's interesting . . . I want a Twinkie."

Miami, Florida

◆

The first night in Miami, I stumble on a high school synchronized swim team practicing in the black-bottomed pool of the Delano Hotel under the cover of a star-filled sky, and I have to laugh. I mean, who's pulling the strings here? Who's been masterminding this trip's quasi-reality? A night-practicing high school synchronized swim team—*ha!* That's the oldest trick in the book, but I'm not that green. I'm not falling for this pool of trouble.

Back in my room, there are several messages from Herm demanding an explanation for the three hundred dollars in additional charges he's been asked to pay to clean up the pajama party hotel room. I e-mail back: *It could have been worse.*

The following morning—Miami, Day One—I find the bus parked, creatively for once, on the beach out in front of our trendy hotel. I step inside and the first person I see is a stupefyingly attractive blonde with the brightest, whitest, most blinding smile I've ever encountered. I congratulate myself on ending the search and spotting Miss Millennium.

Unfortunately, my discovery has already been discovered—is a Playmate, in fact. At least she will be as of the coming issue. Her name is Jamie and she is in Miami cross-promoting her issue with the bus. Obviously, her arrival establishes my dispatch material for the day. Though we've had brushes with Playmates here and there on the road, the featured presence of one on the bus is really a first, and a certain coup for my readership. And, after all I've been through, I know just what to do with her.

"Are you worried about turning into a bitch?" I ask her.

She's from Salt Lake City, was an office manager before coming to *Playboy*, and isn't the sort of person to get naked in front of friends or even her mother. So she was having something of a nervous breakdown about the coming issue—until she finally saw the pictures. Oh, and she was a competitive barrel racer growing up and was voted Rodeo Princess in high school.

As for turning into a bitch, she's hoping that between family and her own brains, she won't let it get to her head. "Now is this interview over?" she jokes.

It isn't. I need to tell her about the weird coincidence, about my thing for clowns and growing up dressing as a clown. Doesn't she see how freaky that is, that she was into rodeo and I was into clowns? After all, there are clowns in the rodeo, and the idea of my being a clown and her being a rodeo princess—isn't that just about the sexiest thing she's ever heard of?

Apparently not, so I suggest she feel free to flip me off if she doesn't like the questions, a Playmate flipping the bird being almost as sexy as the rodeo business. She does flip me off and I swoon.

"What about dating famous people? Are you dating someone famous yet?"

"I'm dating Michael Bay."

"As in the director of one of this year's top-grossing films. That didn't take long."

She flips me off—it's so tingle-inducing—and again asks if the interview is just about over.

"No, actually, this interview is going to take the exact same amount of time as you are on the bus. Isn't that a coincidence?"

It's another lesson learned, what to do with a Playmate. At this juncture in her life, this woman isn't about to be hooking up with an unknown like myself, nor do I have any desire to tell her my deep dark secrets. But that doesn't mean I shouldn't milk the situation for its own strange pleasure, a middle-ground option I wouldn't have appreciated before the trip.

Which leads to my grabbing Jamie's upcoming issue off the table, explaining there's nothing my readers would love more than a shot-by-shot critique of her spread. It'll make us feel like we were there. And she, being the sport she is, or just bored enough to continue, sinks back on the couch with me and gives me little stories behind every shot. Blushingly, she tries to cover up the more revealing photos—for example, Jamie in cowboy boots, sans pants, standing on the lowest fence rail, leaning out over the top, exposed from the back.

There're some stunning photos, the prettiest I've seen in a while, particularly one of just her face, which I honestly admit is my favorite and, coincidentally, hers, too. I must say, this is the way to go through an issue of the magazine, with the Playmate right there, providing color commentary. I mean, imagine if each issue came with its own live centerfold. Now, that would be a way to sell some magazines. The whole thing is so multimedia-interactive, so where-were-you-when-I-was-fifteen, that I finally suggest we close the magazine and—deep breath—put it aside.

Finally, an outside journalist appears on the bus, giving Jamie a break from me. But I'm behind him, peering over his shoulder, flipping her off. And when the guy turns around, almost catching me, she manages to sneak one back. After he's finally left and I have her back to myself, I can't help telling her, "You know, just in the five or six hours I've known you, I have to say, you already seem like more of a bitch."

She laughs.

"Seriously."

She laughs again.

"I'm not kidding."

If Sophia were in Miami, her "cheesy" meter would be going off the charts. Guilty as charged.

*   *   *

That night, back in my hotel room, once again alone, I decide to call Julie, though it's already eleven. But being congenitally disorganized, I have to find her number on a chicken-scratch filled sheet of paper filled with important numbers from the road.

"Hello?" she says.

"Hey, it's me, Leif. Am I waking you?"

"Oh, hey. No, you're not waking me."

"I just wanted to give you a call, say hi. I'm down in Florida, feeling kind of lonely."

"Well, I'm glad you called. How was your Thanksgiving?"

This isn't going well. Asking me how's-your-Thanksgiving when I told her about it last week?—if I want this kind of relationship, I can just date in LA. Ouch.

"What's going on with you?" I ask.

"Not much. Busy. Work, school, you know."

"School? Are you taking a class?"

"Yeah, I'm taking two classes."

You've signed up for two classes since we talked? Something seems off here.

And then I look down at my sheet of phone numbers. There are two numbers with Julie's area code. This isn't Julie, it's some other Georgia candidate . . . Becky, the FedEx employee with the long legs.

"Well, good talking to you. Just wanted to call and say hi, hope you're well. Sorry to call so late, didn't see the time. I guess that about does it, talk to you later."

I'm a *huge* creep with blushing ears. *Yeah, what's up, I was just randomly calling up candidates because I have access to your phone numbers, not to mention addresses.* Man, oh, man, what was she thinking? *Hey, one of those guys from Playboy called at eleven at night to tell me he was feeling lonely.* Big, huge, goofball.

And the next morning, among my dozens of e-mails, is one from the FedEx office in Athens. I'm not sure I can bear to open it, begin reading with one eye closed:

Leif!!!! It was so great to hear your voice. I was thriiiilled that you called. Forgive me for being such a freak on the phone, it's just that there I was under the covers, next to my fiancé, who was extremely curious to know who I was talking to. Hope that explains my bizarre behavior. It's kind of amazing that you called, though, because you were in my dreams the previous night. We went to the same college and I was head over heels for you and you asked me to go flying. And we did, just took off into the air. It was the most amazing sensation, and then I woke up! Leif, when are you going to return and get me out of this place?!

What? *You* were acting like a freak? Fiancé? Flying? Get you out of this place?

It's funny, isn't it? All my agonizing, when it appears I could have been calling women randomly and having as much if not more success. Funny. Ha.

In the Air II

Okay, complete and full disclosure.

The plane ride back to LA is interminable. The movie is over, the lights are off, and most of the plane is sleeping. I'm thinking about Daisy, including her encouraging e-mails. And the thing is, this whole Search experience has swung my libido so far from where I began, I can't turn it off. It seems so degenerate, right here in the seat, even if I am all alone in the row, but I do it—join the Mile-High Club, solo.

Once in the terminal, heading for baggage claim, I discreetly throw the blanket out.

I'm not home a day when among my e-mails there's a note that gives me a Hitchcockian scare: *You should consider doing a column about getting off in unusual places, for instance, I've had some success with airplanes.*

I . . . am I being followed? Seriously, has the government decided I'm subversive and put a tail on me?

I send a note back, creepy as it feels to even make contact, but determined to suss this one out. *What do you mean?* is all I write.

And immediately I get a response: *Yeah, if you wait until late in the flight, when the lights are down, if you're careful, you can use the blanket as a shield and no one has any idea.*

Ick.

Los Angeles, California VI

◆

"All right, Vegas, let's go," Sophia says, taking him by the hand, heading for the Grotto.

It's our first night in LA and we've all been invited to the Mansion Christmas party.

Vegas emerges ten minutes later, wearing a smile that leans toward shit-eating.

"What happened in there was something between Sophia and myself. It was beauty-ful, and special, and none of you will ever get me to betray that moment," the big ham testifies, taking a swallow from his longneck, catching his breath. "I will say this, though, it gave me a tingle."

There's a story circulating tonight about Vegas. Over Thanksgiving break, his wife called Playboy, wanting to know where he was, what this top-secret mission was that Playboy had him on. Rich assured the woman he had no idea what she was talking about, but Vegas wasn't currently under any secret mission for the company. Vegas always told us that his marriage had ended, but that he and his wife remained good friends. His wife seemed to feel differently. If my memory serves, Vegas had raved about spending the Thanksgiving break at a nudist colony.

Most of our talk tonight, though, is about the future. Both Seamus and Butch may be staying on with the company—Seamus as part of the security detail at the Mansion. Butch's position seems a little shakier. He's made the case to me and everyone else who'll listen that what Playboy really needs is to keep the bus going, now that they've invested all this money in the thing. If they do, he suggests, it makes perfect sense to hire him as the permanent driver.

"What *about* the bus, Rich?" Sophia asks. "Is it true that it might ride again?"

Rich's smile fades. "There's talk to that effect."

Apparently the company is considering taking it to the Super Bowl, then possibly to some Spring Break destination. There's also talk about Hef's buying it and using it for his adventures out and about in Hollywood.

"That's great, and you'd keep running it?" Sophia asks, fighting laughter.

"Never. No way," Rich says, chewing on ice from his cocktail. "I know you guys are going to miss it, and I'm sure I'll miss working with you, and maybe someday a long, long time from now I'll look back on this with fondness. But you don't know, you'll never know— for me, that thing was a time bomb on wheels. Being in charge of the bus was no party."

Watching him speak, I see several hairs fading from brown to gray before my eyes.

"What about Fearless? Word is he's going to be the new West Coast editor. Is that true, Fearless?"

"That's what Herm says. We'll see."

"That's great," Rich says. "Just keep in mind, the further in you go, the harder it is to get out."

What I don't mention about my near future is that after Christmas, on my way back to LA from Minnesota, I'll be stopping in Albuquerque, a place I thought I'd never visit again. Daisy called to tell me about getting into med school, nearly a full scholarship, and while I was congratulating her, she invited me to visit.

When I suggested it wasn't a good idea, the age difference, *mumble mumble,* she resorted to Daisy cowgirl toughness, saying she'd already arranged it so her aunt would be out of town, leaving us with the house to ourselves. Besides, she said, this was probably my last chance to have sex with a twenty-year-old. And if I really meant to stick with writing as a career, I'd better start thinking about hooking up with a sugar mama and could do worse than marrying a doctor. It was a bit of logic I had a tough time refuting.

Sophia, who's kicking herself for not shooting more video, will be doing some writing about her Search experiences. She's already received interest from two different women's magazines who want a female take on our journey.

Eventually our discussion winds around to the great unanswered question: What has been the result of this massive multimillion-dollar undertaking, the search for a Miss Millennium? Which lucky young woman is about to be catapulted by the coveted honor into fabulous fame and fortune?

The truth is, we don't know. For my part, all I can contribute to the discussion is what I've seen. There have been ads for the Search in the magazine that read, in part, "We're still looking!" And I've heard from photographer friends that the finder's fee offered to any photographer who brings her in has been increased.

Later, I'll tell my friend Estella about the trip, suggest that perhaps the Playmate of the Millennium doesn't *exist*. But Estella will have none of it, finds the whole suggestion outrageous.

"After all *that*? Not to find her? That's crazy. All those women? What were you looking for anyway, a woman with three boobs?"

She's not far off. Four boobs, actually. Months later, I'll learn that the Playmate of the Millennium will actually be twins—the Peruvian-born but Miami-raised Bernaola twins, Carol and Darlene. They mesh nicely with the two in 2000, as well as with the cultural moment known as the "Latin explosion."

But here tonight at the Mansion, Playmate 2000 discussion over, Rich stares off into space, looking like he's still haunted by the specter of the bus continuing on. The Search has been a coup for him and his rapid rise in the company is assured, but for the moment the man is profoundly shaken.

Finally, Hef and entourage make their appearance, which means it's time to put on my paparazzi hat. I tack through the crowd to Hef's table, where sits the great man himself, his four girlfriends, and a couple of Playmates. Along with Hef's personal photographer, I snap some photos. Hef & Company are bouncing around, mock dancing, and exchanging the occasional kiss. There's much whispering and visual joking, which ignites regular bursts of laughter.

What do you say to the man who's salvaged your sexuality, restored your potency, and seemingly even given you the impossible—formidable anatomical equipment? Besides *thanks*?

Taking my pictures, watching Hef lose himself in all that blonde hair, tan young flesh, and cleavage, I ponder my future. It's a sunny picture: a possible West Coast editor job; the chance to keep the Fearless Reporter alive, thus stay in this world; and the opportunity to rise up the ranks like Rich and engage in many more mini-Hefscapades. Why, then, am I feeling grim?

One of the girls is making the little bunny ears with fingers behind her head, which is picked up by the others. Soon everyone's doing the bunny, fingers to heads, bouncing slightly in their seats, cracking each other up with their efforts, all of which I'm capturing with my camera.

How can I do this? I mean, come on, the bunny-ear gag? It's been done before, I remember, back at the Labor Day party. I'll try anything once for the experience, but twice? Clearly, this is my defect, a flaw in my mental wiring, an inability to go with desire.

Instead, I'm stuck confronting what I know too well will be a lonely, drawn-out compulsion to put this inner monologue down on paper, to try to make some sense of it all and hope it's something that will entertain and stimulate, not just invite ridicule.

Something tells me, as smart as Hefner is, what he's thinking about at the moment—sandwiched in between four girlfriends—is not putting it all in perspective or initiating a dialogue. As he's said lately, his life is an attempt to honor a promise made to the boy within. In the end, there's no escaping it. I'm not Hefner.

The big final stop proves something of a whimper. In LA, it's true, anyone who should be coming by the bus will already have an agent, or at least have already stopped by Playboy's West Coast office.

The last day on the bus, approaching the last hours, there's a surge of candidates—particularly of candidates wanting to flirt. It's a wouldn't-you-know-it situation, the gods having a final bit of fun with me. *Surround him in his last hours on the bus, have everyone pretend like they want him. Yeah, that'll be a hoot.*

I'm not falling for it, see it for what it is. Instead, I'm determined to conduct one good last photo session, my Playboy photography swan song. All that remains is finding the ideal subject, which is what I'm considering when a dimpled candidate named Cleo playfully flashes me, revealing floral-print bustier, matching panties, garter, stockings. And just like that, I—trained professional—know that Cleo is the one.

Unfortunately, Playboy Video wants to share. And though mentally I've already flown the coop, I still feel obligated to work with them. So we discuss what to do. The Hollywood sign is an obvious option, but as the video guys point out, that trip would take us through brutal afternoon traffic. So Vince suggests the Beverly Hills sign. I don't really know what he's talking about, but am willing to give it a shot.

Driving east, riding with Cleo, following the video crew, I start on the questions. She bartends in a tough bar, but makes great money and models occasionally. She grew up in a happy home, leading an idyllic life, until one night in high school, things started shaking. It was an earthquake and brought down half of the house on itself— the half her parents were sleeping in. "There's no going back," she says. One minute you're living a happy life, the next it's just gone and nothing you can do will put it back.

The Beverly Hills sign is a joke. It's this carved wood thing on the side of a busy road that says BEVERLY HILLS. It's barely bigger than a stop sign. Lame. There're so many cars whizzing by, we may as well be on the highway. *Hey, I'm Cleo, standing by my favorite overpass. Welcome to LA. Love ya!* But Vince wants to go ahead with it.

Cleo is a trouper, laughing off the rather uninspiring setup and acquiescing to Vince's suggestion that she tell the camera that LA women are indeed the best. Having made this declaration, she opens her brown suede coat, underneath which she is wearing neither shirt nor bra, and gives a shimmying flash that is much more than Vince deserves, not to mention the ogling motorists.

And that's it. The Beverly Hills sign.

"What?" Collin asks me, now knowing me well enough to see my wheels spinning. "Are you going to do something else with her?"

He's caught me thinking. But at the moment it's just dissatisfaction with what we've done, frustration that I found a classic candidate and we're not rising to the occasion. The muse still hasn't come.

"Naw, let's just head back to the bus."

"Okay. You riding with us?"

"Cleo, do you mind giving me a ride?"

She doesn't need to go back to the bus, and it's not in her direction, but she doesn't have a problem with it. Collin eyes me for a second longer, still sure I'm up to something, but I just shrug my shoulders.

Back in Cleo's SUV, following the video crew through traffic, I ask Cleo if she'd be up for more shooting if I can come up with a concept, and she enthusiastically says yes.

"I wish we didn't have this traffic," I say, thinking about different backdrops—the rooftop of a friend's apartment building, or another friend's swanky home in the hills. Time is my enemy, though. I risk forfeiting the last minutes of the Search.

"Well, first, let's lose the video guys. Up here, at this intersection, as they go through, hang a hard left, but don't signal or let on that we're turning."

My head nearly smacks the window, so sharp is Cleo's turn, but she manages it, sending us down a side street with no possible way of being tracked down by the buzz-crushing video team.

It's panic time, though, my heart starting to pound, the old anxiety rising up. This is where I live, Los Angeles, of all places, there *must* be some perfect final shoot location. But as we drive along, now on a busy street, traffic flying by, heading in the direction of the bus, I look down the quiet side streets at quaint Beverly Hills neighborhoods and experience a twinge. It's that old creep feeling. Here I am taking a candidate to god knows what.

Just spit it out. You know you're thinking of something!

"This may sound strange," I begin, my quavering voice almost betraying me, teetering on the edge of weirdness. "But what would you think about just pulling over, on this busy street with traffic flying past? It kind of seems appropriate, LA in rush hour."

She pulls over, right there on Pico, in front of a Jewish temple. This is perfect, I think. The traffic keeping me from feeling like a creep, and yet traffic as a theme, as the quintessential LA condition. Okay, it's not exactly Nan Goldin, but it'll suffice.

"So," I address Cleo, who is sitting behind the wheel, smiling in an expectant way. "We'll just . . ."

I take a picture of her, sitting there, looking cute.

"You really are lovely. Can you move your seat back as far as it goes?"

She slides her seat back.

"Now do you mind unzipping the top?"

She unzips the top.

"Now recline the seat . . . and stretch out on your side."

She has pretty, smoky eyes and great eyebrows. And as she pulls the coat back and reclines along the seat, her stomach makes all those beautiful lines that a woman's stomach makes, exhibiting both strength and softness.

"Do you want the skirt off?"

Cleo, you adorable thing!

"Why, actually, yes, I do."

Hmmm . . . even better, scanty floral panties riding high on hips.

"Oh, and would it be all right to open the sunroof, so I can shoot down on you?"

There are other cars with occupants parked along this busy stretch of road, those cars you sometimes see containing single men or women, just sitting there, for whatever reason, killing time. And there's the steady blur of traffic out the window. I'm loving this idea of car as mobile photo studio. Just driving along with the Mrs. and suddenly, *Hey, baby, pull over, let's take some dirty pictures.*

"Why don't we try some with you in the backseat now?"

We move the fronts seats up and I wedge myself up against the dash, trying to get as much perspective as possible.

"Right on, Cleo, that's great," I say, as she takes charge, reaches for the handholds on opposite sides of the car, above the back door. She drops her chin naturally, lets her lower lip hang open just enough, ever so wantonly. This shot is going to kill the readers. On top of it all, she has great breasts, just-right, smallish C-cup, strongly defined nipples.

"Are you doing okay?" I ask.

"I'm great."

"Good. Okay, yes, kneel on the seat like that, then let the jacket hang so you're just barely covered. I need to have some shots that cover up."

The interesting thing is, I'm very much turned on by this. Cleo is too much my type and the space too confined not to be. Still, I'm not having that debate about whether this will escalate to sex, or whether I'll need to excuse myself and leave the car. Nor am I feeling as I was in the beginning of the trip, that I have Freon flowing through my veins.

Rather, what I'm experiencing is a creatively fertile lust. And Cleo is responding to it, as well as to the lust of all the other men she imagines connected with that lens. We're both engaging in a nice slow burn. All those forces are there, but it doesn't need to go to the next level. We keep shooting on the side of the road, our vehicle vibrating from the force of passing motorists. Cleo actually sighs from it all.

"I guess," she says, "all women must love this—love having their picture taken."

I wouldn't go *that* far. But having seen what I've seen, I'd say some definitely do. I tell her this, and I also point out that some men love taking a woman's picture. Ultimately, the whole experience has taught me to throw up my hands, because as much as my rational mind could dissect the whole thing, at this particular moment, with my heart pounding, libido racing, and mind fully engaged, I couldn't care less what anyone thinks.

As Cleo and I keep working, scrambling repeatedly up and over seats—like little kids in a fort—as we pursue yet another angle, I notice out of the corner of my eye that we're losing light, that the sun is going down, which strikes me as early even for this late in the year.

But when I look up, I see why. It's the windows. They've fogged over, filtering out the day's remaining rays. Cleo and my fog.

I am, for the moment, a happy man.

Acknowledgments

I might have gone back to selling insurance if not for the help of a small horde of folks, and I'm beyond pleased to be able to thank them.

The list begins with my younger brother and fellow scribe, Sigurd. He has long lent me a fierce and feisty loyalty, much beyond what I deserved, and I've never adequately expressed my gratitude. The rest of my family have all provided similarly heroic support. My mom went to every one of my first, and only, play's performances. My pop transformed himself into a font of encouragement, though the uncertainty of the writing life surely made him unbearably queasy. Brother Scott and Sister Tora have always been there as well, particularly as a first audience—back at the family dinner table that was the proving ground for our version of humor.

This book would have ended up in the half-finished project graveyard if not for the encouragement of two friends, which came at critical times. Jack Murnighan hectored me onward as I was just beginning, and was tempted to keep beginning, and Marshall Boswell was equally vociferous when I had a draft, but might have opted to start over. Both were extremely generous in their interpretation of my efforts, egging me on in ways that I had to take seriously. However, I would have never known how to start were it not for the help of my favorite writing teachers: Ted Braun, Marisha Chamberlain, Dr. James Ragan, John Rechy, Hubert Selby, and Eric Van Lowe.

The leap from experience to manuscript to book was only possible thanks to an alliance of professionals lead by my agent, Laura Dail. Laura embraced *Accidental Playboy* when it was barely an idea (one, incidentally, with a much less appealing title), and she stuck with it through thick and thin and back again. Editor Rick Horgan showed a similarly longstanding devotion to the project, editing the book with a much-needed meticulousness, the sort that those in his profession are said to no longer have time for. Steve Dembitzer and Bob Stein provided exemplary legal counsel, along with much appreciated hand-holding and levity. At UTA, Howie Sanders and Rich Green placed the film rights with flair, and were a pleasure to watch in action. All of these people deserve and have my special gratitude.

I'd also like to thank the people I worked with on the road and those who helped with the daily dispatches. The crew on the bus always supported me in my antics, which was no small part to the success of the website. Mikki Chernoff was a great source of fun and sex appeal at various stops, but due to issues of pace, tragically doesn't appear in the edit. Back in Chicago, Terry Glover and Mike Wasisco made order of what was often chaos, along with Jill Norton, Agnes Galecka, and Linda Steingass. "Herm" and "Sophie" made crucial contributions to this book, long after the end of the trip. I would also like to thank Playboy Enterprises and "Rich" for the job, and the freedom. As for the Playmate 2000 hopefuls with whom I interacted for the website, what can I say beyond the obvious—thanks for your charm, gusto, humor, beauty, and openness.

Rufus Griscom, my bosom pal, and "Burt," my therapist/mentor/ friend, deserve the most credit for helping me to get closer to the person I struggle to be, and for that they deserve all the thanks I'm capable of giving. Friends Murray Oden, Genevieve Field, and Jonathan Rosen steered work my way when it was most needed, and all three did so without being asked. There's a long, long list of friends who, upon hearing that my story would become a book, expressed satisfaction at the news with an intensity rivaling my own. Sorry to leave out every name, but thank you to all my pals, both friends from way back and those from more recent years, all the writers, actors, singers, dancers, and cameramen who continue their own travels down precarious paths.

Then there are the readers, including those who read through to the end of the acknowledgments. Despite my lifelong love of books, previously it never dawned on me that the simple act of reading would mean anything to the author. But of course it does, as I can now see. It means the most of all. Thank you.